Barnes & Noble Critical Studies

General Editor: Anne Smith

Reading the Victorian Novel: Detail into Form

READING THE VICTORIAN NOVEL: DETAIL INTO FORM

edited by

Ian Gregor

Published in U.S.A. by
BARNES & NOBLE BOOKS
81 Adams Drive—Box 327
Totowa, N.J. 07511

Published in U.S.A. by
BARNES & NOBLE BOOKS
81 Adams Drive—Box 327
Totowa, N.J. 07511

ISBN 0–06–492542–0

First published in the U.S.A. 1980

© 1980 by Vision Press, London

Contents

Acknowledgements   7

Introduction by *Ian Gregor*   9

1   Readings of Melodrama by *Michael Irwin*   15

2   Wilkie Collins and the Crisis of Suspense by
     David Blair   32

     Interchapter 1   51

3   'Bound in Moss and Cloth': Reading a Long Victorian
     Novel by *Graham Clarke*   54

4   *The Mill on the Floss*: 'Memory' and the Reading
     Experience by *A. Robert Lee*   72

5   Reading a Story: Sequence, Pace, and Recollection
     by *Ian Gregor*   92

6   'The Past-marked Prospect': *The Mayor of Caster-*
     bridge by *Rod Edmond*   111

     Interchapter 2   128

7   *Jane Eyre* and 'The Warped System of Things' by
     Doreen Roberts   131

8   Reading *David Copperfield* by *Keith Carabine*   150

9   *The Voicing of Fictions* by *Mark Kinkead-Weekes*   168

     Interchapter 3   193

CONTENTS

10 Reading Illustrations: Pictures in *David Copperfield*
by *Stephen Lutman*   196

11 The Portrayal of Death and 'Substance of Life':
Aspects of the Modern Reader's response to
'Victorianism' by *W. L. G. James*   226

12 A Note on Serialisation by *Malcolm Andrews*   243

Interchapter 4   248

13 'The Flash of Fervour': *Daniel Deronda* by *Ruth Raider*   253

14 Beyond the Victorians: *The Portrait of a Lady* by
Stuart Hutchinson   274

15 *News from Nowhere*: Detail and Desire by *Bernard
Sharratt*   288

Interchapter 5   306

Index   311

Acknowledgements

The contributors would like to express their gratitude to those members of the secretarial staff at the University of Kent who helped to make the enterprise of preparing and assembling this book go as smoothly as it did. In particular, they would like to thank Sheila Taylor for her efficiency and interest in dealing with the many demands made upon her and which she responded to with such good humoured patience.

Introduction

by IAN GREGOR

The characteristic stance of the critic to his text is that of the reader over the writer's shoulder. The stance which lies behind the essays in the present volume is better described as the reader looking over his own shoulder. The text, the specific work, is still the unquestioned centre of attention, but it is an attention which has as an inseparable element, the reader's consciousness of himself as reader. It is a shift in emphasis that might seem to imply no more than a call to modesty, but in fact, it is a shift which has a set of precise and significant consequences for the way we can talk about fiction.

The title of the book, *Reading The Victorian Novel: Detail into Form*, expresses the double interest that has helped to give it shape. From one point of view, the book is concerned with the process of reading itself, with the way novels come to us as page by page experience, gathering themselves suddenly and vividly in one place, slowing down in another, changing rhythm, quickening our expectations here, relying upon recollections there. From another point of view, the interest in the present volume concerns reading in retrospect; with the attempt to make a coherent account out of the immediacies of our reading experience, by recollecting the details which seem significant, by finding a suggestive contour in the parts to express the whole. The two interests complement each other, but they are not constant companions and in the essays that follow the emphasis will shift, in varying degree, from one to the other.

It is many years since Percy Lubbock wrote *The Craft of Fiction*, and much has changed in the manner and mode of writing about the novel since 1921, but the opening paragraphs of that book contain a memorable reminder:

To grasp the shadowy and fantasmal form of a book, to hold it fast, to turn it over and survey it at leisure—that is the effort of a critic of books, and it is perpetually defeated. Nothing, no power will keep a book steady and motionless before us, so that we may have time to examine its shape and design. As quickly as we read, it melts and shifts in the memory; even at the moment when the last page is turned, a great part of the book, its finer detail, is already vague and doubtful. . . . The form of a novel—and how often a critic uses that expression too—is something that none of us, perhaps, has ever really contemplated. It is revealed little by little, page by page, and it is withdrawn as fast as it is revealed; as a whole, complete and perfect, it could only exist in a more tenacious memory than most of us have to rely on. Our critical faculty may be admirable; we may be thoroughly capable of judging a book justly, if only we could watch it at ease. But fine taste and keen perception are of no use to us if we cannot retain the image of the book; and the image escapes and evades us like a cloud.

Lubbock describes admirably the volatility of the reading experience of fiction and in stressing the *length* of the novel he is indicating something which has a marked effect on the nature of our reading attention and distinguishes it from the attention we give to poetry or to drama. What Lubbock describes is central to our concerns, but the present book departs sharply from him in that the flexibility and patchiness of the reader's response which, for Lubbock, is a matter for regret is for us indicative of the novel's creative volatility. 'Nobody would venture to criticise a building', Lubbock writes, 'a statue, a picture with nothing before him but the memory of a single glimpse caught in passing . . . how many books can a critic bring into a state of relative stability?' We should remember that unlike a building, a statue, or a picture, a novel exists not in space but in time. It finds a more appropriate analogue with film, coming to us as unfolding process, encouraging a description in terms of pace, sequence and rhythm. Precisely because it is a process, repetition, for instance, can become an important dynamic element in structuring the fiction and not a sign of redundancy. Lubbock's remark implies that if we had total recall we would—theoretically at least—be better, if not perfect, readers of fiction. It would be our contention that such recall would render the reading of fiction impossible. Out of the tissue of things remembered and forgotten, half-remembered and half-forgotten, the novelist weaves his fiction, and though this is a tissue which cannot be consciously aimed at, its creation involves a whole rhetoric of effect—melodrama, suspense, voice, style— which is the result of design and calculation.

These effects are all lavishly present in the Victorian novel and partly for this reason, partly because of the intrinsic attraction that that novel has for us, it became the area which we thought would be most congenial to our present enterprise. It will be readily agreed that the English novel, from the Brontës to Henry James, has a noticeable homogeneity. A quite distinctive equilibrium is achieved between the ordinary and the extra-ordinary; a new congruity is established between the mysterious and the domestic, between the moral and the anarchic. But the most striking common feature, is the confidence with which the reader is addressed, the expectation, built into every narrative, that it will find a complement in *his* wisdom, *his* integrity, *his* feeling heart. It was this dramatic range in content, this openness to the reader, that seemed to offer a range of dynamics much suited to our purpose. Further, to assess the nature and variety of the reading response we needed a collaborative work, and the low and generous threshold of Victorian fiction made easy the accommodation of diverse reading temperaments.

Favourably assisted by a choice of period, the making of a book like the present one could still only have been accomplished in rather special circumstances. Conceived as a collaborative enterprise, the project was first sketched in general terms, then drafts of all the chapters were read and criticised by the contributors, final versions discussed and an order of contents approved.

Such a summary description is misleading in that it suggests a much greater clarity of aim than, in fact, existed. Only as the discussions developed did the route to be travelled become clearer. In the early sketches, the book was divided into two sections. The first was to deal with a number of general themes which would be substantiated by a series of studies of individual novels. The dominant notion behind the division was the relationship of detail to form. As our discussions continued, however, the different nature of our responses made us become increasingly aware, as a matter of experience, of the plurality of reading experience, and this became increasingly central to our concern. It cast fresh light on the reading of individual novels, and it was to lead, at a later stage, to a sustained discussion about the reader's relation to fiction in much more general terms.

The kind of collaboration we undertook was really only made possible by having a group of people living and working in the same place, able to meet easily and at regular intervals. More specifically, it was only possible by a group actively engaged in teaching certain courses and familiar with shared styles of teaching. At the University of Kent fiction has always been taught as a *genre* rather than historically. Currently, the main fiction course happens to deal with the nineteenth-century novel, and this has meant that there are a large number of teachers whose interests lie in that area. Though the present book does not reflect any particular syllabus, it was able to draw on a large pool of contributors, many of whom had already conceived and taught courses jointly. This particular enterprise brought together interests and attitudes which had been built up for some time, and when the idea began to take shape, it was relatively easy to see how it might be developed.

We met at regular intervals from the autumn of 1977 to the autumn of 1978. Most meetings began with a draft of a proposed chapter. Our experience was, however, that again and again discussion took us beyond the immediacies of the particular chapter and developed a momentum of its own. Various themes and problems recurred in a way that made us wish to give them an independent presence. This affected the shape the book was eventually to take. We began to group the essays in a way that would bring out connections between them and allow the emergence of interests held in common. And then, sited at various points between the chapters, we placed a number of interchapters, which would attempt to characterise the grouping, and point outwards to more wide-ranging issues.

We decided to begin the book with chapters on melodrama and suspense, because discussion suggested that what we had originally thought of simply as distinctive elements within a fictional mode, could also be regarded as suggestive metaphors for the reading process in general. The second group of essays dealt most directly with issues raised by the title of the book, and once brought together, seemed to provoke a further set of questions, which the interchapter explored, about that shadowy, and constantly invoked, figure—'the reader'. The third group of essays seemed to display, in retrospect, contrasting critical stances—and the interchapter was concerned with the implications of 'the novel experienced as process' and 'the novel reviewed as a whole'. The fourth group of essays is the most concerned with the Victorian reading experience, and the critical questions revolved about the recoverability of that experience and its value. The final group of essays was concerned with novels which, in a variety of ways, seemed to express dissatisfaction with the Victorian novel. The interchapter explored the tensions and paradoxes which emerged in the process of transition, and also the double vision that is involved in being a reader of a fiction whose modes have been largely abandoned and whose conventions seem so different from our own.

When we started the book we were very much aware of the diversity of the topic and the advantages of collaborative treatment. Events served to confirm those expectations. Different responses began to appear as we discussed the various texts; proportion and emphases shifted; lines of enquiry which looked promising turned out not to be so. Nevertheless, despite the diversity of interests and the plurality of views, the topic itself—the reading process, the articulation of detail into form—remained clear, and especially so in the final stages, when with the drafts of individual chapters completed, new and unexpected views began to open up. The book which began as a study of the reading process, did, in its making, cause us all to *experience* the diversity of that process. In consequence, it is not a book which presses towards a specific conclusion. Rather, it finds its shape and substance in taking a form which will allow it to display the plurality of the reading process, a form which contains its own gesture of self-commentary in a series of interchapters, and most importantly a form which can extend an invitation to the readers of this book to reflect on the volatility of their own reading experiences.

I.G.

1

Readings of Melodrama

by MICHAEL IRWIN

'. . . Art is the secret of how to produce by a false thing the
effect of a true . . .'—Thomas Hardy

Most Victorian novels modulate into melodrama at least occasionally. An author who has seemed to concern himself specifically
with the patterns and pressures of everyday living will suddenly
resort to extravagance. There may be scenes of storm, fire, flood,
murder, last-minute rescue. In episodes of emotional intensity
psychological and descriptive realism may be abandoned. Speech
and gesture become rhetorical; landscape and weather fall prey to
the pathetic fallacy.

Plainly this tendency has much to do with the popularity of
melodrama in the nineteenth-century theatre. The novelists of
the period were reflecting and responding to certain tastes, needs
and capacities that since their day have largely atrophied. It is
arguable that the hyperbolical scenes jarring to a modern reader
represent a serious mode of writing to which we have lost access
and which we are therefore likely to misread.

Peter Brooks has demonstrated that appreciation of the melodramatic element in Balzac and James is greatly enhanced by
reference to stage melodrama.[1] Stephen Lutman's account, in this
book, of the 'syndrome of related . . . forms' that helped to condition the responses of the nineteenth-century reading public does
much to explain why the Victorians might have been able to cope
with abrupt shifts of convention and style that we find it hard to
accept (p. 197). My own immediate interests can't be extricated
from those of Brooks or Lutman, but the emphasis will be rather
different. I will be concerned only indirectly with theatrical history.
Although the adjective 'melodramatic' seems unavoidable I could
write an essay along the lines I have in mind about novels written

before 'melodrama' was invented. *Tom Jones, Clarissa* and *Humphry Clinker* could all be described, for my purposes, as incorporating melodramatic elements. Nor will I have much to say about the Victorian reader. My starting-point is my own reading experience. In teaching courses on nineteenth-century fiction I regularly encounter scenes of such melodramatic lavishness that I cannot decide what the reaction of the discerning critic should be nor even what my own reaction in fact *is*. I can find myself moved emotionally by a sequence that my critical sense denounces as trashy. A particular episode—for example the death of Jo in *Bleak House* or the death of Giles Winterborne in *The Woodlanders*—may be so precariously stylised as to seem triumphantly effective at one reading and preposterous at another.

Any work of fiction requires an alert response to a series of minute signals that cumulatively define the nature and scope of the emerging story—that seem to establish ground rules. The reader who has been persuaded that he is engaged with a realistic novel may well find an extravagant episode not merely confusing but subversive. Gwendolen Harleth's doings have seemed to demonstrate the psychological and moral necessity of grappling with confining realities: Providence will send no romantic rescuer. But then Mirah is providentially, romantically rescued. What is George Eliot about? Has the reader misread the signals? Have the ground rules been changed? Is the author entitled to change them?

My theme will be the relationship, the reconcilability of the realistic and the melodramatic aspects of Victorian fiction. My argument will be discontinuous—a series of stepping stones.

It would be impossible to retrieve the word 'melodramatic' as a critical term. One of the O.E.D. definitions summarises almost adequately what seems to have become the normal and inescapable meaning of the adjective: 'Characterised by sensational incidents and violent appeals to the emotions.' But why would it seem inappropriate to call *King Lear* or *Macbeth* 'melodramatic'? In ordinary critical parlance an incident in a novel will be so described if it is thought to be *unjustifiably* sensational or to involve an *unjustifiably* violent appeal to the emotions. The term thus becomes pejorative.

16

This is a pity, because it would be useful to the critic to have available an adjective which corresponded to the O.E.D. definition. In fact for the purpose of this essay I shall be obliged to use the word 'melodramatic' in just that sense, while keeping it in quotation marks as a reminder that its pejorative connotations are in abeyance. In this revised sense the adjective has a considerably wider range of reference. Many an extravagant episode in Victorian fiction is so stylistically dispassionate as to escape pejorative comment: the sale of Henchard's wife, for instance, or the death of Raffles. Conversely in the novel, as on the stage, everyday happenings could be sensationalised by their presentation. Lucy Snowe is thrown into violent agitation by the receipt of a single letter from Dr John. On what terms can violence or extremity of either kind become an appropriate ingredient in a realist novel?

In Shakespearian tragedy the main characters are so important, if only in an obvious political sense, that sensationalism of incident or language can be held to contribute to an appropriate intensity of effect. Where a scene in a novel is dismissed as melodramatic the likely implication is that there is a discrepancy between the ordinariness of the people concerned and the degree of interest that we are asked to take in their doings. To put the point crudely, for the sake of definition: Cordelia's sufferings seem to be in some sense commensurate with her status as a Princess, while little Nell's seem arbitrarily excessive, because she is an ordinary middle-class child.

The novelist's problem here is one of the many posed by the democratisation of art in the eighteenth and nineteenth centuries. In the first instance the dilemma was in effect a theological one. If an entire crew must drown so that Crusoe may be educatively marooned must not that sinner be a chosen soul? In literary terms the question redefines itself: why should the reader (or spectator in a theatre) feel a powerful sympathetic involvement with the plight of some humble private individual?

Curiously the two most obvious answers are converse. The individual may take on importance as being a representative figure. The stylised and powerfully rhetorical account of Jo's death in *Bleak House* might be justified by the fact that Jo's fate stands for that of the thousands of urchins 'dying thus around us every day.' Less obviously Fanny Robin, whose 'melodramatic' last hour will be discussed later in this essay, resembles many a girl in folk-song or local legend betrayed by a fickle sweetheart. Hardy can risk being exaggerative about his particular case, because through it he appeals to a general sympathy.

The alternative possibility is conveniently summed up in a reflection of Angel Clare's: 'Tess was no insignificant creature to toy with and dismiss; but a woman living her precious life—a life which, to herself who endured or enjoyed it, possessed as great a dimension as the life of the mightiest to himself' (ch. 25). Every individual whosoever must be fervently, must be disproportionately interesting in his own eyes. If the reader can be induced to share the subjectivity of vision of a fictional character he will perceive no incongruity between the ordinariness of that character's doings and the violence of the reaction to them.

All this amounts to a reminder that the novelist who deals with everyday life must take account of the fact that 'extremity' of various kinds is intrinsic to it. For example, in the Victorian period the relationship between middle-class and working-class life fairly invited translation, in fictional terms, into the relationship between the conventional and the 'melodramatic'. Where the amplifier was set to the sound register of bourgeois domestic doings the sufferings of the poor could only emerge as a deafening blare—unless the novelist could make a series of adjustments, carefully timed and controlled. More generally, the life of the most commonplace individual, at whatever social level, is bound to include some passages of 'melodramatic' intensity: episodes of love, or fear, or grief. Henry Fielding, in *Tom Jones*, shows one way of dealing with such difficulties: 'The first Agonies of Joy which were felt on both sides, are indeed beyond my Power to describe: I shall not therefore attempt it' (Bk. XVIII, ch. 10). In the Victorian novel unbearable stress of feeling is often translated into sickness. David Copperfield, Eugene Wrayburn, Pip, Clennam, Rochester, Jude Fawley, Giles Winterborne, Lucy Snowe, are a few of the many characters to undergo what is in effect a nervous collapse. They have been tried beyond endurance. Illness is the melodrama of individual physical existence. In a literary context it is insufficiently expressive. The novelist who invokes it is in a sense, like Fielding, confessing failure; his art cannot record the emotional or moral turmoil that his story has generated.

These considerations do, I hope, suggest one of the criteria by which we instinctively judge the effectiveness of the 'melodramatic' aspects of a realistic novel. The contrast, the balance between the discrepant conventions should seem proportioned to the contrast and balance between those discrepant elements in actual life, whether social or psychological, which the conventions display. By this criterion, at least, the death of Jo or the sleep-walking scene in *Tess* may stand justified: the extremity of the stylisation involved does not exceed the extremity of feeling, in relation to the relevant norms established in the text, that the situation embodies. This would not be true of the arrival of Hetty's reprieve, in *Adam Bede*, or the last minute intervention at the trial in *Mary Barton*. In both cases the kind of excitement that the episode engenders is actually more trivial than the emotion aroused by the main action of the novel.

The criterion proposed, however, has little relevance to those Victorian works that while ostensibly 'realistic' are in fact melodramatic in their very conception—they include *The Old Curiosity Shop*, *Desperate Remedies* and the novels of Charlotte and Emily Brontë. The reader of *Jane Eyre*, for example, cannot well discern the normal or reasonable patterns of behaviour against which the heroine's strange adventures and extreme reactions might be judged. The author presumably intends the whole story to be seen as a transcription of a mental and spiritual conflict. Jane Eyre has to establish her own identity in relation to the opposing claims of reason and emotion, duty and passion, 'sense and sensibility'. The extravagances of the action are means towards dramatising the conflict. Mrs Rochester's rampagings and St John Rivers's Indian mission mark out the sensual and ascetic extremes between which Jane must chart her course. Any middle-class girl of the period might have felt herself divided in this way though she led a quiet life and had no lovers at all. The exotic story is necessary not to create but to express the dilemma that is central to the novel.

It is worth noting parenthetically, that women and children are in general more apt than men to 'melodramatic' treatment, simply because they are more helpless. Even the poor man could strike a blow for himself: the helpless woman had no such resource. In several obvious ways Nell Trent is the counterpart of Oliver Twist, but Oliver at least manages—however implausibly—

19

to knock down Noah Claypole; Nell can only weep. Oliver, like David Copperfield, takes to the road alone when his life becomes unbearable. Nell could not do so because the sexual risks involved would have been too obvious and too appalling. The perils surrounding her must be presented in metaphorical terms. George Eliot, of course, repeatedly complains of the inability of women to *do* anything significant—' "We don't ask what a woman does— we ask whom she belongs to." ' (*The Mill on the Floss*, Bk. 6. ch. 8. The speaker is Mr Wakem). For Sue Lyon she rather desperately contrives a situation in which a suitably striking gesture can be made.

Charlotte Brontë offers an alternative strategem: *Jane Eyre* or *Villette* arguably functions like the sub-text of a George Eliot novel. She presents a portrait of a personality, but it is an anamorphic portrait. Rightly viewed its exaggerations might subside, its distortions vanish, for a coherent image to appear. Even if that potentiality is not fully achieved it remains true that the excesses of the novel enable the author to produce effects and suggestions impossible to more temperate writers. The dilemmas of Elinor Dashwood and Maggie Tulliver are distinctly similar to that of Jane Eyre, but they are more pallidly presented because there is too simple an emphasis on the side of virtue, propriety, restraint. A controlled narrative about a conflict between control and passion is always liable to collude with the former principle and misrepresent the latter.

Where a novel is 'melodramatic' only intermittently there are likely to be notable problems of equilibrium. But there is also a variety of opportunity: a deficiency or an imbalance may be hurriedly adjusted. It becomes easier—at the simplest level—for the novelist to give all his significant characters something sufficiently interesting to *do*. The result may be clumsy on occasion, but at least the narrative line can be kept clear and energetic. It is in this spirit that Arthur Donnithorne is made to gallop in with Hetty's last minute reprieve, or that Biffen, in *New Grub Street*, has to rescue the manuscript of his novel from a fire.

More subtly, a variety of energies accumulated over the length of an extended, quiet narrative sequence can be counterpoised by a single striking incident. It is necessary to the plot of *Far From the*

Madding Crowd that Bathsheba should fall in love with Sergeant Troy. Since, through many chapters, she has resisted the attentions of both Oak and Boldwood, and since Troy has emerged as an uninteresting, not to say a disagreeable figure, this might have proved a tricky narrative corner to turn. The obvious alternative risks were that Hardy would have had to provide lengthy explanations or that Bathsheba's character would have been trivialised. He avoids both, chiefly by means of the 'melodramatic' sword-play episode, which simultaneously accounts for Bathsheba's infatuation and places it. The encounter does not have the reductive effect of a mere seduction scene: indeed it is rich in complex suggestion. It implies attraction of a certain *kind*. (*A Pair of Blue Eyes* features a comparable but more cerebral episode in which the heroine is routed at chess.) By means of a 'melodramatic' chapter Hardy has swiftly, emphatically and delicately established a situation that a more literal novelist could have laboured over for fifty pages.

In this particular instance the author has an advantage: as a soldier Troy is a potentially romantic figure. How, if at all, may a similar point be made about a drabber person? Dickens, for example, frequently sets out to dramatise the doings of the uneducated, the crushed, the taciturn, the physically unattractive. How is he to give a voice to such characters? Where it is, literally, a voice that he provides, the language is likely to be implausibly heightened to do justice to the strength of feeling pressing for articulation. Oliver Twist addresses Sikes with an eloquence and religious fervour which would seem to constitute an unlikely tribute to his own upbringing:

> 'Oh! pray have mercy on me, and do not make me steal. For the love of all the bright Angels that rest in Heaven, have mercy upon me!'
>
> (ch. 22)

More generally, of course, Dickens's humble characters will be displayed in terms of appearance, clothes, possessions. Barkis, who can barely speak, is interestingly portrayed by the contents of his box; Peggotty, in the first half of *David Copperfield*, by the boat in which he lives and by its furnishings. In both cases, but more obviously in the latter, the definition is varied and generous—a powerful latent energy. When Peggotty loses his adopted daughter

21

all this energy must be converted into action. The result, if proportion is to be maintained, must inevitably be 'melodramatic'.

Whether his quest can be taken seriously is another matter. My own reading pulls two ways. I am irritated by David's failure to point out the hopeless impracticality of his friend's mission, and feel that he should be hiring a competent private investigator on Peggotty's behalf. But I am simultaneously aware that this course of action would demean Peggotty, reducing him to a mere victim. My own sympathy for the character makes me ready to accept the far-fetched course of action as expressive of the force and dignity of his feelings.

So with the storm scene where, in quadruple coincidence, David looks on as Ham dies in a vain attempt to rescue Steerforth, whose body is washed ashore amid the wreckage of Peggotty's boat. Dickens is piling it on here and he pays a price for doing so. Some magnificent description is flawed by circumstantial inconsistency. David sees and hears what the 'melodrama' demands, not what the elements would seem to permit. Steerforth's curls and cap, for instance, and Ham's last words, are conveniently distinguishable in the turmoil. But neither the coincidence nor the manipulation of detail seriously affects my response. This culminating episode in a whole family of sub-plots needs to be of a certain scale. And there is a need for Ham to be established as a nobly generous figure instead of a kindly dolt. My reservations, as I read, are theoretical merely. The dynamic of the novel demands a 'melodramatic' scene.

Constable's 'Waterloo' seemed as if painted with liquid gold and silver, and Turner came several times into the room while he was heightening with vermilion and lake the decorations and flags of the city barges. Turner stood behind him, looking from the 'Waterloo' to his own picture, and at last brought his palette from the great room where he was touching another picture, and putting a round daub of red lead, somewhat bigger than a shilling, on his grey sea, went away without saying a word.

The intensity of the red lead, made more vivid by the coolness of his picture, caused even the vermilion and lake of Constable to look weak. I came into the room just as Turner left it. 'He has been here', said Constable, 'and fired a gun'. . . . The great man did not come into the room for a day and a half; and then, in the last moments that were allowed for painting, he glazed the scarlet seal he had put on his painting, and shaped it into a buoy.

Leslie, *Autobiographical Recollection*, I, pp. 202–3

Turner's action was obviously exceptional, or the incident would not have become an 'anecdote'. But one of the points of the story is that it shows how remarkable an effect a great artist can achieve by means of even a single striking highlight. Just as the daub of red lead could modify a score of surrounding colours so a lurid scene in a novel can seem to redefine a predominantly sober context. The author, like the painter, may well be in complete control of what he is doing. It would have been absurd to tell Turner that his red lead was too bright. The excess of brightness was precisely what he sought. In the same way a 'melodramatic' rather than merely a 'dramatic' incident may be exactly what the economy of a novel demands at some particular point.

It would be irrelevant, therefore, to argue that an episode such as the storm in *David Copperfield*, or the stoning scene in *North and South*, or the sleep-walking in *Tess* should be 'toned down'. But to say that is not to deprive the critic of criteria. Turner was taking a risk with his painting: the powerful effect could have gone powerfully out of control. Another of the points of the story is that he was skilful enough to restore the balance. The painting in question, *Helvoetsluys*, is an orthodox representational seascape. Turner could only incorporate the daub of red lead by transforming it into a buoy. In one of his more abstract paintings the spot of bright colour might perhaps have been left more ambiguously defined. In Constable's *Waterloo Bridge* it would probably have been noticeable only as one element in a pattern.

It was characteristic of the stage melodrama of the period that excesses of different kinds could achieve aesthetic equilibrium. Everything depended upon the 'mix'. It was not merely that extraordinary virtue was set against extraordinary malice: there might be proportionately exaggerative friendship, conviviality, domesticity, patriotism. In particular a sardonic humour could be a powerful controlling influence. The requirements of 'realism' made it hard for a novelist to work in quite this way. (Dickens perhaps comes closest, in *The Old Curiosity Shop*, where Nell's cloying sweetness is redressed by the outlandishly sadistic jests of Quilp—but this novel, of course, is far from realistic.) Frequently, however, one extravagant episode was used to counterbalance and mitigate another. The storm scene in *David Copperfield* seems the less implausible in that it follows Peggotty's quest, the machinations of Heep and the odd death of Mr Spenlow. The reader has come to expect something larger or brighter than life. In patterning and colouring *David Copperfield* isn't unlike *Waterloo Bridge*.

An example of a 'melodramatic' episode dangerously isolated like Turner's red lead is to be found in the second Book of *Middlemarch*. It involves, in fact, a melodrama. Lydgate falls in love with a Parisian actress whom he sees murder her own husband on stage. One can grasp the kind of point Eliot wants to make and still feel that the incident is a miscalculation. *Middlemarch* up to this point could reasonably be described by the phrase Leslie uses of *Helvoetsluys*: 'a grey picture, beautiful and true'. The abrupt splash of colour seems merely garish. In the more various and energetic context of the last two books of the novel the episode would seem less crude.

A failure of a different kind is the notorious one of the murder of Jude Fawley's children. At the cost of a bad pun the view of many critics can be summarised in the comment that Hardy has failed to shape little Father Time into a boy. In this case the extravagant episode is not an isolated one. Numerous sequences in the novel have been heightened, stylised. The general critical disapprobation would suggest that the stylisation hasn't succeeded, perhaps hasn't gone far enough. Hardy's admiration for the 'mad, late-Turner rendering' is on record (F. E. Hardy, *Life*, January, 1887). Perhaps *Jude* is too close to *Helvoetsluys* and not close enough to *Rain, Steam and Speed*. The 'mix' is wrong.

A man stands by the deep waters of a weir-hole, contemplating suicide. What checks him is the extraordinary sight of his own counterpart, in life-size effigy, floating below. In summary and out of context the episode sounds grotesquely far-fetched, the coincidence too gross. Full-scale effigies are unusual phenomena. This particular one has been jettisoned in the very river in which the subject proposes to drown himself, and floats into sight conveniently on cue.

Yet when reading *The Mayor of Casterbridge* I find these 'melo-dramatic' happenings perfectly acceptable. They are, of course, causally related. In a sense it is the making of the effigy that has driven Henchard to the brink of suicide. The revellers who carried it plausibly threw it into the river at the approach of the magistrates. This is a novel of remarkable topographical solidity. The river has featured repeatedly in the narrative, and so have its two bridges, one of brick and one of stone. Henchard has been seen haunting the latter, and was in fact lingering by it, listening to the sounds of the weirs, on the night of the skimmington ride. Altogether the scene succeeds as it does partly because it is founded on certain established realities in the text.

A similar defence might be made of numerous 'melodramatic' scenes in Victorian fiction. For example the substitution of Carton for the condemned Darnay does not seem too outrageous because the physical resemblance between the two men has previously been a constituent of the plot. Dickens showed his own concern for adequate planning of this kind when rebutting Sir James Stephen's charge that the collapse of Mrs Clennam's house had been opportunistically based on 'a recent fall of houses in Tottenham Court Road'. He argued that the catastrophe of his novel had been set up long before the accident, that he had approached it 'with a painful minuteness and reiterated care of preparation' (*Household Words*, 1 August, 1857). Every serious reader of *Little Dorrit* knows this to be true. There are numerous scattered references to the decrepitude of the house and to mysterious internal noises.

But it is clear from the article as a whole, that when Dickens refers to his 'reiterated care of preparation' he has in mind something more than circumstantial plausibility. To achieve so much would be the equivalent of Turner's shaping his blob of red lead into a buoy. Leslie's anecdote suggests that Turner superimposed the patch of bright colour on a painting that was effectively complete: no buoy was needed. Dickens shows that the simultaneous destruction of Mrs Clennam's house and of Rigaud had been tacitly established as vital to the system of ideas within *Little Dorrit*. It was intended to seem an inevitable aspect of the novel's structure. In a letter to Bulwer-Lytton he puts forward a similar argument concerning a crucial chapter of *A Tale of Two Cities*.

I am not clear, and I never have been clear, respecting the canon of fiction which forbids the interposition of accident in such a case as Madame Defarge's death. Where the accident is inseparable from the passion and action of the character; where it is strictly consistent with the entire design, and arises out of some culminating proceeding on the part of the individual which the whole story has led up to; it seems to me to become, as it were, an act of divine justice.

(Forster, *Life*, Bk. 9, ch. 2)

The defence from design would need to be peculiarly strong in this case since the crucial confrontation between Madame Defarge and Miss Pross is brought about very laboriously. Dickens has the awkward task of explaining that Miss Pross remains in Paris after her mistress's departure in order that she may then precede her on her journey to the coast. The design is well enough, but it is betrayed by the execution.

The scene of Henchard's projected suicide succeeds on both levels. As Rod Edmond implies, Henchard is repeatedly forced to confront his past self, or past selves (p. 114f). The ex-Mayor draws bitter contrasts between the man he once was and the man he has become. The scene at Ten Hatches weir is an objectification of a metaphor central to the meaning of the novel. But the metaphorical effect is not achieved at too great a cost in terms of credibility.

In serious Victorian fiction, as in Shakespearian tragedy, melodrama normally functions as metaphor. The author finds a vivid equivalent for a reality too elaborate or too extended to be briefly depicted. The flood in *The Mill on the Floss* seems to me to involve an unusual kind of metaphorical failure. There have been several earlier references to the possibility that Maggie might drown; but the implication has been that this danger is merely a figure for the risks that she will run in trying to adjust to a hostile environment or to escape from it. By literally drowning her heroine Eliot turns figure into fact. The metaphor doubles back on itself and becomes meaningless. It is as though Gwendolen Harleth were to be killed in a riding accident; or—to take relevant examples from two other novelists—as though Paul Dombey, or the Stephen Dedalus of *Portrait of the Artist*, were to die by drowning.

Thomas Mann chooses to afflict various members of the Budden-
brook family with tooth decay. The unfortunate Thomas Bud-
denbrook actually dies, in effect, of tooth-ache. Now since this
ailment is in real life so rarely fatal the scene seems designed to
display, for a number of reasons too complex to summarise here,
a contradiction in fictional perspective: a character is killed by a
symbol. There is clearly no suggestion of such artifice in *The Mill
on the Floss*. George Eliot seems to round off her metaphor in default of being able to round off the life-story on which it was
designed to comment.

More characteristically the problem with 'melodramatic' metaphors is one of correspondence. The sequence concerned should
be felt by the reader, either instinctively or upon reflection, to be
faithfully equivalent to the slower, looser reality that is summarised. The 'melodramatic' flight and death of Lady Dedlock is acceptable partly because her metaphorical fate is not essentially at
variance with her prospects as more literally viewed. She can
plausibly feel herself to be hounded, humiliated, destroyed. The
chapters at issue are not a falsification but a transcription. Maggie
Tulliver's fate has no such appropriateness. It is presented as an
escape, a vindication, an answer to prayer; but it involves the
defeat of Maggie by her environment, a meaningless reconciliation
with Tom, and the extinction of the Tulliver family.

I am less concerned to argue the particular case than to make
the general point that many an episode in Victorian fiction attacked
as extravagant is defective rather as involving a failure of equival-
ence. It matters much less that little Father Time is an 'unbeliev-
able' child than that the metaphorical sequence of which he is part
distorts the problems that it purports to demonstrate.

Oliver Twist is a more comprehensive failure of this kind. The
violent indignation that Dickens arouses on Oliver's behalf, and on
behalf of poor children generally, demands a target, someone the
reader can blame. Dickens offers not one villain but four: Bumble,
Fagin, Sikes and Monks. Of these Bumble bears by far the greatest
responsibility for the wretchedness of Oliver's childhood—but he
is allowed to decline into a figure of comedy. The reader is encouraged to direct his resentment against Fagin and Sikes despite
the fact that on Dickens's own showing they must themselves have
been victims of social injustice. Monks, a figure from the melodramatic stage, has nothing to do with social problems or with the

reality of criminal London. His presence and his plotting deflect the reader's response from its original course. The novel that began with bitter social criticism ends with random sensationalism.

Dickens's later novels are very different in this respect. It is a measure of his artistic development that where anything in the activities or the personality of the main characters—Krook, say, or Mrs Clennam, or Jaggers, or Tulkinghorn—is emphatically larger than life the excess of feeling that is generated is directly relevant to the thematic purposes of the novel in question.

It was suggested that *Jane Eyre* (for example) is a totally anamorphic work, consistent in its disproportioning. A sophisticated illustrator of that novel would have to stylise every aspect of his pictures. Greater difficulties are posed by a work which is only in part anamorphic. Holbein's *The Ambassadors* is the most famous painting of this kind. In a context of scrupulous representational accuracy there is a single puzzling detail. It might be taken for a stone or a very large French loaf if either image was relevant or if the perspective made sense. Only when one squints at the picture from a very oblique angle does the disproportioning vanish and the shape transform itself into a human skull. As was not finally the case with Turner's *Helvoetsluys* the discrepant detail is left discrepant. It is of immediate interest to the viewer precisely because it cannot be assimilated into the visual experience offered by the rest of the picture. On the other hand the memento mori, once decoded, *and* the obliquity of presentation together constitute an interesting thematic comment that arguably becomes part of the picture.

It might be held that certain specific 'melodramatic' episodes in the Victorian novel function very much in this way. For example Laure's murder of her husband, in *Middlemarch*, might be felt to be deliberately extrinsic, a calculated exercise in a discrepant mode. Eliot might be telling us that the undramatic stresses of day to day life can be dramatic in their effects. Lydgate's Parisian experience is a premonition, a savage foreshortening, of his own much more leisurely destruction.[2] A similar kind of defence could certainly be devised for the flood-scene in *The Mill on the Floss*.

I acknowledge this aesthetic possibility without believing in it. If the trick works why did Holbein's picture inspire so few imitators? Recognition of the skull and its meaning, recognition of the 'correct' significance of the episode concerning Laure, seem to me to be mere appendages to the essential experience offered by the works of art in question.

I have structured this essay as a series of notes in acknowledgement of the fissility of the topic. The realist writer may use 'melodramatic' effects for a variety of purposes. A given passage of this kind may be defended or attacked from a variety of points of view. I hope at any rate to have demonstrated that to describe an episode in a novel as melodramatic, in the normal pejorative sense, is to say nothing useful about it whatsoever. The judgement implied will need justification—sometimes very complex justification. In these notes I have used a number of terms—perspective, balance, pattern, design, dynamic—that I hoped would have a useful defining force in context, but which imply very different frames of reference. A complete account of any 'melodramatic' sequence would consider all these possibilities. I thought it might be worthwhile to close with a very short (and not, therefore, exhaustive) exercise of this sort in order to isolate a more fundamental problem that the shift of mode poses for the reader.

The episode in question is the final journey of Fanny Robin. In my experience undergraduate readers dislike it. They don't find it believable at the literal level and have not been persuaded to approach it at any other. Yet the sequence can be defended in a number of the ways that have been sketched above. Fanny is in some sense a representative figure—the betrayed lover. That notion should be the more acceptable in that *Far From the Madding Crowd* provides constant reminders of relevant folk-songs and folk-tales. Hardy may well have felt the need to allot some decisive experience to this relatively minor character commensurate with the pain she has been suffering. To omit the chapter would be in a sense to slight Fanny by reducing her to a mere narrative device. And to belittle Fanny would be to diminish Troy and Bathsheba. The journey to the work-house is part of the preparation and the justification for the violent feelings that are evoked when Fanny's coffin is opened.

Nor is the extraordinary journey an isolated extravagance. Hardy constantly made use of the 'melodramatic' in nature. There are a dozen 'naturally' extreme scenes in the novel: the death of Oak's sheep, the sickness of Bathsheba's flock, the near-death of Oak himself, the rick-fire, the storm. The reader should have become acclimatised to strong effects. Moreover it is intrinsic to Hardy's fiction that his characters should be seen as part of nature. Oak's near-death is an accident similar in kind to that which destroys his flock. In a later incident his own hurt feelings are externalised in a wound he inflicts on the sheep he is shearing. Altogether the context is such that Fanny's strange fate should not seem wildly abnormal or improbable.

It could also be argued that the strong response which Hardy is striving to elicit isn't in excess of the simpler facts of the situation. Fanny is *in extremis*. A case could be made that the dog represents, in some very loose sense, the last animal instinct that, when her conscious will has failed, drags her dying body to the work-house. In other words the 'melodramatic' aspect of the scene is equivalent in scale and even, perhaps, in kind to a reality that can be deduced from it. The problem is that a reader may understand this, or be induced to understand it; may see how the episode has been landscaped into the novel, how the red lead has been shaped into a buoy—and yet may still argue that for him the chapter does not succeed. And the disagreement implied here would, I think, be a disagreement of a rather special kind.

The theatrical background provides a clue. Victorian melodrama may still be seen in our theatres occasionally, but the achievement is often slight. It is easy to make such a production enjoyable, but difficult to make it serious. The more characteristic effects are the crude ones. There will always be bad reasons, shallow reasons, for liking melodrama. What matters in the theatre, what can transform an apparently crude text into a powerful and complex theatrical experience, is the performance. Can the producer, can the actors concerned, bring it off? Many an actor who is brilliant in Chekhov or Pinter, is here at a loss.

In the partly melodramatic novel, I take it, the reader is invited to become a performer. The author helps him, prompts him, cajoles him, but it is going to be up to the reader, in a sense, to 'bring off' the death of Jo, the drowning of Maggie or the last hours of Fanny Robin. Almost by definition a 'melodramatic' sequence in a novel must leave work for the reader: work that his tastes, abilities and temperament may or may not qualify him to carry out.

NOTES

1. Peter Brooks, *The Melodramatic Imagination* (New Haven; London, 1976).
2. Stephen Lutman has pointed out to me that this scene is but one of many in Victorian fiction in which a visit to the theatre is the occasion for extravagant doings. In *Villette* Vashti's performance is the prelude to a fire. The climax of *Armadale* is preceded by the pleasing episode where Lydia Gwilt, from a stage box, recognises one of the chorus of Druids, in Bellini's *Norma*, as her former lover, Manuel. (This despite 'the flowing white beard, proper to the character.') It is at a theatre that Agnes Wickfield sees David Copperfield incapably drunk. The romantic adventures of Daniel Deronda's mother and of Mirah seems to derive from the special circumstances of stage life. 'Do you belong to the theatre?' asks Mirah, when Deronda rows up on cue to rescue her, singing an aria from Rossini's *Otello*. Other novels in which theatricals figure significantly include *Mansfield Park*, *Jane Eyre*, *Great Expectations*, and *The Return of the Native*. It's dangerous to generalise, in a footnote, about works so diverse, but one has a sense that these novelists invoke the idea of 'theatre' as a means towards stylistic heightening. They dally close to the medium that would give them greater freedom to dramatise and magnify.

2

Wilkie Collins and the Crisis of Suspense

by DAVID BLAIR

1

A recent article on Wilkie Collins[1] quotes with apparent approval a comment by Alexander Smith writing in the *North British Review* in 1863: Smith claims that in Collins's novels

> every trifling incident is charged with an oppressive importance; if a tea-cup is broken, it has a meaning, it is a link in the chain; you are certain to hear of it afterwards.[2]

This is an attractive and not uncommon half-truth: it might be detected, for instance, in what Trollope writes about Collins in his *Autobiography*:

> Wilkie Collins seems so to construct his [novels] that he not only, before writing, plans everything on, down to the minutest detail, from the beginning to the end; but then plots it back again, to see that there is no piece of necessary dove-tailing which does not dove-tail with absolute accuracy. The construction is most minute and most wonderful. . . . The author seems always to be warning me to remember that something happened at exactly half-past two o'clock on Tuesday morning; or that a woman disappeared from the road just fifteen yards beyond the fourth milestone. One is constrained by mysteries and hemmed in by difficulties, knowing, however, that the mysteries will be made clear, and the difficulties overcome at the end of the third volume.[3]

Trollope's touch of conscious exaggeration seems, however, absent from the modern critic's account of the reader's experience:

> The reader of a sensation novel engages in the discovery of an artificial pattern, and the enterprise need not teach him anything,

even anything false, about the real world. At its best, the sensation novel aspired towards the condition of a crossword puzzle, a system of language which is governed by its own design.[4]

Or as Trollope puts it less portentiously, 'I am . . . quite prepared to acknowledge that the want of pleasure [in such work] comes from fault of my intellect.'[5]

Smith, Trollope and the modern critic are all concerned to see the novel of mystery as a game requiring a distinctive sort of effort on the part of the author and a distinctive sort of attention on the part of the reader, both of which are cerebral, calculating; and this is a game, clearly, in which the relationship between detail and form is crucial. In this account, Collins, for his part, 'constructs' and 'dove-tails' (in a way which Trollope finds alien)[6] while the reader 'remembers' and 'discovers an artificial pattern'. The result is a novel whose economy of detail may be admirable but promises to be finally astringent, even crippling; there cannot thus be in a Collins novel what Rod Edmond implies for *The Mayor of Casterbridge*,[7] namely, an 'essential' structure and, I take it, a corresponding hierarchy of detail—every detail is, by Smith's claim, equally important; the novel's 'form' extends to and petrifies 'every trifling incident' and it becomes so exclusively 'artificial' as to be 'potentially subversive of the belief that fiction is and must be mimetic'.[8]

That the novel of mystery is in part a game can hardly be denied; and more modern practitioners of 'the detective novel' have tended to bring to even greater prominence the sense of the mystery as a challenge to the reader's ingenuity, as a puzzle pure and simple. But the game which Collins plays is a complex one indeed, and one which involves aspects of the novel and of 'the dynamics of reading' which extend well beyond the immediate issues of his own fiction. It is, however, to Collins and to his novel *Armadale* (1866) in particular that the present essay will return in order to focus some of the more complex and self-conscious ways in which mystery and suspense can be brought to bear upon the reader's apprehension of the novel and the relationship between form and detail.

2

Insofar as a novel presents phenomena which appear 'mysterious', it will induce the reader to ask specific questions as to an explanation, a 'solution'. The necessarily imperative nature of such questions will, it seems clear, endow any novel which depends substantially on such mystery with a particularly insistent forward dynamic—the reader will be curious, hungry for a solution: 'I know nothing, in a case of this kind, so unendurable as suspense,' writes Franklin Blake in *The Moonstone* (2nd. Period, 3rd. Narrative, ch. 1) of receiving a mysterious letter; and his impatience, like Gabriel Betteridge's recurrent 'detective-fever' in the same novel, functions in part as a mirror of the reader's own experience, his voraciousness for resolution. Such curiosity, by having a specificity to correspond to the specificity of the questions, becomes potentially a narrowness of focus, just as the form of the novel becomes particularly stark, particularly endstopped, the novel being required only to provide answers to the questions it has induced. Within such a form detail is either contributory or non-contributory, a genuine clue or a potential red herring; and such a novel, if rigorously 'dove-tailed', will indeed devour all of its own detail in the way of which Alexander Smith complains: the broken tea-cup, 'charged with an oppressive importance', will lose any 'teacupness', will become a purely intra-referential component; and the novel, will, accordingly, forfeit its mimetic functions.

Critically this may be attractive as accounting for the 'cleverness' of novels such as *The Woman in White* and *The Moonstone* and as rationalising our sense of the distinctiveness, even of the distinctive inferiority, of the sub-genre; it might even be thought of as in some sense the Platonic Idea of the mystery novel. In practice, however, no broken tea-cup, even in the most sparse of modern detective fictions, ever fails entirely of teacupness; and no reader ever reads, I would suggest, in such a sterile way. This does not secure the mystery novel as a 'serious' novel; but it does allow that, even given its distinctively self-referential and 'closed' structure, it remains, in respect of detail, vitally mimetic.

The fallacy in an argument which seeks to undermine this sense lies in the supposition that the form can control and dictate entirely to detail. On the contrary, the experience of reading novels which involve mystery frequently defies the suggestion that the novel's capacity for a resolution will correspond precisely to its capacity for suspense and that the dynamic between detail and form is purely intellectually experienced. It is, I think, characteristic of such fiction that the insistence of form cannot cancel out exactly our sense of detail.

Nor is this simply because we become involved as readers, in our irresponsible way, in the teacupness of tea-cups instead of recognising 'broken tea-cup' as merely a recurrent verbal signal; although we do this inevitably as our reading life intersects with our non-reading life, and it does endow detail with a kind of extraneous authenticity. But, more vitally, the particular conditions which mystery and suspense impose upon the novel can release an imaginative vitality, a resonance which can be made to enrich and transcend the purely circumstantial identity of detail.

This can be observed particularly clearly in Ann Radcliffe's *The Mysteries of Udolpho*. In this novel the sense of detail and the insistences of form are qualitatively distinct: form, imposing as it does solutions and resolutions, vindicates a rationality which the untutored sense of the unexplained detail—of the 'mysteries'—has undermined or, at least, has failed to arrive at. Form appears here to be intended to act retrospectively upon the heroine's, Emily's, and upon the reader's sense of the detail and to annihilate that irrational fear which might be thought of as the novel's principal incidental design upon the reader:

> Emily could not forbear smiling at this explanation of the deception, which had given her so much superstitious terror, and was surprised, that she could have suffered herself to be thus alarmed, till she considered, that, when the mind has once begun to yield to the weakness of superstition, trifles impress it with the force of conviction.
>
> (Vol. 4, ch. 14)

The reader too is likely to have been acted upon thus by trifles; but Mrs Radcliffe's novel, for all its proto-romanticism, makes the appropriate formally definitive gestures to the eighteenth-century orthodoxies. By its closing flurry of explanations, the novel seeks to 'tick-off', as it were, all the detail which seemed mysterious, and retrospectively to displace the incidental, erroneous sense of the supernatural ordering of that detail with an enlightened sense of its compatibility with a rational universe. This sense is part of the novel's formal insistence, and its confirmation marks, for the reader, the completion of the reading process.

I have met no reader of *The Mysteries of Udolpho*, however, who finds that this cancellation of the sense of detail by the arrival at a sense of form is truly effective. The displacement of the supernatural by the natural may be intellectually sound and may command a kind of assent; but it is imaginatively unsatisfying because the reader's experience of detail is not neutral, 'suspended', but is specific and alternative—he anticipates an alternative vision of the novel, even projects a delinquent sense of form such as is suggested by the life of the detail. There is thus an experience at the heart of the novel as part of the process of reading which may be renegade, but which has its distinctive validity, commands its own kind of assent—the experience which Mrs Radcliffe attempts finally to impose may be 'proper' but is imaginatively less compelling. Thus we find that the sense of mystery outlives for the reader the sense of a solution; a resonance has been released which cannot be dispelled by the novel's final and formal insistence upon rational cause and effect.

What *The Mysteries of Udolpho* suggests is how a novel, by presenting phenomena before it present resolutions, can create an on-going, perhaps spurious, but nevertheless compelling dynamic between details which can undermine the ability of form to impose its particular tyranny on the reader's experience: there is a life in the novel which comes from within. It is clearly open to an author to harness this ambivalence in order to complicate productively the resonances of the novel through a strategic manipulation of the reader's knowledge and expectations. There is a potentially arresting alternative to that voraciousness which only partly defines the reader's experience of suspense: 'detective-fever' is, after all, substantially an appetite for the process of detecting as well as for specific answers; and Collins might be seen as conceding this obliquely but vitally in *The Moonstone* by having his detective be complex, engaging and wrong, rather than simply a mechanism for revealing desired truths: Sergeant Cuff's roses constitute detail which does not, in any 'dove-tailed' way, feed into form.

The most celebrated moment in all of Collins's fiction can be seen to deploy in miniature the ambivalence which *Udolpho* demonstrates on a larger scale:

There, in the middle of the broad, bright high-road—there, as if it had that moment sprung out of the earth or dropped from

36

the heaven—stood the figure of a solitary Woman, dressed from head to foot in white garments, her face bent in grave inquiry on mine, her hand pointing to the dark cloud over London, as I faced her.

I was far too seriously startled by the suddenness with which this extraordinary apparition stood before me, in the dead of night and in that lonely place, to ask what she wanted. The strange woman spoke first.

'Is that the road to London?' she said.[9]

As in much melodrama, and as with Turner's red buoy mentioned in Michael Irwin's essay,[10] primacy is given to effect over logic: the woman is only gradually defined in relation to her surroundings. By creating a *tableau*, a moment of stasis, Collins creates 'pure' tensions, whose suggestiveness is not impinged upon by a restricting awareness of cause and context. Thus the outstretched arm, apparently pointing, in the strange two-dimensionality of the moment, to 'the dark cloud over London', exists for the reader as for the spectator in an experimental vacuum where juxtapositions are purely evocative: the woman's gesture, white towards dark, seems portentous, a warning of evils to come, and not until she asks her question is this tension released.[11] Had she attracted Hartright's attention with the question and he turned to see her thus, the effect would have been by-passed—the influence of question on gesture is reductive. Thus the suggestiveness is enjoyed and vindicated—there is an unconscious truth in the spurious, procured portentousness; and it is notable that, whereas Blake on receiving his mysterious letter was consumed with impatience, suspense being 'unendurable', Hartright is caught up, in contrast, in the pure *frisson*, the woman-in-whiteness, as it were, so that it does not occur to him to crave explanation—the experience of the detail before him is sufficiently engaging, and the enlightened self, looking back, notes the fact almost as requiring justification. For the reader, again this experience is empowered to outlive enlightenment, to evade the tyranny of cause and effect. Indeed, the whole of *The Woman in White* might be advanced as testifying to this ambiguity in the reading experience; for, as *The Times* pointed out at the time of its first publication, the crucial identification of Laura Fairlie by dating accurately her arrival in London was rendered spurious by a complex of errors and inconsistencies on Collins's part; but, as *The Times* itself conceded:

> A plot that is worked out of impossibilities, like that of robbing the almanack of a fortnight, may be treated as a jest; but we vote three cheers for the author who is able to practise such a jest with impunity. He will not have a reader the less, and all who read will be deceived and delighted.[12]

Collins himself echoed this in a letter to his publisher, Edward Marston, instructing him to stop the press pending corrections:

> Shakespeare has made worse mistakes—that is one comfort, and readers are not critics who test an emotional book by the base rules of arithmetic, which is a second consolation.[13]

If a flawed form can be treated thus lightly, perhaps the authority of all form is suspect: the 'true' experience of the novel is, perhaps, after all, the intermediate experience of detail—the delighted *ingenu* and the indignant arithmetician are confronted to the embarrassment of the latter. Thus there is a sense that *The Woman in White* has a kind of 'form' which is alternative to that which is identifiable with plot or structure, and which comprises an orchestration of experiences, evocative often precisely because prior to definitive placement—this the reader's rather than the critic's form.

3

While Collins's novels characteristically show a mastery of intricate and ingenious plotting and have all of the forward dynamic implicit in the generation of suspense, Collins consistently concedes the authority of the 'intermediate' experience of the novel, manipulating pace and broadening the novel's range. His novels are not simply precursors of modern detective fictions; they are not anything simply, but are in the great tradition of the Victorian novel in their insistent generosity. If they fail of flexibility, it is often because Collins's anticipation of the reader's potential responses appears as taut and fussed—they become too articulate about their own processes:

> Am I trifling, here, with the necessities of my task? am I looking forward to the happier time which my narrative has not yet reached? Yes. Back again—back to the days of doubt and dread,

when the spirit within me struggled hard for its life, in the icy stillness of perpetual suspense. I have paused and rested for a while on my forward course. It is not, perhaps, time wasted, if the friends who read these pages have paused and rested too.[14]

Thus again Hartright, his ingenuousness cracking under the pressure of Collins's complex rhetoric of disingenuousness which all of his narrators inherit to a greater or lesser degree.

A major aspect of Collins's constant solicitude for the reader is the provision of agents who guide, reflect and reassure him of the validity of his own responses: we have thus seen impatience and curiosity lived out in Blake and Betteridge in *The Moonstone*, a more receptive bemusement in Hartright in *The Woman in White*; and the range of examples could be extended to demonstrate Collins's consciousness of 'the crisis of pace', as it might be called, that suspense provokes. It is a crisis, as I have been suggesting, between a voraciousness which demands that detail be either vital or wholly irrelevant, and a sensitivity not only to the independent life of detail but to detail which is, to a greater or lesser degree, peripheral; and it is a crisis for the identity of the novel. It is this crisis that Collins places at the heart of *Armadale*, and the novel accordingly poses questions about its own life and identity in an extraordinarily self-conscious way.

The novel brings together improbably two heroes, both in fact called Allan Armadale, but one, the younger, under the alias of Ozias Midwinter. The climax of the novel's 'Prologue' has been the death-bed confession of Midwinter's father that he has murdered Armadale's, and the concomitant prophecy that the two sons may not meet in future life without the direst consequences ensuing; and the outcast and anonymous Midwinter, put in possession of the written account of this confession at the beginning of the novel proper, is thrown into a dilemma between the warmth and redemptiveness of his already close friendship with Armadale and the fear of the fatal consequences explicit in his father's warning. The novel's principal crux occurs, however, when this warning is apparently rendered specific in a dream which Armadale experiences and of which he sets out a written account in the form of seventeen 'points' covering three 'visions' which Midwinter takes as prefiguring his own and a woman's part in the murder of Armadale. As Midwinter asserts when the dream is discussed:

'. . . I believe that coming events will identify the Shadow of the Woman with a person whom my friend has not met with yet; and the Shadow of the Man with myself.'

(Bk. 1, ch. 5)[15]

The woman is already provided for in his father's prophesy as the unnamed young maid who, although then merely a child, played a crucial and calculating part in the events leading up to the murder —she too Midwinter must shun. In contrast, Armadale, not possessed of the murderous secret of the previous generation and therefore not prejudiced to fatalism as is Midwinter, regards the dream as unpleasant at the time but as nothing more portentous, accepting Dr Hawbury's 'medical' account which suggests the dream to have been pieced together by the sleeping mind from insignificant events of the preceding day. This is not simply a crisis of interpretation—are dreams supernatural or natural?—but, vitally for the novel, one of attitude to subsequent events: so Midwinter's experience in the novel becomes one of restless and impatient anticipation of the fulfilment of the three specific visions and a morbid scrutiny of everyone and everything which the young men encounter on their removal to Thorpe-Ambrose:

. . . he could not conquer the latent distrust of circumstances which was now raised again in his superstitious nature—the instinctive suspicion of everything that happened, no matter how common or how trifling the event, on the first memorable day when the new life began in the new house.

(Bk. 2, ch. 3)

The reader too has reason to suspect trifling events: Collins has already 'trapped' him by planting in Chapter 3 of Book 1 the apparently insignificant detail which is vitally resurrected by Hawbury in his analysis of the dream in Chapter 5. It is a game, however, that Collins never repeats; and in the novel Armadale's wholly antithetical response is assailed in vain by Midwinter's 'superstition'. Even the actual apparent fulfilment of the visions of the dream leaves no lasting impression on him as he settles into a life of eminently good-natured but fatuous inconsequence—his appetite for experience is entirely uncritical on any grounds except those of convenience and pleasure.

Clearly, in Midwinter's obsessive questioning of experience for significance and his disinterest in all that does not appear to pertain to the fulfilment of the anticipated doom the reader can find an extreme correlative for his own voraciousness for a resolution, for the impulse towards the realisation of the projected form. Nevertheless, Armadale's whimsicality is equally crucial to his developing experience not only in that it provides a less lurid colouring of detail in the novel but also in that it makes accessible entire areas of detail which are closed to Midwinter and to 'the Midwinter reader'. Thus, for example, on the first morning at Thorpe-Ambrose, Armadale rises more than an hour before Midwinter, and the reader, following him, has been brought into contact with numerous aspects of the Thorpe-Ambrose world, including Miss Milroy and her father, before Midwinter's day begins; likewise it is Armadale who devises and participates in the excursion on the Norfolk Broads, an episode of outstandingly acute comedy which is among the most memorable parts of the novel. From such areas of experience Midwinter demurs.

Midwinter and Armadale, then, enact a crisis between different 'novels'. Midwinter's is, in a classic sense, fraught with suspense—it is dark, doom-laden, sensational; Armadale's is, in contrast, a light, inconsequential social and romantic comedy. In the former, detail is perceived as 'shadowy', as in the dream, its identity curtailed by its predetermined function in the fated drama—there is in the characteristic voraciousness a reductive tyranny and a narrowness of focus; in Armadale's novel, important and unimportant details live in uncritical juxtaposition. At the Midwinter end of the spectrum detail gravitates towards the status of mere signals; at the Armadale end it has become the varied trivia of daily existence.

The duality is a classic one for any Victorian novel of suspense which seeks in any measure to retain the richness and breadth which the Victorian novel characteristically evinces. Midwinter's superstition is a 'heathen belief' (Bk. 1, ch. 2) and 'like a noisome exhalation from his father's grave' (Bk. 1, ch. 4) and his suspicion of Miss Gwilt constitutes ironically 'the one case in which that superstition pointed to the truth' (Bk. 2, ch. 10); but the reader's access to it provides the novel with its initial forward impulse —the reader's belief in artifice or plot is analogous to Midwinter's in Fate. Similarly, Armadale may be a 'booby', as Miss Gwilt is able to call him without much fear of contradiction (Bk. 3, ch. 10), but it is through his agency that the novel gains that range and variety—even that verisimilitude—which it requires.

Collins thus concedes self-consciously the range of 'readings' possible within the novel and insistently jostles the reader across the vast territory that lies between the Midwinter and Armadale poles, complicating his sense of the novel's identity: if the novel is clearly more fraught with tensions and dangers than Armadale's limited intellect allows him to appreciate, equally it is clear that it is not the novel which Midwinter's morbidity anticipates—if the visions of the dream *are* apparently fulfilled, it is not to the end which his prejudice insists upon. The dream itself, after all, in its written form, contains the seeds of its own contradiction; and the reader who gives a definitive authority to the seemingly sinister Point 15—

> . . . the Woman-shadow stood back. From where she stood, there came a sound as of the pouring of a liquid softly. I saw her touch the shadow of the man with one hand, and with the other give him a glass. He took the glass, and gave it to me. In the moment when I put it to my lips, a deadly faintness mastered me from head to foot . . .

—at the expense of the final Point 17—

> I was conscious of nothing more, till I felt the morning sunshine on my face, and heard my friend tell me that I had awakened from a dream.
>
> (Bk. 1, ch. 5)

does so only through that prejudice to which he has access through Midwinter and through his own expectations as to the kind of novel he is reading; indeed, a vital element in the 'true' identity of the novel could be thought of as being foreshadowed in the obscurity of Point 16, that 'interval of oblivion' for Armadale during which, in effect, the drama of Midwinter and Miss Gwilt is intensified and acted through to a conclusion—Armadale is, not insignificantly, asleep as the climax is enacted. The Reverend Brock's faith in divine providence may be able to project a happy ending for events—'YOU, and no other, may be the man whom the providence of God has appointed to save him', as he writes in his dying letter to Midwinter (Bk. 3, ch. 14) and the name of the ship on which father murdered father and on which Armadale has his dream may be, by an unsubtle but unremarked irony, *La Grâce de Dieu*; but such a strain of prognostication coming late in the novel and failing as it does of the specificity of the dream is unlikely to take as serious a grip on the reader's expectations and to defuse the novel—it remains a safeguard, but little more.[16] And so the reader is likely to feel finally that it is Midwinter's superstition, rather than his closing assertion that 'God is all-merciful. God is all wise.' (Epilogue, ch. 2) that is more central in defining his own experience of the novel: of all the 'projected' forms, Brock's culls least support from the apparent life and direction of the detail.

The reader in the process of reading can never wholly share the neutrality of Armadale's experience of detail because the possibility of fatality is more dominant for him than for his 'surrogate': thus suspense acts upon his experience to give 'neutral' detail colouring and resonance. The Norfolk Broads episode provides a fine example of this: while drawn in one direction towards an involvement in the pure comedy of the excursion, the reader's experience is inevitably complicated by a suspicion, which grows to certainty, that the appointment which has been made to meet up with the Milroys' new governess at the end of the afternoon at Hurle Mere is to be the fulfilment of the first vision of the dream with its 'broad, lonely pool' and 'cloudless western sky, red with the light of sunset'. This gives a wonderful richness to detail such as this, encountered as evening comes on:

> Firm as it looked, the garden-ground in front of the reed-cutter's cottage was floating ground, that rose and fell and oozed into puddles under the pressure of the foot. The boatmen who guided the visitors warned them to keep to the path, and pointed through gaps in the reeds and pollards to grassy places, on which the strangers would have walked confidently, where the crust of the earth was not strong enough to bear the weight of a child over the unfathomed depths of slime and water beneath.
>
> (Bk. 2, ch. 9)

This scenario is later to be reworked lavishly by Collins as the Shivering Sand of *The Moonstone*; and here, as there, it suggests in context a precariousness beyond that which properly it threatens; as does the growing unease and undercurrent of querulousness among the boating party against which the admirable Pedgift Junior strives in vain. Such things, of course, have their proper causes and contexts, but here they take on a new tension and suggestive colouring. Armadale may make such areas of the novel available to the reader, but his carelessness cannot dictate their tone. The reader's actual experience of the novel is going to be a complex product of his possible experiences; and this Collins clearly anticipates.

The institution of suspense and the resultant provocation of the reader to scrutiny and anticipation provides a crisis, then, for the identity and 'meaning' of individual details as for the identity and 'meaning' of form. Details which are only signals push the novel indeed towards the condition of a puzzle, a closed system; but in *Armadale* expectations which are by their nature reductive are constantly complicated or frustrated, the boundaries of the reading experience pushed beyond what impatience and 'superstition' may suggest. Armadale's uncritical appetite for detail certainly frustrates, as we have seen, Midwinter's morbidity; but it is Miss Gwilt who inherits the full burden of this crisis, so barely expressed in the initial polarity of the two heroes:

> Can I say I believe in [the Dream] too? I have better reasons for doing so than [Midwinter] knows of. I am not only the person who helped Mrs. Armadale's marriage by helping her to impose on her own father,—I am the woman who tried to drown herself; the woman who started the series of accidents which put young Armadale in possession of his fortune; the woman who has come to Thorpe-Ambrose to marry him for his fortune now he has got it; and more extraordinary still, the woman who stood in the Shadow's place at the pool! These may be coincidences, but they are strange coincidences.
>
> (Bk. 3, ch. 10)

The 'identity crisis' of the novel is, in a sense, her crisis: she is caught between, on the one hand, her apparent identity as a detail, 'the shadow of a woman', in Midwinter's cherished pattern and, on the other, her own sense of her passion and complexity. The pull which Collins has her undergo from the former (in her own and the reader's apprehension) to the latter, leading to a new, intense and wholly unforeseen crisis, is decisive in the novel—it takes her from shadowy detail to substance and takes the novel definitively beyond what the dream appears to predict. Collins bestows elaborate care on the evolution of her position in the novel: it is one from which Armadale can be despised for his fatuousness and to which Midwinter himself is drawn into a more complex identity, no longer mechanised by his fatalism into 'the shadow of a man'. The intensity of Miss Gwilt's self-determination is vital: even in arriving at the pool as the promised Shadow, she does so, we have seen through her letters, by virtue of the strength of her own motivation and Mrs Oldershaw's conspiratorial expertise, and not as the puppet of Fate. The assertion of her independent life creates from within a novel different from and richer than the novel which Fate threatens to create by patterning and manipulation: rather than form dictating the life of detail, Collins has precisely the opposite happen—the life of detail frustrates the various senses of possible or probable forms, and the novel proves to be, in some respects, a labyrinthine hoax. The life of each detail can suggest an alternative focus, the experience of each character an alternative 'novel': it is a flexibility which Collins can be seen to harness in less perplexing form in the narrative method of the two great novels, and perhaps particularly in the more highly evolved voices and the elusive, mystic centre of *The Moonstone*. Meanwhile, *Armadale* insists self-consciously on what *The Woman in White* was able to suggest more mutedly—that the final sense of the novel will be a cumulation of 'intermediate' experiences, coloured but not definitely located by the tensions which pattern and suspense provide.

4

Armadale may irritate or even bore by its insistent equivocations, but any novel which seeks to capitalise on an illegitimate, 'intermediate' sense of detail or possible form must necessarily be at best disingenuous, at worst fraudulent: *The Mysteries of Udolpho* too can be seen as a hoax.[17] The reader's complaint against *Armadale* is more likely to be that it puts its enormous flexibility to no very positive effect: the various senses of the novel aggregate in the reader's mind but do not interact to any end that would excuse the hoodwinking that is going on. It is perhaps to a novel like *Villette* that one needs to turn finally to see how subtly the 'intermediate' sense of detail can be made to provide a productive complication of response and meaning.

The creation and sustaining of the possible supernaturalism of the nun in Charlotte Brontë's novel provides a strain of 'Gothic' experience for the reader which culminates in the positively Radcliffean explanation conveyed to Lucy Snowe in Ginevra Fanshawe's letter (ch. 40) that the 'nun' has been Ginevra's lover, Hamal, disguised as the legendary phantom in order to gain safe passage to and from the school. By virtue of being Radcliffean, the explanation should cancel retrospectively the intermediate, 'suspended' sense of the figure as indeed spectral; and this circumstantially it does: the appearances of the figure in attic and garden (chs. 22, 26 and 31) are picked up and 'cancelled' in Ginevra's letter. The reader's apprehension of the nun, however, is not to be accounted for simply by the quasi-supernaturalism of the episode; rather, the distinctive *frisson* which the nun creates is the product of a complex recognition that such a 'haunting' bears upon Lucy's condition in a more significant way. The crossings of her path by the nun have occurred at moments which circumstantial explanation reveals to have been wholly accidental but which, deprived of such explanation, have seemed portentous. From the moment of the first encounter, when the figure seems an evil influence bent on poisoning Lucy's moment of romantic blessedness with Bretton's letter (ch. 22), through its subsequent manifestations until it is finally brought to Lucy's own bed as if to 'claim' her following the intensification of her isolation through her misunderstanding of the overheard conversation among her acquaintance in the park (ch. 39), the reader is likely to derive a sense that the nun functions in some sense as a kind of *alter* ego of the heroine, a projection of that capacity for self-induced and embittered sterility which is so strong and so destructive in Lucy. Such an involvement in the episode, while clearly specious, has, equally clearly, a value which is congruent with the 'meaning' of the novel and which can evade and survive demystification. And it is a sense that Charlotte Brontë procures at the expense of a considerable degree of narrative fraudulence, in spite of the wonderful capacity of her heroine's rhetoric, in the best tradition of Romantic language, for mimicking rather than recounting past experience.[18]

The loss which demystification entails for the reader of *Villette* is ultimately slight. A second reading may reinforce the wit of Charlotte Brontë's Gothic allusion, but it is equally likely to emphasise its relatively minor role in the dynamics of the novel; and an important aspect of this reinforcement is, perhaps, that it drives a wedge between the reader's perception of that wit and Lucy's consistent and, as it were, 'recurrent' hysteria—the reader's 'voice' has gained assurance and changed tone, while Lucy's has not, and we can see a certain insensitivity to shifting perspectives. An apprehension of the author's gamesomeness thus triggers a new perception of the quirkiness of the fictional voice; and a second reading confirms a constant and determining distance between that voice and the reader.

The suggestive afterlife of suspense in *The Mysteries of Udolpho*, depending as it does on an enjoyable but irresponsible emotional anarchy of which the novel as a whole at least appears to disapprove, might be thought of as evasive or disruptive—certain important moral attitudes are implicit in the form. The example of *Villette*, however, suggests how this afterlife, while by-passing eventual explanation and displacement, can feed back into the novel and even in a way substitute for form. Insofar as *Villette* is logically and 'realistically' plotted, the intermediate sense is delinquent; but insofar as it is, let us say, 'poetic', depending strongly on subjective continuities, then the supposedly 'invalid' understanding becomes an important part of the novel's overall design as well as its intermediate one. It is such a sense of coherence that the reader might miss in *Armadale*, in spite of its lavish awareness of the mechanics of suspense.

The denouement of *Villette* offers us another insight in that Lucy's final encounter with the nun, at which it is decisively exorcised, articulates obliquely a violence which seems latent in the very tension of suspense and release:

> In a moment, without exclamation, I had rushed on the haunted couch; nothing leaped out, or sprung, or stirred; all the movement was mine, so was all the life, the reality, the substance, the force; as my instinct felt. I tore her up—the incubus! I held her on high—the goblin! I shook her loose—the mystery! and down she fell—down all around me—down in shreds and fragments—and I trod upon her. . . . The long nun proved a long bolster dressed in a long black stole, and artfully invested with a white veil.
>
> (ch. 39)

The demystification is a form of attack, a dismantling. But that Lucy is thus brought into violent collision with another 'self' is interesting; for if this violence can be taken as reflecting a latent violence for the reader in the process of enlightenment, so there is a sense that that violence too is intestine, one reading 'self' being brought into conflict with another. The procedure can be as antithetical as in *The Mysteries of Udolpho*, where the rational and irrational selves glare at each other across Mrs Radcliffe's decorous equivocations; or it can be as muted as in the modulation from suspicion into certainty as the true relationships between characters are confirmed in *Bleak House*; or as startling as for Franklin Blake in *The Moonstone*, who discovers that he himself committed the crime which has so perplexed him—again a collision of 'selves', each self implying retrospectively an entirely different emphasis among the detail which has preceded. That the reader becomes divided against himself in the novel of suspense, even if only to the extent that one reading self will resist the very fact of enlightenment, let alone its specific insistences, is again the primary concession that Collins seems to make in *Armadale*, where the two Allan Armadales, the obsessive and the uncritical, seem to be two halves of a single self. Whatever truce the reader of *Armadale* or any other Victorian novel of suspense may eventually compact with himself, both 'selves' will exercise a distinctive pull on his experience; and the novel will, correspondingly, both concede and complicate its own artifice—its capacity for being merely a calculating puzzle will not, hopefully, seek to dictate to the capacity of detail for malleability and, indeed, for superfluity.

NOTES

1. Walter M. Kendrick, 'The Sensationalism of *The Woman in White*', *Nineteenth Century Fiction*, vol. 32 (1977–78), pp. 18–35.
2. 'Novels and Novelists of the Day', *North British Review*, February 1863, p. 184. Quoted by Kendrick, p. 21.
3. Anthony Trollope, *An Autobiography*, ed. F. Page (London, 1950), p. 257:
4. Kendrick, p. 21.
5. Trollope, p. 257.
6. Trollope makes this point clearer in discussing his own *The Eustace Diamonds*. See *Autobiography*, p. 344.
7. Edmond, p. 111.
8. Kendrick, p. 21.
9. *The Woman in White*, 'The First Epoch', 'The Story Begun by Walter Hartright', iii. Because of their cumbersomeness references to *The Woman in White* will be confined to footnotes.

10. Irwin, pp. 22–3.
11. The art here is perhaps comparable to that discussed in this book by Stephen Lutman in relation to the *David Copperfield* illustrations, where accidental spatial relationships between, say, the (permanent) objects in a room and the (temporary) situation of its occupants are created in a way which endows them with a dimension of necessity and significance. See for example the discussion of 'Traddles and I in Conference with the Misses Spenlow' (p. 218) and of the pointing boy in 'Our Pew at Church' (p. 213).
12. *The Times*, 30 October 1860. In Norman Page (ed.), *Wilkie Collins: The Critical Heritage* (London, 1973), p. 103.
13. Quoted in Kenneth Robinson, *Wilkie Collins: a Biography* (London, 1974), p. 136.
14. *The Woman in White*, 'The Third Epoch', 'The Story Continued by Walter Hartright', viii.
15. My references to *Armadale* follow the notation of the first and subsequent editions—Prologue + 4 Books + Epilogue: the original serial in *The Cornhill Magazine* was in 5 books, the first comprising what subsequently became the Prologue.
16. The specificity of the reader's possible anticipations is crucial in defining the 'fiction of suspense' and in defining suspense against, let us say, a less urgent interest or curiosity as to how a fiction will proceed. A specific anticipation will have a more powerful hold on the imagination in that it will relate more particularly to elements already present to the reader's experience: thus the third vision of the dream in *Armadale* is easier and more inviting to project than a vatic pronouncement that all will turn out well (somehow) in the end: it gains imaginative assent. The ultimate example of this is a fiction with a corpse and six suspects: any 'projected form' must imply a specific rearrangement of relationships between these elements; the author must not produce a resolution by introducing a new and unforeseen villain although he will and must shift the balance of specific probabilities: the reader must feel that he is in possession of the solution.
17. Such fraudulence is implicit in the creation of suspense, whether directly authorial or transferred to a narrator, and Kendrick (*art. cit.*, pp. 34–5) accuses Collins of being little better than Glyde and Fosco. But Collins at least brings the problem out into the open by having his narrators explicitly contracted to an editor to tell only what they knew at the time: as a result there is a constant 'had I known then what I know now' tone to the narratives; and in *The Moonstone* Betteredge and Miss Clack both register regret or protest that they cannot use their retrospective knowledge and Miss Clack actually enters into a correspondence with the editor, Blake, on this subject. Collins claims in the 'Preamble' to *The Woman in White* and elsewhere that this method is used in the interests of clarity, but it in fact operates in the interests of strategic obfuscation.
18. The 'fraudulence' in *Villette* is particularly pointed and potentially discomfiting in Chapter 22, when the 'nun' is first encountered in the

grenier. Here Lucy's necessary retrospective knowledge that the nun is no nun is suppressed in a barrage of rhetoric. I am thinking particularly here of the retrospective switch over the letter—'Dr John, you pained me afterwards . . .'—which actually emphasises that such knowledge is available to the 'voice'—and of the three juxtaposed questions—'Are there wicked things. . . ? Are there evil influences. . . ? What was near me. . . ?'—which follow and lead up to the 'sighting'. A second-time reader might feel that the 'truth' of Lucy's experience was being given a slightly unfair hold over the 'voice's' responsibilities to its auditors.

Interchapter 1

The two preceding essays seek to initiate the underlying debate in this book because melodrama, and to a lesser extent suspense, offer, in miniature, an intensification of the way any novel is structured. They also suggest a kind of latitude and longitude within which the reading response operates. Melodrama as Michael Irwin uses the term, with its emphasis on local effects and energies, lends itself as a synecdoche for the way in which a novel gravitates into episodes. Suspense underlines the trajectory of the novel, its essential sequentiality.

When we begin to look at the criteria for success in these modes, discussion opens up. Michael Irwin's essay argues that melodrama succeeds when it establishes equivalences, when, vivid as the detail may be (Turner's red blob), it can be re-assimilated so that an aesthetic equilibrium is established (the blob becoming a buoy). What about suspense? We can make a comparison with being aboard ship. The travellers may have widely different attitudes to the voyage, varying from those most conscious of their destination to those for whom the pleasure lies more in the agreeable duration of the journey than its completion. Suspense, like travel, is best enjoyed when some happy blend is struck between the varying attitudes—so that even the most purposeful of travellers may enjoy the incidental pleasures of the journey, even those most willing to be detained by the pleasures of the cruise, take satisfaction from onward movement and the prospect of arrival. Suspense can be successfully created in a variety of ways—but a common element in that variety is that moment when we are made to feel, in a sharp and pleasing way, an interlinking between the immediate pleasure and the total design.

'We are made to feel'—that is the phrase that we find melodrama and suspense encouraging us to write again and again. The text seeking the help of the reader to bring it off, seeking a natural completion beyond itself. Here we are in the presence of that

51

element of volatility which though considerably heightened in a consideration of melodrama and suspense, is a central element in all our reading of fiction.

We can see this more clearly if we turn to a literal dramatisation of the relationship between the text and the reader. It is Dickens reflecting on his readings as a public performer:

> When I first entered on this interpretation of myself (then quite strange in the public ear) I was sustained by the hope that I could drop into some hearts, some new expression of the meaning of my books, that would touch them in a new way. To this hour that purpose is so strong in me, and so real are my fictions to myself, that, after hundreds of nights, I come with a feeling of perfect freshness to that little red table, and laugh and cry with my hearers, as if I had never stood there before.
>
> (Dickens to Robert Lytton: 17 April 1867)

'Some new expression of the meaning of my book'—Dickens seems to see his novels as palimpsests, the text at once secreting and revealing fresh meanings in the context of each encounter with it. The occasion writes large what is usually writ small; namely, that reading is 'an elaborate and ever shifting construct made up of diverse elements'; the physicality of the book, type, binding, layout, illustrations; a text, a storehouse of feelings and reflections; a reader, marked by temperament, self-conscious about his own activity. Moreover, public reading, which so often finds in melodrama and suspense its characteristic material, dramatises in a particularly vivid way the kind of trust that must be created between reader and writer, if the text is to be successfully conveyed. It is a trust diffused by the text— bringing assurance that the author has found 'a voice' for his fiction and his reader 'a voice' for communicating it.

The emphasis on the importance of the reader's role must inevitably raise a worry about making the experience too subjective an affair, *too* much a matter of individual temperament. We must, however, make some discriminations. In the middle of a reading, if asked for a reaction, we can only offer unformulated expressions of liking or disliking, our immediate experience being, almost of necessity, too confused and perplexing. The impulse to talk about a text is provoked precisely by that confusion, we want to know what has happened to us. When we discuss a novel it is only partially to hear another person's 'view', it is much more to find out what we ourselves think *in order to possess the text more completely*. Such a possession is then a composite one, it is the book itself *and* the articulated reaction to it. So vivid can be the latter that it is not uncommon to find that the pleasure survives the cause; some novels seem more enjoyable to talk about than to read.

When we seek public expression for our reactions we usually find we are in need of a *persona*, which for convenience, we call 'the reader'. That *persona* may, or may not, have a close relationship with the actual reader. If 'the-reader-in-an-essay' speaks invariably in the imperative mood—'the reader *must* feel,' '*must* be aware', '*cannot* fail to notice',—it is not because he is assuming a prescriptive account of how the novel should be read, but because he wishes to dramatise the directions of his engagement with the activity in hand. It is a rhetoric of persuasion for a specific occasion. The present instance is with the immediacy and fluidity of the exchange between writer and reader, and in underlining that, melodrama and suspense provide a critic with valuable bearings.

3

'Bound in Moss and Cloth': Reading a Long Victorian Novel

by GRAHAM CLARKE

1

Once upon a time there lived in Berlin, Germany, a man called Albinus. He was rich, respectable, happy; one day he abandoned his wife for the sake of a youthful mistress; he loved; was not loved; and his life ended in disaster.

This is the whole of the story and we might have left it at that had there not been profit and pleasure in the telling; and although there is plenty of space on a gravestone to contain, bound in moss, the abridged version of a man's life, detail is always welcome.

Nabokov's deceptive story-like opening to *Laughter in the Dark* makes the reader peculiarly aware of the fiction he is about to enter and creates an uneasy (and problematic) relationship between the 'whole story' told to us in forty-four words and the 'welcome detail' to follow in the remaining one hundred and eighty or so pages. While the reader may know the story, he has committed himself to reading and following the fiction through to its end; one that he knows will, in turn, be an 'abridged version' of Albinus's life. As the opening announces, the fiction, whether 'bound in moss' between the dates on a tombstone or 'bound in cloth' (or paper) between the covers of a book, can never be final but is rather a process created in and limited by the space of the pages to follow. Rarely, upon opening a Victorian novel, does the authorial voice question the veracity of the fictional world in the way that Nabokov does here. Rather, the characteristic 'welcome detail' of such novels assumes a necessary spatial and temporal freedom which gives way to an almost innate dependence on length, size, and *bulk*.[1] If the opening to *Laughter in the Dark* makes the reader conscious of the arbitrary nature of the fiction in a way that Dickens for example, does not, it also makes him aware of the way that the length of a novel affects the way he reacts to it in the reading process; his approach to it and his expectations of it as a reading experience. My interest in this essay is to suggest how a reader's response to what I want to call the 'long Victorian novel', is affected by length and how it determines the kind of fictional experience that such novels encourage and engender. Length, I want to suggest, has a peculiar significance for the reader of a Victorian novel and especially so if we are concerned with an awareness of it as a *book*; a physical object held in the hands. Clearly, there are different kinds of length just as there are different kinds of long novels and I am not suggesting that it is a quality peculiar to the Victorian period. *Don Quixote* and *Tom Jones* are as long as anything by Dickens, Eliot, Trollope or Thackeray just as are any number of twentieth-century novels. And yet the fictional assumptions inherent in Victorian fiction and the reading experience that they evoke distinguish length as a critical factor which deserves more attention than our accounts are usually willing to admit. A more conscious awareness of it will help us towards a more open sense of what it *feels* like to read a Victorian novel.

In *Villette*, Lucy Snowe, after receiving a letter from Dr John opens it to establish its size, its length: 'Will it be long—will it be short?' she asks, to find, with relief, that 'it was long.' Only afterwards does she begin to read, to find out whether its tone and content are 'cool' or 'kind'. Before this Lucy had simply fingered the envelope to establish the *thickness* of the package. Her expectations rise when she discovers that 'it felt, not flimsy, but firm, substantial, satisfying.'[2] Lucy's reaction is a telling one, for it is a commonplace in our reading experience that the physical nature of a book is intimately connected with the pleasure—or dislike—that it stimulates; of the expectations and anticipations we have in relation to its size and thickness. And yet that sense of 'firm, substantial, satisfying' marvellously evokes the feel of a Victorian novel; the object as an equivalent token for the world of the book. To read Dickens, for example, in a nineteenth-century edition is to be aware of its physical and fictional bulk; the book itself seems appropriate to the fictional experience, to its Victorianness.

For a reader like Lucy, James's description of nineteenth-century novels as 'large, loose, baggy monsters' would be far from a negative one, for it is wonderfully suggestive of the kind of fictional energies, the reading experience that such novels offer and create. Their dependence on and encouragement of largeness and looseness are qualities fundamental to their peculiar nature; qualities which seek a density and thickness that we rightly recognise as Victorian. Surely, central to our reading of them is an awareness of patterned imaginative energies which, unlike Nabokov's skeletal beginning, acquire and eschew printed space, of verbal structures that commit themselves openly to length. Yet, as distinct from their eighteenth- and twentieth-century counterparts, they both use and require length to portray, to the reader, an adequate and achieved image of a social world that they explore, inhabit, and, in the greatest of them, imaginatively control and transcend. Their subject matter demands that the author assume fictional perspectives which, seemingly, create an ever expanding canvas through which a 'substantial' and 'satisfying' sense of the novel's world is given to the reader. The 'welcome detail' is not a question of padding (although at times we might reserve our judgement), it is an integral component of the novel's texture, of the reading experience it seeks to offer.

Certainly 'length', in the way I have been suggesting, can be seen as one of the positive aspects of the reading experience, of the novel's design and effect upon the reader. It makes of it more than a casual factor in our approach, of so many pages to be read. When Morris, for example, has a character in *News From Nowhere* declare that his 'story' will be 'short' even though it could be 'spun out into a long one, as used to be done with such subjects in the old novels'[3] the attempt is to deliberately reduce the way length is used in, say, Dickens or Eliot. Morris's jibe, its narrowness, sees length only in terms of 'story' and of the author spinning words onto the page in order to fill the available space. It is more appropriate to the world of Reardon in *New Grub Street*[4] than to the long novels of Dickens or Eliot. The distinctive achievement of novels like *Bleak House* and *Middlemarch* is an expanding density and complexity towards the creation of a realised and felt fictional world. Their imaginative breadth demands both a spatial freedom and temporal capacity equal to the creative intention. Indeed, such novels are impossible to think of as having *less* pages—their particular essence, the alchemy of effect, lives precisely in their thickness and bulk.

Much of this effect lies in the *detail* that such novels give the reader. It is what Pevsner, in speaking of mid-nineteenth-century English painting has called the 'accurate rendering of observed life',[5] a characteristic, surely, of the particular reading experience that so many long Victorian novels evoke. Indeed, to think of the Victorian novel as a painting from the period suggests a sense of length in the way I am concerned to define it. Frith's *Paddington Station* (1862) and *Derby Day* (1858), for example, may be seen as offering a visual equivalent of a long Victorian novel's composite achievement. To look at these paintings is to feel a realised and defined image of the totality of a novel's effect, of the reading experience. They reveal a detail, variety, and comprehensiveness redolent of Dickens. It is as if the temporal process of turning page after page has been caught and transmuted into a single, but complete, picture of the novel's subject: its size and imaginative space flattened and opened out into a massive, but conclusive 'page'. Yet, as we read them, both paintings deny a single perspective on the subject, an easily determined structure or focal point for the reader to settle upon. Their very length forces the eye to move from detail to detail, character to character, scene to scene, and story to story. The complexity and multiplicity of effect, while held together by large structural motifs and experienced 'serially', emerges as a shaped and achieved image of nineteenth-century English society; an image compounded by the very *length* of the paintings themselves. Indeed, they give the impression of being limited only *by* their frames and yet their veracity, their presence and effect, is dependent on the length and space that Frith has available for the depiction of his subject. The panoramic sequence, the long canvas are used to create an appropriate fulness, a 'bulk' whose effect is held, finally, in the *size* of the object itself—the painting or book whose silent sentience awaits the movement of the eye over and through it. The reward, and the experience, is the encompassing of an Englishness caught within the substance of the artifact: a social landscape that we rightly recognise as 'Victorian'.

Clearly, such a landscape demands length and space in which the artist can indulge the propensity for detail and solidity of effect; qualities distinctive, in different ways, of Eliot, Dickens,

Thackeray, and Trollope. The intention, as with Frith, is the creation of a fictional world equal to the novel's task. Length and thickness are used to define and make knowable the nature of a society through a language which constructs an equivalent physical and social reality 'on the page'. Consider, for example, the opening two paragraphs of *Bleak House*:

> LONDON. Michaelmas Term lately over, and the Lord Chancellor sitting in Lincoln's Inn Hall. Implacable November weather. As much mud in the streets as if the waters had but newly retired from the face of the earth, and it would not be wonderful to meet a Megalosaurus, forty feet long or so, waddling like an elephantine lizard up Holborn Hill. Smoke lowering down from chimneypots, making a soft black drizzle, with flakes of soot in it as big as full-grown snowflakes—gone into mourning, one might imagine, for the death of the sun. Dogs, undistinguishable in mire. Horses, scarcely better; splashed to their very blinkers. Foot passengers, jostling one another's umbrellas in a general infection of ill temper, and losing their foot-hold at street corners, where tens of thousands of other foot passengers have been slipping and sliding since the day broke (if this day ever broke), adding new deposits to the crust upon crust of mud, sticking at these points tenaciously to the pavement, and accumulating at compound interest.
>
> Fog everywhere. Fog up the river, where it flows among green aits and meadows; fog down the river, where it rolls defiled among the tiers of shipping and the waterside pollutions of a great (and dirty) city. Fog on the Essex marshes, fog on the Kentish heights. Fog creeping into the cabooses of collier-brigs; fog lying out on the yards and hovering in the rigging of great ships; fog drooping on the gunwales of barges and small boats. Fog in the eyes and throats of ancient Greenwich pensioners, wheezing by the firesides of their wards; fog in the stem and bowl of the afternoon pipe of the wrathful skipper, down in his close cabin; fog cruelly pinching the toes and fingers of his shivering little 'prentice boy on deck. Chance people on the bridges peeping over the parapets into a nether sky of fog, with fog all round them, as if they were up in a balloon and hanging in the misty clouds.

The first word, 'London', announces the initial 'canvas' of the novel. Dickens turns the noun into a verb and uses the full stop and capital letters to hold within them the immensity and complexity of the novel's action and scope as the omiscient voice of the author assumes an aerial perspective in an all-knowing, all-seeing process. The reader, like the Chancellor, may be sitting, but the syntax moves outwards and beyond in an encompassing inclusiveness at it moves towards its primary verbal icon: London, England, 'Bleak House'. While, as with Frith, the material is held together by large structural motifs, the realisation of this physical and social world is, once again, dependent upon length; a plenitude of detail, character, and scene which offers the reader an equivalent experience of that world. Thus, in the sequence here, objects have a tangibility, an extension and solidity that gives them a weight and place within the text. We do not come upon them as symbols; rather, there is an assumed relationship between word and thing which, through the accretion of language, seeks a world of nouns and objects—the *density* of the novel's texture.

Length, however, assumes a further (and crucial) aspect in a novel like *Bleak House* in what it reveals about the relationship between author and text, text and world, which allows the writer to seek the totality of his vision, a moral vision which impinges upon the reader through the novel's capacity for proliferation, voraciousness, and density. Like Frith, the novelist assumes that his art can fathom and define a particular social fabric and forge relationships between private and public worlds. *Bleak House* may begin with fog and it may be a mystery story, but its declared intention is towards clarity and definition, finding and revealing the connections between the 'tens of thousands' of people who, in the opening passage, move unknowingly about the chaos of London. The novel's task, like Inspector Bucket's, is to go into the well of its society, to move through a world others cannot enter or understand. It leads the reader out of the fog and gives meaning and shape to the puzzle. The author's omniscience places him at the centre of this knowable world just as space and length allow him to imaginatively possess it. Clearly, such a process distinguishes the typical Dickens novel from, say, *Moby Dick*. Where Dickens uses length to build, so Melville uses it to break-up any fixed sense of a fictional world in the reader's mind. Equally, it is what distinguishes a novel like *Bleak House* from *The Pickwick Papers*. The picaresque perspectives of *Pickwick* use length to keep the adventure going, allowing Dickens to meander and digress at will just as Pickwick does on his travels through England.

Isn't this distinction, this sense of the novel's task, what James so admired when he declared that *Middlemarch* was a 'picture—vast, swarming, deep-coloured';[6] a view echoed by Eliot when she announced that: 'I don't see how I can leave anything out, because I hope there is nothing that will seem to be irrelevant to my design. . . .'[7] The novel's capaciousness spreads, like the Frith examples, into a patterned complexity necessary to its intention. Dickens's density may be the teeming solidity of an urban world; Eliot's is a gradual and subtle moral patterning which extends over the surface of England. In Eliot we move through a natural and social landscape of town and country, of historical process in space and time, whose perspective announces a canvas so large that England itself is to be encountered and subsumed into the creation of a 'felt' life. The intention, as she makes clear in *Middlemarch*, is to make known the 'intimate relations' of a 'living structure' (ch. 15). Clearly such a premise demands length and space for everything *is*, potentially, material for the novel if it is to achieve any genuine breadth and panoramic inclusiveness. The early critic who suggested that had Eliot 'left out the secondary characters' *Middlemarch* 'would have been half the length'[8] ignored and misread how crucial such qualities are to the reading experience that the novel offers. They form part of the 'finer texture' of the novel's substance; a landscape adequate to 'a study of provincial life'.

2

The Victorian novel, then, assumes through its length the possibility of a completed and enclosed fictional world. The reading experience, through a linear and sequential development will be, quite obviously, distinct from, say *Ulysses* or *Finnegans Wake*. It is what Josipovici has called the 'swelling continuity' of Victorian narrative, a form which encourages a particular kind of reading response:

> Reading an intricately plotted nineteenth-century novel is very much like travelling by train. Once one has paid for one's ticket and found one's seat one can settle down in comfort and forget all everyday worries until one reaches one's destination, secure that one is in good hands.[9]

The narrative conventions encourage the reader to 'settle down', just as those 'good hands' suggest an implicit faith in an authorial voice which offers ease and comfort. There is almost a sense of paternal wisdom which moves beyond omniscience. Our faith in the 'security' of the text relies precisely on that welcoming attitude which invites us into its 'warmth'. The reader can relax and look forward to a reading experience unimpeded by fragmentation, compression, or ambiguity. As a travelling companion the author, and the text, will rarely involve the reader in any kind of compromising discussion. We can, literally, put the book in our pocket and take it out when we want a 'good read'. Unlike Nabokov's conscious duplicity the reading will be enclosed within a fiction that moves reassuringly towards its inevitable 'safe' end. Rarely are we asked to question the nature of the fiction, or of the way we read, as Fowles does in *The French Lieutenant's Woman*. There the reading experience is of a calculated 'mix' between a deceptively safe Victorian narrative and its undercutting by the author. The reader is led into a false ease which Fowles clearly intends him to question. Dickens, in contrast, allows the reader to indulge in his fiction, in its detail and length, safe in the knowledge that the fat book in the hand is a friend he will come to know and trust as he moves through it on his journey.

Yet if the metaphor of the train journey suggests the assumptions we make about long Victorian novels, of what we expect from them, and of the way we approach them, it surely doesn't adequately convey the variousness of the individual reading experience, of the fluctuating response that the reader has to a text during the time he spends with it. Of course our general sense of a novel works through a linear and expanding reading experience but the magic playfulness between eye and word, reader and page, between what has been read against what remains to be read, exists in a more shifting, ineffable, and relative state of flux than the rather linear and static metaphor of the journey implies. Our awareness of a developing structure and determined progress through a novel is caught, affected, and changed in relation to the shifting psychological relationship that the reader undergoes as he moves through 'all those pages'. Every journey is uneven, and while we may take pleasure in its length, comfort, and ease we inevitably alter our mood during it (we will be bored, tired, excited, impatient, and irritable) just as the landscape through the window, or the companion in the compartment will vary in their claims upon our attention. Indeed, it is surprising the extent to which this reaction on the part of the reader is generally ignored in our critical accounts of a novel's effect. We rarely seem to consider how our sense of a novel is affected by moments (or periods) of boredom, impatience or downright frustration. Rather, we speak as if the novel extracts from us an invariable pitch of attention and involvement, of concentration and excitement.

Clearly some novels, in retrospect, will evoke a sense of constant expansion and imaginative activity. We all have texts that we were unable to 'put down'. And yet with the long Victorian novel to ignore an inevitable lapse or variation in our reading response is surely to do violence to the true nature of the original reading experience. With a long novel the sheer length of the journey, of the time it takes, makes this shifting relationship unavoidable. Quite obviously the mood in which we take up the text will often alter and determine our reaction to it and yet clearly the novel itself will create a change of mood in us—will encourage a sense of boredom, mental tiredness, and irritability. As against an episode in the novel which offers a sudden increase in pace, a sudden but distinctive melodramatic scene or sequence, or the reappearance of a 'favourite' character, the reader might find himself in an area of flatness where his attention is drawn more to the number of the page, of the pages still to go, rather than the narrative landscape. Our boredom at such points, our awareness of the novel as a book rather than a fiction, can engender a feeling of frustration where its length becomes so much space and time to be filled and traversed. Our concentration wavers and wanders:

> Pay attention to it, or you will be all aboard, when we get deeper into the story. Clear your mind of the children, or the dinner, or the new bonnet, or what not. Try if you can't to forget politics, horses, prices in the city, and grievances at the club. I hope you won't take this freedom on my part amiss; it's only a way I have of appealing to the gentle reader. Lord! haven't I seen you with the greatest authors in your hands, and don't I know how ready your attention is to wander when it's a book that asks for it, instead of a person.[10]

Collins here directly appeals for the reader's attention, warning him that he must concentrate on the narrative. Yet there is a peculiar sense here as if the author knows that his reader might be bored, that he must nudge him back into the text. Indeed, and particularly in *The Moonstone*, Collins reveals a peculiar awareness of how a reader might *feel* as he moves through the novel. It is as if he admits the impossibility of the author creating an even tempo and intensity of effect and interest, just as it is impossible for the reader to always 'pay attention' through such a mass of pages and detail. Invariably a long novel will fall away into flat or flagging areas which, initially at least, have the effect of disrupting and distorting the reading experience. Like James we have all felt an 'occasional tendency to skip' as we seek a turn in narrative pace, a climactic moment to recharge and refocus our involvement with the text.

But we should not be too dismissive of such 'flat' areas or of our reaction to them. One of the great strengths of the long Victorian novel is that it can consciously create a pattern of variable intensity within the accumulative density of its effect. Inevitably so much of a novel's texture is lost, its 'finer detail' reduced to a vague shadow that we place against our memory of particular passages that have been marked by the pencil. It is these, invariably, to which we return when, in retrospect, we seek to shape the novel for ourselves. Yet surely, if we are to remain faithful to the novel's patterned movement and to our original reading experience, we should remember that such passages and episodes exist within the expanding flux of its six or eight hundred pages. Not to be aware of the space and (reading) time that surrounds them is to distort their place within the novel's overall timbre. Flat areas are quite crucial to a long novel's life; its high points depend for their very resonance on the space that the author (and reader) has at his disposal, high points that retain their sincerity precisely because of a variable pace and pitch within the reading experience. It is this aspect of the Victorian novel that Barbara Hardy has called its capacity to suggest 'the ordinary life between crises', the 'necessary illusion of a slow movement of time and a natural unfolding of character and action.'[11]

And yet this variation in pace and tone equally works towards the reader's sense of variety and complexity. As the fiction seeks largeness and looseness so its energies refuse, more and more, to be caught or fixed into a final form within the reader's mind. The

c

63

pattern of the novel constantly changes as the reader moves through it. The complex plots of, for example, *Vanity Fair* and *Little Dorrit* fall away from the memory just as, by the end of *Bleak House*, we cannot recall the names of all the characters or place each of the scenes in a distinctive sequence. But isn't this part of the process? Like the Frith paintings, there is a sense in which the substance of the novel in the reader's mind has been achieved through the overwhelming proliferation of detail, character, and scene— a temporal and relative experience that we carry with us as we move through it. It is the general *effect* that these novels have upon their readers; an alchemical solidity and sureness so that we rightly speak of an author's *world*, an imaginative texture which retains an innate existence and immutability of its own.

The question of length, then, is a complex one and involves aesthetic, critical, physical, and psychological aspects that are further complicated by the conventions of the genre itself. And yet if one is concerned to establish its credence in the individual reading process it seems inevitable that we should ask ourselves how a Victorian reader might have viewed a 'long' novel as he moved through it. It is with this in mind that I want to look briefly at *Wuthering Heights* which, while not a long novel in itself, offers us a dramatic example of a reader 'reading'. Lockwood is not only the narrator, to us, of Heathcliff's story, he is also the listener, (or *reader*) of Nelly Dean's narrative, a narrative which he approaches as a book. Indeed, Lockwood reveals to us how and why he reads and while his position involves, inevitably, questions about his role as narrator, his relationship to Dean's narrative tells us much about the way a 'novel' is received and restructured in the mind of the reader. It is almost as if Lockwood is the reader who is 'himself a novelist'.[12] He creates, distorts, and distills a form of the original narrative in his own mind, through his own voice.

Dean's narrative, then, may be seen as a long text and her subject, like Nabokov's, as the 'abridged version' of a man's life. In this sense the beginning of her 'story' is like Lockwood opening a book at its first page taken up, as he tells us, out of boredom and loneliness. Lockwood, the reader, clearly wants to be entertained, to escape into the 'novel'. Like Nabokov, Dean declares in the opening sequence that she could tell her story, 'all that you need know' in half a dozen words (ch. 7) but Lockwood insists that she tell it slowly and 'minutely' for this is the method he likes:

You've done just right to tell the story leisurely. That is the
method I like; and you must finish in the same style. I am interested in every character you have mentioned, more or less.

(ch. 7)

Lockwood encourages the development of length and detail, he
wants a long novel. And thus he continues to read his 'neighbour's
history' at different sittings which, in turn, he relates to us as a
'little condensed'. This accumulative sense of Lockwood's reading
creates a wonderful awareness of a novel being read, reflected upon
and restructured in the reader's own mind: a process which, in
Lockwood's case, involves boredom, memory, and even physical
and mental tiredness. At the end of Chapter nine, for example,
he decides to close the story (book) for the night:

> At this point in the housekeeper's story, she glanced towards the
> time-piece over the chimney, and was in amazement, on seeing
> the minute-hand measure half-past one. She would not hear of
> staying a second longer—in truth, I felt disposed to defer the
> sequel of her narrative myself; and now that she has vanished to
> rest, and I have meditated for another hour or two, I should
> summon courage to go also, in spite of aching laziness and limbs.

He leaves the next 'chapter' until the morning when, once again,
out of a sense of listlessness and boredom he recalls the 'chief
incidents' and resumes 'reading'. The story is not received at one
sitting and his relation to it, as the reader, varies as much with
the way he feels as does his interest in the subject. What we have
is the sense of a book being taken up and put down, of being
opened and closed and as it is opened so the energies of the text
are put in motion to reveal the complex *frisson* and magical fluidity of the novel's verbal patterns which holds so much of its inde-
finable nature. A mercurial tension is created in the space between
Lockwood's reaction to Dean's story and the original text: her
narrative behind Lockwood's version.

The final sense is of a tension between the 'whole story' and the
'detail'; between a book, fixed and bound, and the imaginative
space of the opened and turned pages. And so Lockwood completes
his reading yet by 1802, when he returns to the area, he admits
that the details are 'dim and dreamy'. How appropriate then, that
at the end of *Wuthering Heights*, after hearing (or reading) a
sequel to the original story, we have Lockwood looking at Heath-

cliff and Cathy's tombstones, the detail now 'bound in moss' and the book closed; surrogate tokens holding within them the energies of the text itself.[13]

3

Lockwood's position in *Wuthering Heights* suggests much about the process of reading a 'long' novel and the extent to which time, memory, attention, and the way the reader creates his own text all play a part. Yet if the story had been received at a single sitting how different the sense of it would have been, for Dean's tale is essentially a long one in the time sequence it covers, the detail it involves, and the complexity of its substance just as in the time it takes to tell (or be read). But to think of long Victorian novels simply as single books is to ignore the original reading experience that they offered the Victorian reader. As Tillotson has shown, the 'publication of a new novel in one volume was rare.'[14] Novels would be published in two or three volumes which displaces our usual sense of the novel as a single object. We may finish a volume but we have not necessarily finished the novel. But clearly of more significance for the reading process is the extent to which so many major Victorian novels were first published (and written) as serials.[15] What developed was a very different relationship between author and reader, reader and text than the kind when we hold the finished work 'in our hands'.

Without a book before him the reader could not fix a sense of the novel in his mind, could not measure, as Lucy did her letter, his awareness of the novel in relation to its thickness, its size, or of the pages still to be read. With the serial form the novel as an object is dissolved and any spatial relationship made fluid and diffuse because the reader could not look ahead or contemplate the novel as a whole. Indeed, and crucially so, the serial form took the control of the novel away from the reader and left him in an *imagined* space that could not be thought of in terms of the physical space still to be read. At the end of each instalment the reader would contemplate a vacuum, an 'end' which looked forward to a continuing verbal space which he could not measure. He might speculate but he could not know. Although, as Tillotson admits, the Victorian novelist intended his novels to be 'read and reread in book form'[16] much of the timbre, tone, and original energy of the fictional process is quite dependent on the serial form. It encouraged a reading experience lost upon the modern reader when he confronts those thick, almost brick-like paper-back editions in which he is most likely to read Dickens and Thackeray.

Yet how can the modern reader possibly recover the original kind of relationship, the original reading experience that the serial form created? How different a sense of a novel's 'meaning' is one given if you share in, say, a Dickens novel taking shape over some eighteen months, of reading one instalment and of having to wait perhaps a month for the next? What happens to the 'finer detail', the continuity, with that kind of time span? The modern reader rarely, if ever, comes upon a long Victorian novel like this. More often than not his experience of the novels will be in a rapid sequence of parts, of great gulps, perhaps two or three hundred pages at a time which clearly alters the original 'feel' of them. Even in many modern editions serial endings are not indicated so that the reader passes on, unaware of the break, the gap that ex-isted for the Victorian. A relationship to the text which depended on a slowly developing sense of the novel is lost in a rapid move-ment through it in a form and at a speed that was not the original intention of reading them. With a much slower pace the reader had to let what had been read settle in his mind and achieve a more leisurely proportion and shape. Keith Carabine's attempt to read *David Copperfield* 'serially' is an important one for at least something of the original reading pattern is restored.[17] Perhaps the nearest the modern reader can come to this sense of a novel's development is in the recent television serialisation of nineteenth-century novels. To follow those is to take part in a public event, to comment upon them and to live with them as we are forced to wait a week before we know 'what happens next'.[18]

It is, then, impossible for the modern reader to enter fully into the kind of relationship between reader and text, reader and author that serialisation created; but we can sense some of the feeling that developed as the novels took shape and achieved their form. Dickens, for example, in his 'Preface' to the first edition of *Nicholas Nickleby* (1839) speaks for both himself and the reader when he announces his 'feeling of regret' after leaving a 'pursuit that has long occupied our thoughts' and that on the first of next month (his readers) may miss his company at the accustomed time as something which used to be expected with pleasure; and think of the papers which on that day of so many past months they have read, as the correspondence of one who wishes their happiness, and contributed to their amusement.

Again, in the 'Preface' to *Martin Chuzzlewit* (1844) Dickens 'lingers' after reaching the end 'anticipated through twenty months, yet sorrowfully penned at last. . . .' Time and time again there is a sense of a performance and friendship coming to a close, of a final curtain that neither reader or author wants. It is remarkable how often Dickens refers to his novels as a journey where the participants have developed a bond to be broken once they leave the travelling compartment. It is, most obviously, the emotional tenor we miss here, of an event shared that we can no longer partake of. But it isn't just this, for in coming upon these novels 'cold' we miss much of the original sense of exploration, of creating 'form' that author and reader shared. As the novel developed so they both experienced a common journey, an immediacy in the growing and unfolding pages, a process that would often encourage what has been called at its best 'brilliant resourceful improvisation'.[19]

This historical relationship, then, is an important one but one which, in its original intensity, the modern reader can only be aware of rather than share in. And yet, in the experience of moving through so many pages, a bond *is* developed between reader and text, of an acquaintance with the book which partly grows out of the time (and investment) we are forced to give it and partly with a growing sense of familiarity as we map our way through it, come to recognise the voice (or voices) of the landscape and settle into the narrative canvas. If we see the Victorian novel in this way, attempt to come to terms with the novel as both book and text, then hopefully we will give to our reading response a greater sense of freedom in relation to both the individual experience and the Victorian nature of the effect; an effect, I have suggested, that is in important ways dependent upon length. When we next open another long Victorian novel we might well recall Alice's encounter with the Mouse:

'Mine is a long and a sad tale!' said the Mouse, turning to Alice and sighing.

'It is a long tail, certainly,' said Alice, looking down with wonder at the Mouse's tail; 'but why do you call it sad?'[20]

NOTES

1. The word 'bulk' in the way that I use it here was first suggested to me by Gabriel Pearson in his introduction to *Dickens and the Twentieth Century* (London, 1962). For a positive response to these qualities *see* Barbara Hardy's *The Appropriate Form* (London, 1971).

2. *Villette* (Everyman), chs. XXI and XXII. I am, of course, ignoring its place in the text.

3. *News from Nowhere* (London, 1977), p. 353. For a further discussion of the implications of this see Bernard Sharratt's chapter on the novel, below, esp. pp. 289–91.

4. I am thinking, for example, of the following: 'The second volume ought to have been much easier work than the first; it proved far harder. Messieurs and mesdames the critics are wont to point out the weakness of second volumes; they are generally right, simply because a story which would have made a tolerable book (the common run of stories) refuses to fill three books. Reardon's story was in itself weak, and this second volume had to consist almost entirely of laborious padding. If he wrote three slips a day he did well.' *New Grub Street*, George Gissing (Penguin edition), ch. 9.

5. *The Englishness of English Art* (Harmondsworth, 1964), p. 39.

6. *Galaxy*, March 1873 in *Middlemarch*, ed. P. Swindon, Case-book Series (London, 1972), p. 62.

7. George Eliot to John Blackwood, 24 July 1871. *Ibid.*, p. 31. It is remarkable how many early impressions of the novel saw it in terms of a large picture. In Blackwood's letter to Eliot on 20 July 1871 he notes that 'it is a most wonderful study of human life and nature. You are like a great giant walking about among us and fixing every one you meet upon your canvas.' (*Ibid.*, p. 30). Again, in the *British Quarterly Review*, 1 April 1873, an early review comments on the 'delicacy of detail and completeness of finish—completeness as regards not only the individual figures, but the whole picture of the rural society delineated—and for the breadth of life brought within the field of the story.' (*Ibid.*, p. 68).

8. T. Bentzon, *Revue des Deux Mondes*, February 1873. *Ibid.*, p. 56.

9. 'Modern Literature and the experience of time' in *The Modern English Novel: the reader, the writer and the work* ed. G. Josipovici (London, 1976), pp. 257–58. The book and the journey is of particular significance for an aspect of Victorian reading. The subject is too large for no more than a cursory glance, but R. K. Webb notes the following:

'Travelling had become easier, and railway journeys required a particular kind of light reading which W. H. Smith and Son provided in the "yellow-backs", cheap light novels directed specifically at the traveller.' 'The Victorian Reading Public' in *The Pelican Guide to English Literature 6*, ed. B. Ford (Harmondsworth, 1958), p. 209.

10. Wilkie Collins, *The Moonstone* (Penguin edition, 1966), p. 62. Collins is often peculiarly aware of the demands of length upon the reader and the reader's awareness of the novel as a work. In *The Moonstone* we are asked to be 'pleased to jog on a little while longer' with the knowledge that we will be 'in the thick of the mystery soon'. At other points we are asked to 'read on . . . as patiently' as we can. Should we be flagging there is the promise of 'another new chapter'.

11. *The Appropriate Form*, pp. 16 and 17.

12. The phrase is Lubbock's from *The Craft of Fiction*.

13. Lockwood is a 'bookish' man: 'No books!' I exclaimed, 'how do you continue to live here without them? If I may take the liberty to inquire—Though provided with a large library, I'm frequently very dull at the Grange—take away my books, and I should be desperate.' (ch. 31). Significantly, on his return to the Heights, Lockwood sees the remainder of the story as 'the sequel of Heathcliff's history' as if it were, so to speak, another volume in the 'saga'. (See ch. 32).

14. *Novels of the Eighteen Forties* (Oxford, 1956), p. 23.

15. *See* Tillotson, especially Part One. We tend to forget in our critical response to the nineteenth-century novel, how many 'major' novels first appeared in serial form. A few examples only must suffice. Dickens, of course, is the primary example. *David Copperfield* was published in nineteen parts between May 1849 and November 1850. Thackeray published *Vanity Fair* in monthly parts between January 1847 and July 1848. Eliot published *Daniel Deronda* in eight parts between February and September 1876, Collins *The Moonstone* between January and August 1868, and Trollope *The Prime Minister* in eight parts between November 1875 and June 1876. Hardy published *The Mayor of Casterbridge* in serial form of which we read in *The Life of Thomas Hardy* (London, 1962) that 'it was a story which Hardy fancied he had damaged more recklessly as an artistic whole, in the interest of the newspaper in which it appeared serially, than perhaps any other of his novels, his aiming to get an incident into almost every week's part causing him in his own judgement to add events to the narrative somewhat too freely' (p. 179). In his 'Preface' James tells us that *The Portrait of a Lady*, like *Roderick and The American*, was 'designed for publication in *The Atlantic Monthly*, where it began to appear in 1880. . . . It is a long novel, and I was long writing it. . . .' My emphasis has been on the reading rather than writing of serials although the two are, quite obviously, intimately connected.

16. *Novels of the Eighteen Forties*, p. 40.

17. *See* Keith Carabine's chapter on *David Copperfield*, below, p. 150.

18. Near the end of *Changing Places* David Lodge has one of his characters offer a significant comment on this question: 'mentally you brace

yourself for the ending of a novel. As you're reading, you're aware of the fact that there's only a page or two left in the book, and you get ready to close it. But with a film there's no way of telling, especially nowadays when films are much more loosely structured. . . . There's no way of telling which frame is going to be the last.' We might also think, in relation to the reading of a Victorian novel, of the endings to *The French Lieutenant's Woman* and the warning at the beginning of the book where, in bold type, we read: 'The author and publisher assure the reader that there are no pagination errors in the final chapter of this story.'

19. The phrase is J. I. M. Stewart's from his introduction to the Penguin edition of *Vanity Fair*, 1968.
20. *Alice in Wonderland* (London, 1966), p. 32.

4

The Mill on the Floss: 'Memory' and the Reading Experience

by A. ROBERT LEE

1

Shortly after George Eliot's death in 1880, in issuing their Standard Edition, Blackwoods appended to her *Westminster Review* and other Essays a miscellany of jottings under the general heading 'Leaves From A Notebook', one of which, 'Story Telling', contains the following:

> The only stories life presents to us in an orderly way are those of our autobiography, or the career of our companions from our childhood upwards, or perhaps of our own children. But it is a great art to make a connected strictly relevant narrative of such careers as we can recount from the beginning. In these cases the sequence of associations is almost sure to overmaster the sense of proportion.[1]

Whether George Eliot had *The Mill on the Floss* in mind with these remarks we can't know, but they bear very helpfully on what it is to read her second novel. They underline the challenge of writing so personal a narrative, for *The Mill on the Floss* engaged the profoundest and most sensitive reaches of her memory, much as *David Copperfield* had for Charles Dickens. Certainly the novel's better-known autobiographical elements—Maggie as an incarnation of Mary Ann Evans, Tom and Mr Tulliver as respectively her brother and father, the world of the Floss, Dorlcote Mill and St Ogg's as a recast version of her Midlands upbringing—report little more than the surface of things, although it might fairly be said that in Maggie Tulliver George Eliot was seeking to re-create a childhood through which to understand herself better as an artist and as a 19th-century public figure and woman.

More than any of George Elliot's novels, *The Mill on the Floss* touched an inward nerve. But could she write disinterestedly where this personal well-spring of feeling was involved? She showed herself aware of the difficulty when she confided to her French correspondent, Mme Eugène Bodichon, as *The Mill on the Floss* was in the first stages of composition:

> at present my mind works with the most freedom and the keenest sense of poetry in my remotest past, and there are many strata to be worked through before I can begin to use *artistically* any materials I may gather in the present.[2]

In attempting to make art of materials taken from her 'remotest past', and which called upon the remembrance of earliest pains and crises, George Eliot faced a familiar problem in autobiographical writing. How, in her own terms, to make her novel always 'strictly relevant' and to maintain the right imaginative balance between 'the sequence of associations' and the 'proportion' of the whole? For her sterner critics, she by no means succeeded. The marvellous opening two Books, in which Maggie and her realm are put before the reader with astonishing authority, fail to get sustained. They offer far richer fare than the rest of the novel. Once Maggie has grown to young womanhood, the argument runs, her colloquies with Philip sound staged, too evidently the set-pieces of Victorian moral debate. Further, with the introduction of Stephen Guest, the narrative gives way to haste, and to a climax all too recognisably that of nineteenth-century melodrama.

For other readers, and I include myself, the novel does not so fail, or at least it stays in the mind as something different and finer. Despite the evasion of expectations arguably aroused by the early Books about a life as vital and inherently interesting as Maggie's, or about the starkness with which the misalliance with Stephen brings the novel to a close, *The Mill on the Floss* withstands these reservations. How it withstands them is the subject of this essay. My contention will be that the novel has an affective power which transcends mis-givings about 'proportion' and the novel's ending, and which summons the reader into a world remembered in a way that recalls *The Prelude* or *Jane Eyre*.[3] More precisely, I believe that George Eliot implicates her reader in a quite unique idiom of memory and that her achievements with this idiom make the novel the distinctive reading experience it is.

By 'memory' I want to suggest several things. Firstly, from its opening pages, *The Mill on the Floss* calls in an especially intimate way upon the author's own memory. We meet it in the poignancy of much of the novel's tone, and in the kinds of detail George Eliot pauses over, directs us towards, and frequently makes the occasion of commentary. At another level, as we read past the first Books, it becomes clear that all the Tullivers carry within them the memory of their origins inside the domain of the Floss and the Mill. As readers, we cannot but be involved in the process and directions of these rememberings. They establish a rhythm, a characteristic motion to the novel. Then, too, even more relevantly for my purposes, the reader builds up, and finds himself asked to activate, his own reading memory. The names of the landscape, or Maggie's flights and later unhappinesses, or Tom's actions, these and other lines of detail remind us of earlier occasions and places in the Tulliver realm, the novel's world of first experiences and affiliations.[4] All these elements of 'memory' tend to coalesce, often overlapping and fusing. Such a varying register of recall, if I can term it that, solicits from the reader a willingness to recognise, and corroborate, the kind of reading experience *The Mill on the Floss* offers.

For the novel is nothing if not an invitation to meditate upon a way of being, a remembered landscape of 'places', human feeling, a childhood.[5] I do not mean to imply that the novel doesn't arouse other interests or provoke other kinds of response—to the moral question of Maggie's call to duty, say, or to St Ogg's as a portrait of nineteenth-century provincial manners, or to a love-story of sorts. Nor do I wish to under-stress how fine a gallery of minor figures George Eliot offers in the Dodson clan, or the important role of the debates in the Red Deeps. But the response I am anxious to identify, and which I think most typical, derives from the novel's powers of creating a mood and the promptings it makes to contemplation. For all that the reader's interest is engaged in what will happen to Maggie, to her Great Expectations, the propulsive energies of the story bear us irresistibly into the past, and as the novel develops, into its lengthening shadow. That 'past' is both Maggie's, and as the novel moves towards its end, ours. We respond to it much as George Eliot's narrator, at the outset, remembers in a dream, the little girl gazing into the Floss's waters and the enclosing 'geography' of the Mill, the countryside and St Ogg's.

2

George Eliot is often quite explicit about the appeal she is making to her reader in *The Mill on the Floss*, and about the idiom in which the novel is cast. Let me offer three examples. In Book 2, having set Tom Tulliver to be the Rev. Stelling's pupil, she offers a wry portrait of a country boy wholly unsuited to Latin and Euclid, homesick and impatient for the holidays. In his anxiety to be free of a life of books, and re-united with his family at Dorlcote Mill, he calls to mind 'the bright light of his parlour at home', the smiles and embraces of his kin, and the Tulliver hearth with its familiar grates and fire-irons and rug. These, in a phrase which again recalls Wordsworth, George Eliot suggests to have been 'first ideas' in Tom's life. The boy's remembering she glosses with these observations:

> There is no sense of ease like the ease we felt in those scenes where we were born, where objects became dear to us before we had known the labour of choice, and where the outer world seemed only an extension of our own personality: we accepted and loved it as we accepted our own sense of existence and our own limbs. Very commonplace, even ugly, that furniture of our own early home might look if it were put up at auction; an improved taste in upholstery scorns it; and is not the striving after something better and better in our surroundings, the grand characteristic that distinguishes man from the brute. . . .? But Heaven knows where that striving might lead us, if our affections had not a trick of twining round those old inferior things—if the loves and sanctities of our life had no deep immovable roots in memory.
>
> (Book Second, ch. 1)

Tom's 'old inferior things', the Mill, its grate and fire-irons, are precisely of the kind George Eliot thinks 'twined' in the intimate tissue of affection. They serve Tom as a species of mnemonic, releasing in him the terms of his boyhood and of a life lived inside the Tulliver family and the Mill, and with Luke and with his dog, and to the natural rhythm of the year. Tom, so to speak, 'reads' his remembered things, completes the mnemonic by his own confirming memory. They serve Tom, just as places like the Red Deeps, the Great Ponds, or Dorlcote Mill and the Floss serve the reader. The world Tom remembers 'places' the busy gentility of the Dodsons, the ill-spirited legal wrangles of Mr Tulliver with Lawyer Wakem, and even the loss of ownership of the Mill. In speaking of 'the ease we felt in those scenes where we were born', and of 'the sanctities of life' and 'the deep immovable roots of memory', George Eliot directs us to far more, however, than a process being enacted in Tom Tulliver's mind. Built into the telling of her tale is the author's awareness of the reading experience it offers.

In Book 1, 'Boy and Girl', we encounter a similar pointer to the novel's manner of using the idiom of memory. Tom and Maggie have gone fishing. True to form, Tom takes charge, the experienced hand guiding the novice. The occasion, and the context in which it takes place, George Eliot describes with perfect sureness:

> It was one of their happy mornings. They trotted along and sat down together, with no thought that life would ever change much for them; they would only get bigger and not go to school, and it would always be like the holidays; they would always live together and be fond of each other. And the mill with its booming—the great chestnut-tree under which they played at houses—their own little river, the Ripple, where the banks seemed like home, and Tom was always seeing the water-rats, while Maggie gathered the purple plumy tops of the reeds, which she forgot and dropped afterwards—above all, the great Floss, along which they wandered with a sense of travel, to see the rushing spring-tide, the awful Eagre, come up like a hungry monster, or to see the Great Ash which had once wailed and groaned like a man—these things would always be just the same to them.
>
> (Book First, ch. v)

'These things would always be just the same to them': the note is a typical one for Tom and Maggie, and also for the reader. The tone is affectionate, seeking the reader's participation in a time and experience lovingly recalled. The features of the 'world' in which the expedition takes place, even as early as this in the novel, the reader can feel to be wholly familiar, the booming Mill, the chestnut trees, the Ripple and the banks which 'seemed like home', and above all the Floss, entering and defining the lives of the Tulliver children and their family like a life-force. George Eliot makes her emphasis plain in an accompanying comment:

Life did change for Tom and Maggie; and yet they were not wrong in believing that the thoughts and loves of these first years would always make part of their lives. We could never have loved the earth so well if we had had no childhood in it—if it were not the earth where the same flowers come up again every spring that we used to gather with our tiny fingers as we sat lisping to ourselves on the grass. . . .

The wood I walk in on this mild May day, with the young yellow-brown foliage of the oaks between me and the blue sky, the white star-flowers and the blue-eyed speedwell and the ground ivy at my feet—what grove of tropic palms, what strange ferns or splendid broad-petalled blossoms, could ever thrill such deep and delicate fibres within me as this home scene? These familiar flowers, these well-remembered bird-notes, this sky with its fitful brightness, these furrowed and grassy fields, each with a sort of personality given to it by the capricious hedgerows—such things as these are the mother tongue of our imagination, the language that is laden with all the subtle inextricable associations the fleeting hours of our childhood left behind them. . . .

(Book First, ch. V)

This passage again conveys the characteristic accent of *The Mill on the Floss*. Its first sentence underlines that, whatever the novel's subsequent 'story' of Maggie's life, and of all the Tullivers, the determining influence upon their lives resides in 'these first years', and in the 'earth' which has initially formed and nurtured them. Maggie's and Tom's 'day out' memorialises a far larger round of life, just as the familiar and 'well-remembered' May flowers and song-birds do for the narrator. In speaking of a 'language that is laden with all the subtle inextricable associations the fleeting hours of our childhood left behind them', George Eliot might properly be thought to have described the idiom of *The Mill on the Floss*. It is an idiom the novel continues to 'speak' well after we have forgotten the story of Maggie's drowning.

The arrival of change into Maggie's world, and it arrives in the course of Books III and IV with the downfall of Mr Tulliver, frames Maggie's first years even more sharply. The opening two Books have portrayed a childhood in such opulent fulness, and with so convincing a stress upon the child's point of view, that we think of it as a time complete in itself. Here is Maggie's reaction, the third of my three examples of the novel's idiom, to the demise of the family as she has known it before her father's bankruptcy:

Maggie's sense of loneliness, and utter privation of joy, had deepened with the brightness of advancing spring. All the favourite outdoor nooks about home, which seemed to have done their part with her parents in nurturing and cherishing her, were now mixed up with home-sadness, and gathered no smile from the sunshine. Every affection, every delight the poor child had had, was like an aching nerve to her. There was no music for her any more—no piano, no harmonised voices, no delicious stringed instruments, with their passionate cries of imprisoned spirits sending a strange vibration through her frame.

(Book Fourth, ch. III)

The 'past' invoked here, in which Maggie ran free and which we as readers have built into a complex 'memory', is rightly said to act with the force of 'an aching nerve'. The familiar 'nooks', Maggie's every 'affection', the 'music' of her early life, all refer us to a time richer than her present. The language in which she looks back, cadenced, insistent in its rhythms, reflects the novel's general idiom of memory. The 'outdoor nooks' call to mind the 'landscape' of the Deeps, the Ponds, the bankside world of the firs and the Great Ash, to which Maggie has often fled, or simply wandered. The 'music' of her life, and she's associated with music throughout the novel, belongs with the small girl who fashioned stories of the insect world, or took pleasure in the boom of the Mill-wheel, or could tell Mr Riley about the water witch, the child gifted with a great and various fund of creative vitality. A phrase like 'imprisoned spirits' recalls the other dimension of Maggie's early life, the child of contrary impulses, often vulnerable and easily moved to tears of frustration. To think of the vulnerable Maggie is to remember the girl who cut off her luxuriant hair in spite, or let Tom's rabbits die in excitement at his return from school, or denied him a share in her jam-puff, or knocked over the pagoda of playing cards, or listened to her Uncle Deane's music-box only to arouse Tom's anger by her caress, or threw her cousin Lucy into the mud out of anger. Above all, we remember Maggie as a 'life' figure, the novel's Cissy Jupe or Eppie, against whom the Dodson aunts, busy and quick with opinions, represent the human spirit grown solemn. Behind this, as in the other passages, the reader detects, once more, the novel's general inflection.

3

So far I've been suggesting that *The Mill on the Floss* engages the reader most characteristically as 'memory', and I now need to make that contention stronger by considering the novel in three further ways, as 'geography', as 'society' and as 'family'. From the start, the novel offers the Tulliver geography as special, far more than a mere sense of place, or lightly etched background to the life and destruction of the novel's heroine. George Eliot guides her reader to an increasing recognition that this is a world of nooks and places which glistens with the affectionate sheen of memory. The novel's idiom 'speaks' through the Tulliver place-names, as I have indicated, the Floss, the Ripple, Dorlcote Mill, the Red Deeps, the Round Pools, the Great Ash, and the different chestnut trees and firs. As we read through the first two Books, to Maggie's meetings and debates with Philip in the Red Deeps, to the loss of the Mill and, ultimately, to the flight with Stephen, these places become aids to the reading memory, a litany of recollection. Similar places —Dunlow Common where the gypsies camped and Maggie hoped to see their queen, Garum Firs where the Pulletts live, the St Ogg's wharfs where Bob Jakin takes his new wife and Tom learns business—each marks a crucial moment in the Tulliver fortunes, and secretes the memory of a previous time and experience. No less than the better-known ones, these places help to create a landscape which exists as a place to be contemplated and a tone of voice to be heard by the responsive reader.

We first meet the novel's 'geography' in the following fashion:

> A wide plain, where the broadening Floss hurries on between its green banks to the sea, and the loving tide, rushing to meet it, checks its passage with an impetuous embrace. On this mightly tide the black ships—laden with the fresh-scented fir-planks, with rounded sacks of oil-bearing seed, or with the dark glitter of coal—are borne along to the town of St. Ogg's, which shows its aged, fluted red roofs and the broad gables of its wharves between the low wooded hill and the river brink, tinging the water with a soft purple hue under the transient glance of this February sun. Far away on each hand stretch the rich pastures and the patches of dark earth, made ready for the seed of broad-leaved crops, or touched already with the tint of the tender-bladed autumn-sown corn. . . . Just by the red-roofed town the tribu-

tary Ripple flows with a lively current into the Floss. How lovely the little river is, with its dark, changing wavelets! It seems to me like a living companion while I wander along the bank and listen to its low placid voice, as to the voice of one who is deaf and loving. I remember those large dipping willows. I remember the stone bridge.

And this is Dorlcote Mill. I must stand a minute or two here on the bridge and look at it, though the clouds are threatening, and it is far on in the afternoon. Even in this leafless time of departing February it is pleasant to look at—perhaps the chill damp season adds a charm to the trimly-kept, comfortable dwelling-house, as old as the elms and chestnuts that shelter it from the northern blast. . . . As I look at the full stream, the vivid grass the delicate bright-green powder softening the outline of the great trunks and branches that gleam from under the bare purple boughs, I am in love with moistness. . . .

The rush of the water, and the booming of the mill, bring a dreamy deafness, which seems to heighten the peacefulness of the scene. They are like a great curtain of sound, shutting one out from the world beyond. . . .

Now I can turn my eyes towards the mill again, and watch the unresting wheel sending out its diamond jets of water. That little girl is watching it too; she has been standing on just the same spot at the edge of the water ever since I paused on the bridge. . . .

Ah, my arms are really benumbed. I have been pressing my elbows on the arms of my chair, and dreaming that I was standing on the bridge in front of Dorlcote Mill, as it looked one February afternoon many years ago. Before I dozed off, I was going to tell you. . . .

(Book First, ch. 1)

Here, as emphatically as anywhere in the novel, is the tone George Eliot invites her reader to hear and ponder. Her narrator's 'voice'—companionable, fond, contemplative—is the voice of retrospect. It establishes the Tulliver landscape and the past to which it has been witness as parts of a loved memory. It isn't difficult to understand why Proust, seeking to introduce his reader to another landscape of memory, might have seen in the opening chapter of *The Mill on the Floss* the model for *Du Côté De Chez Swann*. 'Dreamy deafness', 'a great curtain of sound shutting one off from the world beyond', arms grown 'benumbed' under the influence of reverie—such language establishes the way to an understanding of the novel's emotional temperature. For the 'geography' of *The Mill on the Floss* creates no one landscape in particular, nor a myth of region in the manner of Hardy's Wessex or Faulkner's Yoknapatawpha, but rather a realm and a climate where landscape has become saturated with feeling. Time and human experience, in the novel, are to be measured not as clock time, but in the measure set by the murmuring Floss and the booming Mill-wheel and the deliberate sweep of the narrator's gaze.

Aptly, the scene's detail is seen as a view from the bridge, a vantage-point which affords distance, yet an ease of vision and the promise of further familiarity. The narrator has wandered inside, and through, this landscape, listening as an intimate to the sounds of the Floss and Mill. Guided by his (or her) idiom, we can hardly do otherwise. Our gathering response is thus organised several ways: we are led from outside to inside the novel, made conscious of a 'now' and a 'then', and offered an idiom which asks the reader to recognise and affirm its individual resonances.

If the 'geography' of *The Mill on the Floss* could be said to possess lines of longitude and latitude, they would undoubtedly be formed by the Mill and the Floss. Both represent central points of reference for the narrative, and the reader encounters them most vividly when 'twined' in the idiom of remembered affection. In Maggie's case, we can think of the refuge she derives from the Mill, especially in the episode where her father refuses her permission to collect Tom from school and she vents her unhappiness on the doll. She turns from her despair back to the Mill, of which the novel offers this description:

> Maggie loved to linger in the great spaces of the mill, and often came out with her black hair powdered to a soft whiteness that made her eyes flash out with new fire. The resolute din, the unresting motion of the great stones, giving her a dim delicious awe as at the presence of an uncontrollable force—the meal for ever pouring, pouring—the fine white powder softening all surfaces, and making the very spider-nets look like a faery lace-work—the sweet pure scent of the meal—all helped to make Maggie feel that the mill was a little world apart from her outside everyday life.
>
> (Book First, ch. IV)

We hear in this, assuredly, the Mill's most affirmative meaning for Maggie (it holds other, less agreeable, meanings for her),

its role as a retreat, a sanctuary, a place of restoration for her
wounded spirit. From its grain she draws 'new fire', nourishment
for her identity and creative needs, so easily and often threatened
by her brother and the 'outside everyday life' about her. In its din,
its rhythmic power in pouring forth the ground meal, in the scent
and 'the unresting motion of great stones', we are made aware that
what Maggie seeks, and frequently, as here, secures, from the Tulliver Mill, is the energy for life.

For Tom, too, the Mill stores a way of being, an affirmation of
family and tradition. Nowhere more poignantly does he recall the
Mill than in Mr Stelling's study as he labours gracelessly over his
books. But perhaps the most affecting instance of the Mill's role as
'geography' is Mr Tulliver's remembrance on his sickbed of what
it has meant to him and his family. The idiom again directs the
reader towards the past, into memory:

> But the strongest influence of all was the love of the old
> premises where he had run about when he was a boy, just as Tom
> had done after him. The Tullivers had lived on this spot for gener-
> ations, and he had sat listening on a low stool on winter even-
> ings while his father talked of the old half-timbered mill that had
> been there before the last great floods which damaged it so that
> his grandfather pulled it down and built the new one. It was when
> he got able to walk about and look at all the old objects, that he
> felt the strain of this clinging affection for the old home as part
> of his life, part of himself. He couldn't bear to think of himself
> living on any other spot than this, where he knew the sound of
> every gate and door, and felt that the shape and colour of every
> roof and weather-stain and broken hillock was good, because his
> growing senses had fed on them.
>
> (Book Third, ch. IX)

George Eliot's use of the Floss also seeks special acknowledgement. At one level it shares with other rivers in fiction explicit
thematic functions. Where Mark Twain uses his arterial Missis-
sippi as both a route to freedom and the savage reality behind the
slave-phrase 'sold down the river', or H. G. Wells his Thames in
Tono-Bungay as a means of helping the reader judge the tide of
Edwardian social change, or Joseph Conrad his Congo to express
the serpentine twists and coils Mr Kurtz believes the 'heart of
darkness', his 'Africa', George Eliot similarly uses the Floss as both
a literal power, 'a rush of water', in the opening chapter's phrase,

and a pervasive source of imagery for the novel's main preoccupations. It expresses the 'tide' of Maggie's destiny. To St Ogg's it supplies a myth of origin. Luke Moggs, Bob Jakin, and Mr Tulliver to a lesser extent, see in it a wealth of folklore and superstition. To the author it is always on hand as a means to closing the narrative by having Maggie 'tumble in', as Mrs Tulliver's too blatant warnings have prophesied. History, and the flux of human change, are also bound up in the motion of its waters. From the outset, it appeals as a river in whose ebbs and tides there resides a complicated evolution of trade, battles, settlement. The Floss, as it were, has 'deposited' its historical sediment at the threshold of St Ogg's. Its currents have clearly been witness to generations of human history, and have watered 'the patches of dark earth' with their bankside crops and trees back into forgotten time. To the Tullivers and their Mill, it acts literally as a life-source. In all these manifestations the Floss marks a central coordinate, the animating presence in the novel's 'geography'.

Just as the Floss establishes a 'measure' for the natural world of St Ogg's and the Tulliver realm, it gives to the reader, too, his 'measure' in reading the text. It suggests initially that we read at a pace which will allow us to gather into ourselves how this world has evolved. Once Maggie enters the picture it plays an even more complex role. At one moment it serves as a kind of counterpoint, a commenting 'tide' on her different perplexities and upsets. Eventually, when Maggie encounters her final disgrace and the turbulent feelings of loss which drive her back to Tom and the Mill for a last time, the novel enacts the turbulence by making the Floss into the destructive power it has always threatened. In this, both the Floss and the narrative blend into one, a shared 'tide' to be understood in a shared rhythm by the reader.

4

If I choose not to emphasise St Ogg's and its society as an instance of how often, and successfully, the nineteenth-century English novel depicts provincial society, that is not because I think *The Mill on the Floss* unconcerned with showing a wholly particular town and its culture. The society in which the Tullivers, the Dodsons (especially Messrs Clegg, Pullett and Deane), the Wakems and the Guests make up different class strata and interests, George

Eliot offers as perfectly individual to her novel. Arguments about national questions of Reform and the Catholic Vote, as well as about local business and law matters, authenticate very persuasively the novel's sense of period and place. But St Ogg's carries about it other resonances, of a kind which invite us to think the town emblematic of a far older human order.

St Ogg's, the novel takes care to stress, has variously been pagan and Celtic, Roman, Saxon, Danish, Norman, and known a Cromwellian and eighteenth-century history. These accretions of time and successive layers of human presence are not merely asserted, however. They seem remembered in the Floss's ebbs and tides, in the landscape's changing seasons, in the dialects and folklore and the social parlance of the community. We sense a community grown familiar and inward through long practice. The apparent contemporaneity of St Ogg's, as a rising business centre and small port and as a network of small-town manners (its nuances, nevertheless, not yet those of the town of Middlemarch) masks a far older social reality. For St Ogg's, together with the outlying farms and water-mills and tenancies, is made to echo with the footfalls of these earlier histories. The reader builds his sense of St Ogg's not only from the doings of a Mr Deane, or the landed manners of Stephen Guest and his sisters, or the peddling of Bob Jakin, but from the different 'pasts' the novel calls attention to— the past of St Ogg's in Saxon legend, or the past of St Ogg's under the Roundheads and Cavaliers. George Eliot offers her town as a storehouse of past as much as present existence, the inheritor of an established continuity of human habitation. We feel in George Eliot's idiom again the voice of an older world brought close by being remembered through time.

Maggie's experience at the bazaar, where Dr Kenn perceives 'the expression of pain on her beautiful face' (Book Sixth, ch. 9), offers a case in point. This is St Ogg's in public dress, capable of tattle and injuring whisper, as Maggie will discover to her cost when she is judged to have flaunted accepted standards by her behaviour with Stephen. Dr Kenn, whose voice is as close as any in the novel to George Eliot's own, recognises that eventual judgement to be merciless. The account of Stephen's attentions to Maggie, especially the fevered need he feels for her, and the attempted flight and Maggie's anguish, are contemporary enough. But George Eliot uses the bazaar to make us think a more emblematic drama is being played towards its conclusion. The bazaar, set in the town's armorial hall, with its built-in history and its booths and gossip, acts as a theatre-in-small of all such behaviour. It might well suggest to the reader a pageant show, a species of Vanity Fair. Before us is a house of manners far older than nineteenth-century St Ogg's. George Eliot's description of the hall typically takes us back into time:

> All well-dressed St. Ogg's and its neighbourhood were there; and it would have been worth while to come, even from a distance, to see the fine old hall, with its open door and carved oaken rafters, and great oaken folding-doors, and light shed down from a height on the many-coloured show beneath: a very quaint place, with broad faded stripes painted on the walls, and here and there a show of heraldic animals of a bristly, long-snouted character, the cherished emblems of a noble family once the seigniors of this now civic hall. A grand arch, cut in the upper wall at one end, surmounted an oaken orchestra, with an open room behind it, where hothouse plants and stalls for refreshment were disposed: an agreeable resort for gentlemen disposed to loiter, and yet to exchange the occasional crush down below for a more commodious point of view. In fact, the perfect fitness of this ancient building for an admirable modern purpose, that made charity truly elegant, and led through vanity up to the supply of a deficit, was so striking that hardly a person entered the room without exchanging the remark more than once.
>
> (Book Sixth, ch. 9)

The hall, as it were, stores the town's past. The human parade of St Ogg's has passed here before. If what is to happen between Stephen and Maggie re-enacts other and previous illicit relationships, where better than in 'this ancient building'? Certainly, the irony of conducting 'charity' which will ultimately be denied to Maggie, belongs with far older habits of human conduct. George Eliot's idiom again is one of memory, of other bazaars and other falls from grace. St Ogg's expresses at once a contemporary self and its many prior incarnations.

5

Similarly, we respond to the Tullivers as a family, and as heirs to a rootedly English way of life, in terms which cannot but acknowledge their particularity. Where more vitally does one meet an individual family in the Victorian novel? But in creating them, George Eliot was again creating something far more. She was remembering the face of all 'family': the conflicts of youth with age, offspring with parent, the sheer energy of the domestic round. In Mr Tulliver she created a daughter's protector, a first 'lover', the father who wards off the Dodson bad spirits and the opprobrium Maggie brings upon herself by her flight to the gypsies or the mutilation of her hair. But Mr Tulliver is also a typically weak father, the dupe of foolish prejudice. In depicting his idiosyncrasies—over water rights or lawyers—George Eliot suggests a father's familiar and representative foibles. Mr Tulliver embodies both the literal master of Dorlcote Mill and the typology of the 'father' or 'husband'. Similarly Mrs Tulliver: she is wholly individuated as Maggie's mother, and as the weakest of the Dodson sisters, but she embodies, too, a kind of hapless loyalty, a simple and often infuriating standard of wifely and maternal well-meaning. In Tom Tulliver, we respond, probably without affection, to the brother who draws Maggie's love to himself, and again to a more representative presence, the sibling male striving for his own implacable style of authority. George Eliot remembers in Tom Tulliver not only the boy who will endure a sour passage to manhood as the redeemer of his father's curse, but as variously the bully and oaf, and the Tom Sawyer figure easily amused by Maggie's or Philip's stories and the flashing sword at Mr Stelling's. When read with Maggie herself and the gallery of Dodsons and Mosses, these latter poor relatives *par excellence*, the novel's world of family takes on a quite figurative notation. The novel offers an undoubtedly actual family, and the personification of 'family' itself.

The memory of the Tulliver domestic round is held secure by the loving creation of detail. There is the Mill itself, seen from the inside, a vividly recalled interior of attics and front parlours, as well as the identifying furniture and rugs, the pots and pans and linen, summoning up in the reader the memory of all such first homes. Then, too, the manner in which George Eliot depicts family life in process, the meal-times, the visits, the petty flare-ups and rows, the outings and Dodson–Tulliver conferences, the unceasing hum of a family about its daily business, these, too, assume an almost typological power. Yet Tulliver family life is perceived overwhelmingly through Maggie's viewpoint. She experiences life in the Mill as wholly individual drama. Our reading response, accordingly, is intensely local, yet alert also to the larger human round signified in Maggie's life and in the Tullivers' way of being as a family. We read of the Tullivers and respond to an idiom which carries other and more representative stores of memory.

6

A 'world apart', 'memory', 'geography'—these are terms apt to the discussion of most novels, but they bear singular relevance to *The Mill on the Floss*. They indicate, I hope, that though the novel might be thought to resemble other classic Victorian novels of memory, *David Copperfield* pre-eminently, *Jane Eyre*, or even so studiedly idyllic a work as Charles Kingsley's *The Water Babies*, it differs markedly in texture and in the reading response it seeks. *David Copperfield*, for instance, marvellously transforms childhood experience, but from its celebrated first sentence, its dynamic is all into onward movement, into how matters will turn out. With *The Mill on the Floss*, as I have emphasised, the dynamic is retroactive. George Eliot's novel first creates, then moves forward, by continuously consulting the past. One could almost go as far as to say that the novel makes little impact as an unfolding tale and that its failures of 'proportion' derived from an irreconcilability between the 'picture' established in Books 1 and 2 and the 'drama' that was to emerge out of it. For all these reservations, in most readers' estimation, the novel does not fail. Assuredly it weakens as we move into the later Books, but that is the result of the novel's being caught up in an impasse between recollection and the active resolution of all that has passed in Maggie's life.

George Eliot was aware of the problem. Replying to her publisher John Blackwood, on 9 July 1862, about a 'critical letter' from Sir Edward Bulwer-Lytton, she found herself allowing two faults (it is the letter in which she defends her conception of Stephen Guest), the first Maggie's passivity in the Red Deeps quarrel, the second:

> that the tragedy is not adequately prepared. This is the defect
> which I have felt even while writing the third volume, and have

87

felt ever since the MS left me. The *'epische Breite'* into which I was beguiled by love of my subject in the first two volumes, caused a want of proportionate fulness in the treatment of the third which I shall always regret.[6]

Henry James, too, in what remains one of the most generally perceptive accounts of the novel, could not resist the thought that George Eliot had overplayed her hand with the opening Books and that the subsequent narrative, most especially the ending, simply evades the implications of the portrait so far presented to the reader:

> As it stands, the *dénouement* shocks the reader most painfully. Nothing has prepared him for it; the story does not move towards it; it casts no shadow before it. Did such a *dénouement* lie within the author's intentions from the first, or was it a tardy expedient for the solution of Maggie's difficulties?[7]

James goes on to disclaim any objection to floods *per se*, or earthquakes, but finds himself dismayed by the flood in *The Mill on the Floss*. Spinsterhood, or the return of Stephen into Maggie's life (there are grounds for thinking that George Eliot might have continued the story as one in which Maggie's love had an ameliorating impact on Stephen), offer stronger possible endings to the novel. Such, one can't help remarking, indicates how James would have written the novel, especially given interests which led to *The Portrait of a Lady*. But Maggie is not an Isabel Archer, or for that matter a Dorothea Brooke, or a Daniel Deronda, for all that James might have liked her to be. The 'portrait' of Maggie Tulliver, a portrait of a childhood and its world, is always circumscribed by the Floss and Mill domain. Most readers wish Maggie free of the tide which takes her to her death, but to think of her with a destiny like Isobel Archer's, or Daniel Deronda's, seems to me alien to the whole reading experience represented by *The Mill on the Floss*.

Which is not to contend that the novel's ending isn't problematic. But in a number of ways it can be said to 'complete' the earlier Books. The Floss, despite Henry James, has always threatened as an instrument of Maggie's death. More centrally, does not Tom's final 'Magsie' direct us to the novel's portrait of the Tulliver childhood? Similarly, do not the clasped arms of the brother and sister take us back to Maggie's first ever memory, of walking hand in hand with Tom by the Floss? Whether we construe Maggie's return to Tom as the Great Reconciliation, or as the selfless act Maggie's debates with Philip have long prepared her for, or as the last strand in a pattern to Maggie's behaviour which, rightly or wrongly, has always made her seek out Tom as the decisive presence in her life, her journey calls on almost *every* element of our reading memory from the novel. When she asks, as her life collapses about her: 'Where am I? Which is the way home?' (Book Seventh, ch. V), she returns to her only 'home', Dorlcote Mill, and *via* the Floss and the Ripple and through all of the 'geography' which has enclosed and defined her life. The journey she undertakes is a call to memory for the reader. She passes first St Ogg's, its houses and rooftops, then the bankside willows and chestnuts, then the warehouse where Tom has worked. In rowing onward to the Ripple, she sees for a last time the Scotch Firs and the Deeps. Amid the storm and the river-flood, they loom before her like spectral ghosts, presences from a time long ago which have never ceased to haunt her. The appeal the narrative makes to the reader throughout these closing scenes is as much to the reading memory as to any inherent sense of 'drama'—to the memory of a time and a world the novel has always kept in view. Even at a risk of sentimentality, the note sounded in the last paragraph is appropriate, a remembrance of where Maggie's life has been lived most vividly and where we, as readers, have been most engaged by the novel:

> The boat re-appeared—but brother and sister had gone down in an embrace never to be parted: living through in one supreme moment the days when they had clasped their little hands in love, and roamed the daisied fields together.
>
> (Book Seventh, ch. V)

At one level, this ending can rightly be thought perfunctory, 'Victorian melodrama'. At another, it underlines precisely what *The Mill on the Floss* has meant as a reading experience. For it functions as a species of cryptic recall, a directive back into the novel's past. In recalling this past, the ending of the novel achieves two essential things. It testifies to George Eliot's authorial confidence in the 'memory' her novel has created and to an equal confidence in her reader's ability to call that memory into play. The effect, then, is to merge the memory-in-the-text with that memory-in-the reader which lingers long after the actual reading experience is over.[8]

NOTES

1. *The Works of George Eliot* (London, 1883). Standard Edition. Essays, pp. 299–300.

2. J. W. Cross (Ed): *The Life of George Eliot* (London, 1885–87), 3 Vols. Vol. III, pp. 128–29.

3. Wordsworth very clearly shared with George Eliot a belief in the restorative powers of 'memory', as this celebrated passage confirms:

> There are in our existence spots of time,
> That with distinct pre-eminence retain
> A renovating virtue, whence, depressed
> By false opinion and contentious thought.
> Or aught of heavier or more deadly weight,
> In trivial occupations, and the round
> Of ordinary intercourse, our minds
> Are nourished and invisibly repaired;
> A virtue, by which pleasure is enhanced,
> That penetrates, enables us to mount,
> When high, more high, and lifts us up when fallen.
>
> (The Prelude, Book XII, lines 208–18)

4. Something of what I have in mind about the power of landscape is conveyed in the following passage where Maggie remembers the Red Deeps of her childhood and sets that memory against her present feelings:

> In her childish days Maggie held this place, called the Red Deeps, in very great awe, and needed all her confidence in Tom's bravery to reconcile her to an excursion thither—visions of robbers and fierce animals haunting every hollow. But now it had the charm for her which any broken ground, any mimic rock and ravine, have for the eyes that rest habitually on the level; especially in summer, when she could sit on a grassy hollow under the shadow of a branching ash, stooping aslant from the steep above her, and listen to the hum of insects, like tiniest bells on the garment of Silence, or see the sunlight piercing the distant boughs, as if to chase and drive home the truant heavenly blue of the wild hyacinths.
>
> (Book Fifth, ch. I)

5. The kind of novel *The Mill on the Floss* offers itself as being is admir-

ably perceived by John Freeman: 'George Eliot's Great Poetry', *The Cambridge Quarterly*, Vol. V, No. 1, Spring–Summer, pp. 25–40.

6. Cross: *Life, Op. Cit.* Vol. III, pp. 317–18.

7. 'The Novels of George Eliot', *Atlantic Monthly*, 18, October 1866, pp. 127–28.

8. In the B.B.C. adaptation of *The Mill on the Floss*, it is striking how—for all the fine acting—the book's contemplative tone has been lost. Maybe the medium, because of its instantaneous nature, can't reproduce the written text's deliberate play of memory.

5

Reading a Story: Sequence, Pace, and Recollection

by IAN GREGOR

1

Some two hours after beginning *Wuthering Heights*, the reader arrives at one of the most well remembered exchanges in the whole range of Victorian fiction. It is Nelly Dean 'catechising' Cathy about her proposal to marry Edgar Linton and her spirited reply:

> My love for Linton is like the foliage in the woods. Time will change it, I'm well aware, as winter changes the trees. My love for Heathcliff resembles the eternal rocks beneath—a source of little visible delight, but necessary. Nelly, I *am* Heathcliff—he's always, always in my mind—not as a pleasure, any more than I am always a pleasure to myself—but as my own being. . .?
>
> (ch. 9)

Like the speeches that surround it—and 'speeches' seems a more appropriate description than conversation—it is highly wrought, lavish in metaphor, emphatic in rhythm with its balanced cadences and dramatic pauses—far away from the idiom of a young country girl quizzed by her companion-housekeeper. But as these pages sweep by, that kind of 'realism' seems far away.

The exchange between Nelly and Cathy occurs at a point mid-way through Chapter 9, and to see it in the context of that chapter is to see that it stands in marked contrast to the pages that immediately precede it and those that follow. The chapter opens tumultuously, but it is the tumult of activity rather than speech. Hindley returns to the Heights, drunk, 'vociferating oaths dreadful to hear'; Nelly desperately tries to protect Hareton from his rage by hiding him in the cupboard. A fierce argument breaks out between Hindley and Heathcliff, but Nelly remains unmoved by the violence and wrath which surrounds her:

> '. . . with the help of Satan, I shall make you swallow the carving knife, Nelly. You needn't laugh . . .' 'But I don't like the carving knife, Mr. Hindley', I answered, 'it has been cutting red herrings —I'd rather be shot if you please'.
>
> 'You'd rather be damned!' he said, 'and so you shall. No law in England can hinder a man from keeping his house decent, and mine's abominable! open your mouth.'
>
> He held the knife in his hand and pushed its point between my teeth: but, for my part, I was never much afraid of his vagaries. I spat it out, and affirmed it tasted detestably—I would not take it on any account'.

It is an extraordinary account and even granted that it is Nelly who is narrating the tale and thus taking every opportunity to present herself favourably, the tone of the passage, conveying Hindley's baffled rage and Nelly's unflinching gentility, comes close to black comedy. Certainly, it is totally different in mood from the conversation between Nelly and Cathy which follows. It is that conversation which Heathcliff overhears, and so learns that Cathy intends to marry Linton. He then disappears into the storm. The chapter concludes with a staccato recital of events—Cathy's grief and Heathcliff's departure, her subsequent fever and convalescence, Linton's wooing, their subsequent marriage and departure to the Grange, followed later by Nelly herself.

However we choose to describe the different elements in this comparatively short chapter, we have to conclude that they are very different in kind: a vivid scene of melodramatic action, a conversation of lyrical intensity, a swift laconic recital of events which happen over a three-year period which then establishes the narrative pattern of the rest of the book. In summary, those are the elements in the chapter, but when read in context not only are we not conscious of the severity of these transitions, but the chapter seems entirely homogeneous in mood and structure. The ninth chapter of *Wuthering Heights* is a good instance of the importance of *tempo* in reading, for we can see clearly enough in this case, not only is it tempo which catches us up in the narrative, but in fact it defines the nature of that narrative.

I take this chapter from *Wuthering Heights* as a starting point

93

in a consideration of what might be described as the dynamics of reading a literary text. It is customary in discussing novels to try to convey the overall impression by isolating a number of passages and to urge their representative effect. The very length of the novel form makes such a procedure inevitable, but we should be aware that it is a procedure which can carry with it certain presumptions about the nature of fiction. They are presumptions which relate both to the text and to the reader; to the text in that they can imply a homogeneity which suggests that the whole can always be felt in the part, and to the reader in that he is treated as an observer rather than a participator. In practice, of course, things are not as strict as this, we go to some trouble to 'set' passages in a context, the observer allows his concern to show, but the grain of the activity is continually to 'objectify' the text, to presume disinterested scrutiny.

If, however, we feel the novel to be composed of very diverse elements and energies, and that the reader is involved in a continually shifting relationship with the text, then although we may still have to adopt as a basic procedure a selection of passages, we will try to treat them in a way which will bring out, as a central concern, their dynamic relationship with an unfolding text. And far from presenting the reader as a transparent figure, his *shifting* responses will be seen as an integral element in any 'reading' of the passages. The recognition of the diversity and plurality of the novel, the explicit role that the reader has to play—these are complementary concerns, the one intimately related to the other. What this kind of interest looks like in practice is suggested in Virginia Woolf's description of her response to Jane Austen:

> She is a mistress of a much deeper emotion than appears on the surface. She stimulates us to supply what is not there. What she offers, is, apparently, a trifle, yet it is composed of something that expands in the reader's mind and endows with the most enduring form of life, scenes which are outwardly trivial. . . . The turns and twists of the dialogue keep us on the tenterhooks of suspense. Our attention is half upon the present moment, half upon the future. . . . Here, indeed, in this unfinished and in the main inferior story, are all the elements of Jane Austen's greatness.[1]

Such a description conveys with lively directness the volatility of the relationship between the reader and the novel—the concealed source of the feelings which are present, the text which hints as much as reveals, the reader continually pressed into service, filling in, anticipating, remembering—and the work gradually coming to life in this constant interplay.

What Virginia Woolf does is to indicate the nature of an activity and to give an impression of a particular instance. What I would like to do is to indicate the elements that lie behind that activity, to suggest that in the process of reading a story, a wide variety of different responses are called into play. My particular instances will be drawn from Hardy and George Eliot, but I would like first to resume the discussion of *Wuthering Heights* with which I began.

I broke off the discussion with the contention that the tempo at which we read Chapter 9 is such that its heterogeneous elements not only escape notice, but seem to become an integral part of the imagined world opening to us. This tempo is not just a matter of the reader's involvement, but derives from the fact that Emily Brontë has created a narrative which has managed to establish its own unquestioned authenticity. That she has been able to do this is part of her genius, but by turning back to the opening chapters of that novel we can watch the way in which Emily Brontë sets about creating that authenticity not only by introducing us firmly, but unobstrusively, to the substance of her tale, but to the way it should be read.

'1801—I have just returned from a visit to my landlord . . .' the opening sentence of *Wuthering Heights* is one of the most evocative beginnings in nineteenth-century fiction. 'Once upon a time' is made precise. '1801'—not the present time but not exactly the past either; the reader is an auditor already late upon the scene, 'I have just returned from my landlord. . . .' Many novels end with a vibration; this novel begins with one. We visit the Heights with Lockwood, we feel a similar bewilderment and try to piece together the scene—who is related to whom, why is the man so violent, the woman so withdrawn, the place so neglected and chaotic? With Lockwood's second visit, the questions only increase—and deepen. We read Catherine Earnshaw's diary over Lockwood's shoulder in the same spirit of curiosity. Narrator and reader blend into one. It is a crucial identification, giving Lockwood's nightmare a disturbing intimacy:

As it spoke I discerned, obscurely, a child's face looking through the window. Terror made me cruel; and, finding it useless to attempt shaking the creature off, I pulled its wrist on to the broken pane, and rubbed it to and fro till the blood ran and soaked the bedclothes . . .

The horror of Lockwood's dream is then continued in front of his eyes:

(Heathcliff) got on to the bed and wrenched open the lattice bursting, as he pulled at it, into an uncontrollable passion of tears. 'Come in! come in!' he sobbed. 'Cathy, do come. Oh do—*once* more! Oh! my heart's darling! hear me *this* time—Catherine, at last'.

The two scenes mirror each other, the nightmare is both within the narrator and then observed by him. The questions prompted by the first visit are overwhelmed by the second, and like Lockwood we confusedly leave the Heights and seek to understand what has happened. Snow outside; warmth and refreshment within; Lockwood and the reader are prepared to give absorbed attention to the tale Nelly Dean has to tell. By the beginning of the fourth chapter we are habituated to a *range* of effects which seem demanded by the events they seek to explain. With a bold economy of effect Emily Brontë has got us 'inside' her tale—and keeps us there.

By the time the reader arrives at Chapter 9, he is attuned to the severest shifts in narrative tempo, and in many ways that chapter echoes elements present in the opening chapters. Hindley's violence recalls Heathcliff's; Cathy's dream, relating her being thrown out of heaven, reminds us of her diary; the swift, clipped recital of Nelly filling in the years between reminds us of Lockwood's 'commonsensical' tone as he makes his way back from the Heights to the Grange. I don't want to suggest, in any way, that Emily Brontë smooths out the diverse elements in her narrative by echo and allusion. The roughness is always there, the harsh transitions are an integral part of the tale that is told, but in the process of reading we accept it because the dramatic experience has been attested to and validated from the outset.

'I have said somewhere', Thackeray once observed, 'that it is the unwritten part of books that would be the most interesting', and however he may have intended the remark, it is suggestive in relation to *Wuthering Heights*. The acceptance the reader gives to the world evoked in that novel is obtained as much by what Emily Brontë leaves out as by what she puts in. There is the simultaneous awareness of vivid and memorable detail set in great space, both literal and metaphorical. The Heights and the Grange are sharply present as houses, but we see them at a sharp angle, they fall rapidly into shadow; the road between them is precisely measured, but beyond the houses, it runs into vacancy; the dates have meticulous precision about them, but they exist like those in a loose-leaf calendar, able to be composed in their own order; the genealogical tree is fastidiously detailed, but it grows in space, the Lintons and the Earnshaws divide the world between them.

This imagined world is made continuous by its indifference to *why* things should be as they are, the propulsion of the narrative erases the questions it proposes. Lockwood's initial puzzlement is ours, but the questions aroused by his visit to the Heights can only be 'answered' in terms of story-telling. Built into the act of narration itself, whether it is Nelly speaking, or Lockwood, or a more 'authorial' voice, is a residuum of the mysterious, an instinctual wonder. If a characteristic movement of the tale is the swift enclosure of vivid detail in space, then it is a movement reinforced by the inherently ambivalent presence of a story-teller within the novel. The 'story' summons us endlessly to listen, to meditate, to interpret, but always the events are kept at one remove, autonomous, the preserve of a particular voice of whose authority we can never be certain. In *Wuthering Heights* the act of narration becomes itself mimetic of what it conveys. The mystery is there, without question, in the event, whether it is Heathcliff bursting open the lattice and calling to the empty moors, or Cathy's strange cry of identity, 'I *am* Heathcliff', or Lockwood's nightmare, but it is there no less there in the narrative medium itself with its abrupt transitions, its diverse tones, and in the inevitability of its exclusions. We can take the measure of our involvement when, suddenly, the story-teller falls silent and, even as we continue to read, we are made to stop:

> At this point of the housekeeper's story, she chanced to glance towards the time-piece over the chimney; and was in amazement, on seeing the minute hand measure half past one. She would not hear of staying a second longer—in truth, I felt rather disposed to defer the sequel of her narrative, myself: and now, that she

is vanished to her rest, and I have meditated for another hour or two, I shall summon courage to go, also, in spite of aching laziness of head and limbs.[2]

Nelly had gone, Lockwood feels 'disposed to defer the sequel', and the reader finds that Chapter 9 is now behind him.

2

I have been attempting to suggest ways in which the unfolding narrative of *Wuthering Heights* creates its own manner of attention, a manner involving the reader in a highly concentrated suspension of judgement. The novel may alter in narrative tempo in the second half, but it continues to require the kind of absorbed curiosity which prompted Lockweed to demand that Nelly begin her tale. *Wuthering Heights*, however it may appear in retrospect, demands a reading of the utmost intensity, the feeling present in the writing seems to seek a matching response in the reading. If we turn from the story that Emily Brontë tells to the kind of story that Hardy tells, we find a markedly different kind of reader being called into being, a reader who is to be drawn not so much into an intensity of response, but rather into a continual oscillation between intensity of involvement and contemplative detachment. We can see what this means in practice if we look at two novels which have been discussed elsewhere in this volume from a different point of view.

Chapter 40 of *Far From the Madding Crowd* can be thought of as the longest chapter in nineteenth-century fiction, not in terms of pages, which are few, but in terms of the experience it conveys. The chapter describes Fanny Robin's fateful journey on the Casterbridge highway to the lying-in hospital, and which, together with Troy's sword-play, the shearing supper and the great fire, make it one of the scenes that remains most vividly in the memory when the reading of the novel has been completed. It is not difficult to see why. It is deeply felt and intensely visual: the lonely girl '*in extremis*', half-walking, half-crawling, to the hospital, and then helped in the desperate, final stage by a friendly dog. With such elements the scene is almost cut free from its context to be offered as a suitable subject for a genre painting, with some title such as 'Deserted' or 'The Only Friend'.

But such an activity of detaching and framing is the scene viewed in retrospect; it is not how it strikes the reader coming to it fresh from the renewed quarrel between Bathsheba and Troy in the previous chapter. The breakup of the marriage is becoming evermore certain, the question is simply how it is to be brought about. It is now that Fanny, after a long absence from the novel (several weeks for the first readers of the serial) makes her dramatic re-appearance. The reader's attention is quickened not simply by the recognition of the destructive agent, but by being made to remember again Troy's fickleness and Bathsheba's infatuation. Equally, the reader is being made to anticipate, through Oak's apprehensions, Bathsheba's reaction to Fanny's situation. In reading the story, as distinct from recollecting it, the reader travels through Chapter 40, vivid as it is, with memories freshened by the past and with renewed anticipation of what is to come.

Michael Irwin has discussed the melodramatic effect of the scene and pointed out that though an individual scene may be simple in the response it seeks, its effect in the emotional pattern of the unfolding drama can be complex.[3] Certainly this is true of 'On the Casterbridge highway'. Hardy obtains through Fanny's plight a sharp injection of feeling into the novel through her isolation, through the way in which Fanny endures the sheer difficulty of her journey. The *deceleration* of pace allows the feeling to intensify and infiltrate the narrative. But Hardy in doing this is working not so much on behalf of Fanny as on behalf of Bathsheba. The reader has to be made to see the depth of her infatuation for Troy, never more present than when she has lost him. That, for Hardy, is to be the dramatic climax of the scene, not any revelation about Fanny or her child. When that revelation comes we sweep past it in a way that makes us almost surprised that we have done so, 'her tears fell fast beside the unconscious pair in the coffin'. The way is now clear for the real climax, not the effect on Bathsheba of 'the unconscious pair', but the effect on Bathsheba of Troy's reaction to that pair. This is what consumes her in the desperate cry, 'Don't don't kiss them. O Frank, I can't bear it—*You will, Frank, kiss me too?*' Rhythm, punctuation, underlining, all indicate and convey the intensity of emotional pressure behind a scene which modulates out of an explicitly melodramatic mode into a dramatic one. All the pathos of the desperate journey on the highway can now be drawn upon to generate the tragic feeling present in Bathsheba's recognition that her marriage to Troy is now truly at an end.

In the reading experience of the novel, Fanny acts as an emotional surrogate for Bathsheba, taking our thoughts away from individual caprice towards that universal woe attendant on the frustrations of love, no matter to whom it occurs. But if Fanny's destiny is to allow a deepening of feeling both by, and for Bathsheba, it is a destiny which has, in the dramatic economy of the novel, to be swiftly performed and not allowed to linger in the memory. It is crucial to Hardy's purpose that when the hospital door closes on Fanny, it should close also on the reader's memories of her. However sad Fanny's fate has been, it cannot be allowed to distract attention from Bathsheba; Hardy's management of this leads us to consider the function of Chapter 42, 'Joseph and his Burden—At the Buck's Head'.

At first sight that chapter seems something of a digression, not in Poorgrass's journey, but in the extended conversation at the inn. In fact, the whole scene has a precise dramatic role to perform. Poorgrass oppressed by the burden of bringing Fanny's body back from Casterbridge makes a grateful pause at 'The Buck's Head', where he finds Coggan and Mark Clark already installed:

> What's yer hurry, Joseph? The poor woman's dead, and you can't bring her back to life, and you may as well sit down comfortable, and finish another with us.

That is the tone that characterises the chapter. No longer are we to think unduly about the death of a particular individual, however distressing it may have been, but more of death as an inevitable, and daily, occurence in the life of any community. It is to be an occasion for Coggan to ponder the conditions for entry into heaven, to be unimpressed by the claims of the elect, and to favour the practical charity of Parson Thirdly, regardless of his ultimate destination. By the time Oak arrives, they all have 'the multiplying eye'. Just as Hardy uses the pathos of Fanny's journey to intensify and extend feelings present elsewhere, so now he uses comedy to allow that feeling to subside. Through the amiable generalities of the company in 'The Buck's Head', the poignant memory of Fanny's death is allowed to fade. Poorgrass's deserted wagon, at rest between 'The Buck's Head' and the churchyard, reminds us of that larger perspective which connects the living with the dead, and in that larger perspective Bathsheba's grief will be softened too. As the talk at 'The Buck's Head' goes on, the pathos and the melodrama begin to disappear, and Hardy modulates his story in a way that will allow him, with ease and tact, to resume his main narrative journey in a novel which is to end, some ten chapters later, on a note of quiet resolve and harmony.

Taken together, 'On The Casterbridge Highway' and 'The Buck's Head', are instances of the way pace is used dramatically, to guide our response to the narrative. Both chapters exert a marked effect of deceleration, but where the first works to intensify the feeling, the second works to defuse it. This emerges clearly only when we see the effects made by the chapters in sequence; in isolation, their dramatic function is obscured and they emerge simply as 'scenes' classified as 'melodrama' and 'latterday pastoral'. The notion of sequence is, of course, inseparable from the activity of the reader who is continually filling in, and, in a sense akin to music, arranging the scenes in a way that makes him as mindful of the gaps between them as of the scenes themselves. Hardy's stories, unlike Emily Brontë's, ask to be read in a way which works through the interplay of sudden involvement followed by sudden detachment; we are made to *walk* with Fanny, we are made to look *at* Poorgrass, Coggan, and Clark, and simultaneously, we are made aware of the contemplative vision which holds both together.

If sequence can be thought of literally and locally, located in a continuous series of chapters it can also be thought of diffusely, creating effects which are spread throughout an entire novel. It is this effect I want to examine by looking at *The Mayor of Casterbridge*.

In a recent T.V. adaptation of the novel, faithful and felicitous as it often was in detail, the total impression created seemed alien to the novel. An outdoors novel had become an indoors one, there was a sense of unremitting gloom and claustrophobia, and the determining forces at work seemed to have more in common with Zola than with Hardy. The adaptation continually excised incidents and episodes which, in themselves, seemed to sit lightly to the main narrative but, taken cumulatively, enable us to understand its significance. It is these details which safeguard the novel from being thought of as *The Life and Death of Michael Henchard*.

To see this kind of diffusing detail at work in the main narrative, we can turn to a point almost exactly halfway through the novel.

It is Chapter 23 when Farfrae is calling at High Place Hall to renew his meetings with Elizabeth Jane. To his great embarrassment he meets, for the first time, Lucetta. The scene is short, but it is a crucial moment in the unfolding story, seeming to mark an end of Farfrae's relationship with Elizabeth Jane and initiating another relationship. In the middle of this chapter, however, the main narrative pauses, and the reader follows the gaze of Farfrae and Lucetta through the window into the market place:

> It was the chief hiring fair of the year, and different quite from the market of a few days earlier. In substance it was a whitey-brown flecked with white—this being the body of labourers waiting for places. The long bonnets of the women, like wagon-tilts, their cotton gowns and checked shawls, mixed with the carters' smock-frocks; for they, too, entered into the hiring. Among the rest, at the corner of the pavement, stood an old shepherd, who attracted the eyes of Lucetta and Frafrae by his stillness. He was evidently a chastened man. The battle of life had been a sharp one with him, for, to begin with he was a man of small frame. He was now so bowed by hard work and years that, approaching from behind, a person could hardly see his head. He had planted the stem of his crook in the gutter and was resting upon the bow, which was polished to silver brightness by the long friction of his hands. He had quite forgotten where he was, and what he had come for, his eyes being bent on the ground. A little way off negotiations were proceeding which had reference to him; but he did not hear them, and there seemed to be passing through his mind pleasant visions of the hiring successes of his prime, when his skill laid open to him any farm for the asking.

In *Far From the Madding Crowd* Hardy set up a narrative rhythm which was propulsive and overlapping, Bathsheba's anxiety and disillusion about Troy being present as a persistent undertone in both Fanny's journey and also at 'The Buck's Head'. In *The Mayor*, the narrative rhythm is such that it can accommodate a marked shift in pace without ever disturbing the strong sense of continuity. Hardy creates in that novel a contemplative mood, a habit of mind, which will allow, with the minimum of adjustment on the reader's part, a move forwards and backwards between characters and incidents of no importance at all. Major and minor, background and foreground, these distinctions are irrelevant to the manner of regard we bring to this novel. For the space of the page on which they appear, the shepherd, his son, and 'the crook polished to silver brightness by the long friction of his hands', have as much independence and life as Lucetta and Farfrae, and, were he to appear, Henchard himself.

The dramatic vignette has, of course, its function in the main narrative, enabling Hardy to quicken the feelings between Lucetta and Farfrae, as well as allowing the reader to be aware of their rather facile emotionalism. But the significance of the episode lies not inside High Place Hall, but outside. It is there to remind us— and in this it is representative of many such moments in the novel —of a world elsewhere, of characters indifferent to Farfrae and Lucetta and Elizabeth Jane, and even to Henchard himself, of stories which remain untold. The hiring fair brings the market place into the novel—'the whitey-brown flecked with white'—and it brings too a sense of the passage of time both in the general passing of the seasons and in the juxtaposition of youth and age.

Reading *The Mayor of Casterbridge* has something in common with Henchard 'reading' the face of his sleeping daughter: 'He steadfastly regarded her features. . . . In sleep there came to the surface buried genealogical facts, ancestral curves, dead men's traits, which the mobility of daytime animation screens and over-whelms. . . .' Such a 'regard' makes no distinction between 'surface' and 'depth'; it is akin to 'reading' a situation. Rod Edmond, in his essay on the novel, talks about the 'layering' of time in the novel, and although that is true, the layers have a transparency about them in our actual reading that makes us continually see the pres-ence of the past in the present and the present terms of the past.[4] It is this which gives resonance to the main narrative, so that stark as Henchard's story is in many of its aspects, it is always seen with a compassionate gaze which softens and transforms it.

I suggested earlier that the reading attention we give to a Hardy novel was a matter of oscillation between involvement and detach-ment, but as my remarks on *Far From the Madding Crowd* and *The Mayor of Casterbridge* suggest, it is an oscillation which can take different forms. With the earlier novel we are sharply aware of local intensities, local withdrawals, whereas in *The Mayor*, there is a persistent duality of effect which gives that novel an overall im-personality we associate with epic, but containing within it moments which glow with lyric intensity. Between the reader and the tale we feel the absorbed intentness of the narrative voice, which creates a mood hospitable to generalities and reflections, but which, at a shift in tone makes us aware of the immediacy of detail, its firm contingency. The final sentence of Chapter 23, blends, in cadence and substance, the duality of mood this novel so effortlessly solicits and satisfies, 'Her emotions rose, fell, undulated, filled her with wild surmise at their suddenness; and so passed Lucetta's experiences of that day'.

3

'What she offers is something that expands in the reader's mind'. Virginia Woolf's remark about Jane Austen has particular significance when we come to consider the ending of a story. Endings have received a good deal of attention in recent years, but the interest has been more metaphysical in character than aesthetic, and the impact an ending makes on the reader's attention has been neglected.

In looking at *Wuthering Heights* I tried to suggest ways in which Emily Brontë had, from the beginning of that novel, set up a narrative rhythm which encouraged not only immediacy of involvement in the story but an involvement so complete as to dispel any scepticism on the part of the reader about the credibility of its occasion. In *Far From the Madding Crowd* and *The Mayor of Casterbridge*, Hardy created a more contemplative mood for his tale, but a mood always open to the sudden access of feeling, always capable of responding to a switch in narrative intensity. In both Emily Brontë and Hardy, however, attention to the process of reading gives a heightened awareness of the way in which the narrative medium itself, with all its shifts and turns, can help to enact the story it relates.

Nowhere is the sense of medium felt more strongly, even by the casual reader, than in a story about to end. For the novelist the problem is no longer how to tell his tale, but how to close it down; how to switch imaginative energies which have been used in sustaining the tale, into energies which will not just stop it, but will resolve it. The process of telling must be made to predicate its own conclusion. For the reader, in sight of an ending, the mode of attention shifts, the rhythm alters, and a pressure of significance begins to build up behind the closing chapters. The pace of the narrative begins to slow, the 'ever after' looms, past and present emerge in ever sharper juxtaposition. It is this heightened attention

to the medium that characterises the ending and we are not surprised to find that for some novelists 'endings' seem to play false
to the narrative which leads to them. 'Conclusions are the weak
points of most authors', George Eliot wrote, 'but some of the fault
must lie in the very nature of a conclusion which is at best a
negation'.[5] To consider the final chapter of *The Mill on the Floss*
is to have precisely that heightened sense of a medium, a medium
no longer fully under control of the author, but eloquently suggestive about the nature of the story drawing to a close.

In the present volume we have two markedly different responses
to that chapter. Robert Lee argues that Maggie's drowning has been
prepared for throughout the whole novel; he describes how the
Floss insinuates itself into her life at all its crucial stages, 'She returns to her only "home", Dorlcote Mill, and *via* the Floss and the
Ripple, and though all of the "geography" which has enclosed and
defined her life. The journey she undertakes is a call to memory for
the reader.'[6] For Michael Irwin the final scene is a failure. 'By literally drowning her heroine Eliot turns figure into fact. . . . George
Eliot seems to round off her metaphor in default of being able to
round off the life-story on which it was designed to comment.'[7]
From the point of view of one writer, Maggie's end is implied in
her beginning, from the other, the end exists only as a metaphorical
assertion, the continuity of the story has been broken.

I am not concerned here with commenting on these critical reactions as such, but rather with seeing them as suggestive about
our response to endings in general and to the problem of the ending of *The Mill on the Floss* in particular.

I suggested that the juxtaposition of past and present—made
sharp by the absence of a future—is characteristic of an ending.
As the unread pages get ever fewer and there are no further links
in the chain of causality, no further incidents, the resolution becomes imminent, and the reader is increasingly moved into a response which is also a judgement. In these two responses to *The
Mill on the Floss*, the first inclines to lay emphasis on the past,
the second on the present. The first is more ready to assume the
present into the past to bring out the sense of continuity, the
second to see the present as emerging from the past, a continuity
in name only. Because reading an ending makes us so self-conscious
of 'the past' of the narrative and of 'the now', our judgements are
affected, and where, as in the case of *The Mill on the Floss*, we

have an ending where the tale wavers and becomes curiously irreso-
lute, then those judgements will seek expression in terms of the
seemingly rival claims of past and present. What seems to be at
issue is not so much 'the ending' itself, as the continuity it has
with what has preceded it; it is there that the link between past
and present has to be established.

Towards the end of the last chapter in *The Mill on the Floss* the
reader arrives at the following sentence: 'More and more strongly
the energies seemed to come and put themselves forth, as if her
life were a stored-up force that was being spent in this hour, unneeded for any future'. The contrary motions, so characteristic
of the chapter as a whole, are vividly on display. There is 'energy',
there is 'life', there is 'stored-up force', but it is to be 'spent in this
hour', it is 'unneeded in any future'. Maggie's life, rich in promise,
is at an end; and by extension, the sub-text runs, the novel itself still
rich in life, is at an end also. The story of the final chapter is the
story of George Eliot's effort to justify these contraries.

The author has set herself a double task. She must reveal in all
its fullness the 'life' that is in Maggie, and she must reveal, without
in any way lessening its quality, that it is a life which can have no
future. Maggie, in her rescue of Tom is to perform the decisively
selfless act, and it is through Tom's eyes that we see she gets the
recognition she deserves and needs:

> It came with so overpowering a force—it was such a new revela-
> tion to his spirit, of the depths in life, that had lain beyond his
> vision, which he had fancied so keen and clear—that he was
> unable to ask a question. They sat mutely gazing at each other:
> Maggie with eyes of intense life looking out from a weary, beaten
> face—Tom pale with a certain awe and humiliation. Thought was
> busy though the lips were silent: and though he could ask no
> question, he guessed a story of almost miraculous divinely-pro-
> tected effort. But at last a mist gathered over the blue-grey eyes,
> and the lips found a word they could utter: the old childish—
> 'Magsie!'

Silence, contemplation, awe, these are the words which serve to
create for Tom, for the author, and it is to be hoped, the reader,
'the intense life' which shines in Maggie's eyes. For Tom such
recognition is beyond speech; only 'a password' can make the past
present—'Magsie'. 'Magsie' is a recognition too, on the part of the
author that in renewing access to the past she is acknowledging

the source of her own creativity. We are taken back to where the story has lived most intensely for her too. George Eliot now seeks to complete the meaning of that recognition on the level of action. 'The overpowering force' becomes actual. 'The next instant the boat was no longer seen upon the water and the huge mass was hurrying in hideous triumph'. Life is to be found in death, '. . . brother and sister had gone down in an embrace never to be parted; living through again in one supreme moment, the days when they had clasped their little hands in love, and roamed the daisied fields together'.

To isolate sentences from the final chapter is as distorting to the impression it makes in context as to play a record at the wrong speed. The pace of the chapter, and indeed the whole last section, 'The Final Rescue' is extremely rapid; far from being elegiac and nostalgic the tone of the last chapter is one of verve and energy.

In substance and in mood we have an ending at odds with the tale, and the effect on the reader is that of a reverse thrust. We have a heroine who is capable of a heroic act of selfless surrender, and in her rescue of Tom, Maggie is made to reveal the quality of her inner life. But she is also a heroine without any further role to play, 'the life as a stored-up force . . . unneeded for any future', and the absence of that role is certainly inscribed as deeply into the text as her heroic gesture. Maggie's isolation has been created as powerfully as anything else in the novel, and by the end she is completely alone. There is a gravitational pull in the novel which takes Maggie back to her past, so that any kind of 'positive' ending, such as we find in *Middlemarch* or in *Daniel Deronda* would be quite alien to its imagined world. To think of this in terms of 'evasion' or 'regression' is to fail to take adequate account of the depth of Maggie's isolation, to muffle the tragic end George Eliot sees as inevitable. For the author the tragic end is not Maggie's death, so much as her 'unused life'. *The Mill on the Floss* has led George Eliot into a calculated ambivalence which neither she, nor the form of the novel she was writing, could adequately resolve. If she was careful to avoid the danger in her later novels, we could argue that *Middlemarch* and *Deronda* for all their 'resolved' endings lack the genuinely disturbing effect that the irresolution and dislocation which *The Mill*, uniquely in her work, brings with it. To see why this should be so, it is worth looking at the nature of the dislocation more closely.

The dominant mood of the final chapter is one of plangent ex-
hortation and elegy:

> . . . Maggie walked back to her lodgings, through the driving rain,
> with a new sense of desolation. She must be a lonely wanderer . . .
> she must begin a new life . . ., and she was so unspeakably,
> sickeningly weary.
>
> The long past came back to her, and with it the fountains of
> self-renouncing pity and affection, of faithfulness and resolve.
>
> 'I will bear it, and bear it till death . . . But how long will it be
> before death comes! I am so young, so healthy. How shall I have
> patience and strength? Am I to struggle and fall and repent again?
> Has life other trials as hard for me still?' With that cry of self-
> despair, Maggie fell on her knees against the table, and buried
> her sorrow-stricken face.

The unequivocal abstractions find expression in ritualised and
and exclamatory rhythms, 'desolation', 'faithfulness and resolve',
'the lonely wanderer', this is the natural idiom of these paragraphs.
Isolated from the context, the language is overwrought and sentimental, but for the reader coming with Maggie's life fresh in his
memory, it expresses an irresistible pathos. Certainly, it is feeling
without a focus, yearning without an object, but that is precisely
the nature of Maggie's tragic dilemma, and only in words drawn
from her past, in the remembered cadences of Thomas à Kempis, is
she capable of expressing it. In this mood of reflective pathos, per-
vaded by unchecked memories, Maggie's prayer ends, ' "O God, if
my life is to be long, let me live to bless and comfort. . . ?" At that
moment, Maggie felt a sudden cold about her knees and feet: it
was water flowing under her'. It is a startling transition. The problem of the ending, the continuity, is brought to a fine focus—in the
gap between the sentences. The prayer and the 'answer' to the
prayer, if it can be described in that way, belong to different
worlds.

It is not difficult to see that the novelist is in considerable difficulty at this point, the story has become fractured, 'events' and
'discourse' have become separated out. What is more difficult to
judge is the extent of the damage. I would contend this is considerably less than might formally be supposed and that this should
be so is due, in large measure, to the peculiar nature of the story
George Eliot has to tell.

If Maggie's 'prayer' and 'the flood' can hardly be accommodated within a single imagined world, then the reason touches on changes which extend beyond the immediacies of this particular fiction. The world of the flood, with its biblical overtones, belongs to an older order, an order of demonstrable cause and effect, one which seeks narrative expression in a fiction of causality and conclusion. It is within this perspective that we say the flood had been 'prepared for' throughout the novel. If, despite that, we feel there is something random, something 'forced' about the flood, it is because we are aware of another, different, narrative strain running through the novel. This is to be located not so much in the events, or in their continuity, but in what the events point to, in the unfinished rather than in the finished business. Within this perspective, Maggie's life is less 'une éducational sentimentale', rooted in St Ogg's and The Red Deeps, with an expected climax in happy marriage, than a moral pilgrimage, through which the self might be transcended. Where one strain in the narrative seeks resolution and finality, the other seeks openness, and resists completion. The themes of the novel close, but the experience behind them continues to expand. *The Mill on the Floss* is a novel very much of its period, but by the end George Eliot has taken her novel to a point of emotional complexity which overlooks, without being able to enter, the world that is to be made familiar in *Jude the Obscure* and *The Rainbow*.

From the reader's point of view the ending of such a novel must make a complex impression. It is both unsatisfactory and appropriate. Unsatisfactory in that Maggie's final situation has been inadequately explored, appropriate in that any 'adequate' exploration would have destroyed the novel in which she has her particular being. A later generation of novelists might, for instance, have found in suicide the gesture where Maggie could have both affirmed and destroyed herself, but such a gesture would have been meaningless in the world of *The Mill on the Floss*, though the impulse that could lead to it is latently present within the novel.

Sequence, pace and recollection—I have used these terms as a means of trying to give shape to a sharper apprehension of reading a novel as an unfolding process, a form having within it diverse energies, creating diverse effects, and because of its nature and length, involving the reader in a constantly varying relationship with the text. The terms I have chosen have a fugitive life, prompted simply by local effects, beginnings, continuities, endings; they can all be subsumed in a more inclusive term—rhythm. If a writer has to find a rhythm if his novel is to come 'right', a rhythm which he may well discover in the rhythm of an individual sentence, then likewise a reader has to find a corresponding rhythm in his reading, which may equally well be discovered in responding to local effect. The intimacy of this relationship between writer and reader is well caught in a recent observation made by Graham Greene, 'Novels should always have, if not dull, then at least level patches. That's where the excessive use of film technique, cutting sharply from intensity to intensity is harmful. . . . The writer needs level passages for his subconscious to work up to the sharp scenes . . . and the reader needs those level patches too, *so that he can share in the processes of creation*—not by conscious analysis, but by absorption?'[8] (my italics). To reflect on the wide-ranging effects of rhythm in reading would seem to be one way of making a start on tracing that obscure route that leads from 'absorption' to 'conscious analysis'.[9]

NOTES

1. Woolf, *The Common Reader* I, 1966, p. 148.
2. *See* p. 65 where Graham Clarke uses this passage in his discussion of the long novel.
3. Irwin, p. 29.
4. Edmond, p. 123.
5. George Eliot, Letter to Blackwood, 1 May 1857, *Letters*, ed. Haight.
6. Lee, p. 89.
7. Irwin, pp. 26–7.
8. *The Sunday Times*, 12 March 1978.
9. There have been, in recent years, a number of essays which have discussed the role of the reader in fiction and though their emphasis is rather different from mine, I would like to acknowledge a debt to various essays by Wolfgang Iser, brought together in *The Implied Reader* (1974), and to an essay by J. Hillis Miller, 'Indeterminacy and the Reader's Response', *English Institute Essays*, 1971. I would also like to draw attention to a stimulating essay by Barbara Hardy on 'Narrative', published in *Novel*, Autumn, 1968.

6

'The Past-marked Prospect': Reading *The Mayor of Casterbridge*

by ROD EDMOND

1

Most of Hardy's writing is preoccupied in some way with the past, with history and memory. There is the deeply personal sense of the past, and the private memories that go with it, of the Poems of 1912–13, some of which finds its way into *A Pair of Blue Eyes*. There is the historical past which figures in novels as dissimilar as *The Trumpet Major* and *Return of the Native*. There is the recurring use in his fiction of the settings and remains of ancient civilisations and the remote past to explore continuities and ruptures between past and present. *A Laodicean* and *The Well-Beloved*, among others, use details of the past in this expressive way.

But it is *The Mayor of Casterbridge* in which these issues of the past, of history and memory, have their most concentrated expression, and are brought into a complex relationship with the present which gives the novel an integration, thematic and structural, not found elsewhere in Hardy's fiction. As a result it offers a special kind of reading experience, and it is this which I want now to explore.

2

The morning after Susan and her daughter arrive in Casterbridge, Elizabeth-Jane is seen at the hotel window looking down on to the High Street (ch. 9). The story is poised, ready to move forward again after the detailed descriptions of the previous day which have run over six chapters. Elizabeth-Jane sees Henchard greet

Farfrae, and watches the two men walk off together up the High Street, leaving her saddened at Farfrae's departure and failure to say goodbye. Inside the hotel room Susan is undecided whether or not to approach Henchard, a dilemma solved for her by the sight of five large wagons laden with hay and bearing Henchard's name going past the window. She decides that for the sake of her daughter she must go through with her plan, and Elizabeth-Jane is sent off with a message which will imply that its bearer is Henchard's daughter. What is being set going here is the interplay of past, present, and future, which the novel explores on a much larger scale and indeed expresses through its very structure. The conversation between Henchard and Farfrae results in the latter staying on in Casterbridge as Henchard's manager. Elizabeth-Jane's interest in Farfrae looks forward to their eventual marriage; Susan's hesitations go back almost twenty years; the calculated misunderstanding her message and its bearer will produce looks back to the sale of Susan with which the novel begins, and forward to Henchard's rejection of Elizabeth-Jane and his own lonely death.

All this, of course, only becomes clear to the reader in retrospect. I am here finding one of those 'suggestive contours' which as Ian Gregor suggests in his introduction can only be discovered by viewing the novel, the *finished book*, as a whole.[1] And yet even in the process of reading *The Mayor of Casterbridge* Chapter 9 introduces a marked deceleration. The previous day, spread over six chapters, has been one of activity and discovery. Casterbridge has been entered, but at dusk, and the focus of our attention has narrowed to Henchard and Farfrae. Now, in the clear light of the following morning, Casterbridge is to be seen and contemplated in a more leisurely manner, setting and action are to assume a more equal significance, alerting the reader to the function of certain kinds of significant detail in the growth of the novel.

As Elizabeth-Jane walks slowly up the High Street towards her meeting with Henchard, she looks idly around her.

> The front doors of the private houses were mostly left open at this warm autumn time . . . Hence, through the long, straight, entrance passages thus unclosed could be seen, as through tunnels, the mossy gardens at the back, glowing with nasturtiums, fuchsias, scarlet geraniums, 'bloody warriors', snapdragons, and dahlias, this floral blaze being backed by crusted grey stone-work remaining from a yet remoter Casterbridge than the venerable one visible in

112

the street. The old-fashioned fronts of these houses, which had older than old-fashioned backs, rose sheer from the pavement, into which the bow-windows protruded like bastions, necessitating a pleasing chassez-dechassez movement to the time-pressed pedestrian at every few yards. He was bound also to evolve other Terpsichorean figures in respect of door-steps, scrapers, cellar-hatches, church buttresses, and the overhanging angles of walls which, originally unobtrusive, had become bow-legged and knock-kneed.

(ch. 9)

This passage is characteristic of Hardy in the unusual angle from which things are seen, the finely observed detail and sense of solidity, its touch of quaintness, and its odd blend of objectivity and humour. It has a double movement, down the passages to the stonework of ancient Casterbridge and then back to the street and the more recent but still venerable house fronts, which in turn protrude into the daily activities of mid-nineteenth-century Casterbridge, acting picturesquely as a brake. ('Time-pressed' is doing a lot of work in this context.) The reader discovers that everything in Casterbridge has something older behind or beneath it; for example, the ancient door with its chipped, leering keystone is found at the back of High-Place Hall (ch. 21). The history of the town seems visibly layered, from remotest Casterbridge at the backs of the houses to the 'present' life of this busy early Victorian town in the streets and market place. There is nothing incidental about this passage, charming as it is. The whole of Chapter 9, from its opening with Elizabeth-Jane at the window to her arrival at Henchard's yard, has been constructed with a view to the novel's overall design, and detail of this kind is integral to the way in which past, present, and future are being inter-woven.

'Casterbridge announced old Rome in every street, alley, and precinct' (ch. 11). This opening to the description of the Amphitheatre in which Henchard and Susan meet again is, like other settings of prehistoric earth forts, barrows, the Roman-British burial ground, the Franciscan Priory and mill, much more than 'background detail'. Throughout the novel significant action is held within some context of the past, gripped by it in a way which comes to alert the reader to the work that such detail is doing. The view from the cottage Henchard hires for Susan while they prepare to remarry is an example of this kind of placing.

113

> Beneath these sycamores on the town walls could be seen from the sitting room the tumuli and earth forts of the distant uplands; making it altogether a pleasant spot, with the usual touch of melancholy that a past-marked prospect lends.
>
> (ch. 13)

This 'past-marked prospect' is both historical—the earth forts and the Roman wall on which the trees are growing—and personal, the melancholy coming not just from the historical perspective but also from Susan's own history which she contemplates now that Henchard prepares to set right his guilty act of twenty years earlier. It is the past-marked prospect in fact, which becomes for the reader an image of the novel as a whole.

Individual experience in the novel is rarely located simply in the present. Instead the reader normally views the events of the novel in the context of an ever lengthening past which moves back through the living memory of the community and the recent historical past of a relatively static pre-capitalist rural society, to the middle ages, Roman Britain, and prehistoric times. The movement, as in my opening example, is a double one, first backwards and then forwards, so that the recurring effect is one of shrinking and enlarging. In other words the reader is constantly having to refocus as character and action are first sited within an ever lengthening past, and then brought close again, as for instance when Henchard and Susan meet in the physically and historically dwarfing context of the Amphitheatre, confront their own past and plan their remarriage.

The reader experiences a similar kind of double movement *within* the lives of most of the main characters. Farfrae is the notable exception, Henchard the most fully developed example, and the opposition is significant. Henchard carries his history with him, most obviously in his memory of the sale of Susan and his consequent pledge of abstinence, but also in other, more detailed ways, which lead the reader to see him in this light. Waking the morning after the sale of his wife Henchard looks down on to the village of Weydon-Priors and across the surrounding countryside.

> The spot stretched downwards into valleys, and onwards to other uplands, dotted with barrows, and trenched with the remains of prehistoric forts. The whole scene lay under the rays of a newly risen sun . . .
>
> (ch. 2)

New mornings bring their own promise, but cannot wipe out the past; an intimate connection is being established between Henchard's life and the past-littered landscape he inhabits. His past now clings to him like heavy mud to wet boots. The furmity woman reappears in the court Henchard is presiding over, and the sudden surfacing of his past, which has the effect of seeming to bring it close, completes his downfall. He returns to the places of his past, most notably Weydon-Priors. The associations of the past are too strong for him; he finds it impossible to refuse Lucetta's request for the return of her letters because the place she has chosen for the meeting, the Ring, is filled with the memory of his wronged wife and her return. And it is the Ring from which Henchard first spies on the meetings of Elizabeth-Jane and Farfrae on the Budmouth Road, the setting in this case working on the reader to heighten and dramatise the sense of Henchard ignoring the lessons of the past and once again acting in ways which will lead to his rejection and isolation.

This use of setting to induce the reader to recollect and make connections is developed in the scenes where Henchard spies on Elizabeth-Jane and Farfrae from the prehistoric fort of Mai Dun.

> Two miles out, a quarter of a mile from the highway, was the pre-historic fort called Mai Dun, of huge dimensions and many ramparts, within or upon whose enclosures a human being, as seen from the road, was but an insignificant speck. Hitherward Henchard often resorted, glass in hand, and scanned the hedgeless Via—for it was the original track laid out by the legions of the Empire—to a distance of two or three miles, his object being to read the progress of affairs between Farfrae and his charmer.
>
> (ch. 43)

Mai Dun functions like the Ring to shrink character and action by placing them in a setting redolent of the past. It is as if the reader looks back down the other end of the telescope at Henchard and sees his individual significance temporarily diminished in this lengthened setting. At the same time it works to remind the reader of Henchard's relationship to his own past. He is spying on Farfrae, his supplanter he cannot forgive, and Elizabeth-Jane, his substitute for the daughter he once lost whom he is now losing 'again'. Looking through his glass Henchard sees a male figure approaching.

It was one clothed as a merchant captain; and as he turned in his scrutiny of the road he revealed his face. Henchard lived a lifetime the moment he saw it. The face was Newson's.

(ch. 43)

'Lived a lifetime' is precise. The reader shares Henchard's shock of recognition, sees Henchard's past coming at him irresistibly, and with it the destruction of his relationship with Elizabeth-Jane. It is that evening Henchard leaves Casterbridge.

These general terms in which the reader is persuaded to see Henchard are constantly particularised through detail which itself expresses this larger meaning. Henchard's 'wardrobe' is a case in point, the clothes he wears being one of the specific ways in which the interplay of past and present in his life is expressed. The contrast between the fustian and corduroy of the hay trusser and the evening suit, jewelled studs, and heavy gold chain of the Mayor of Casterbridge which hits Susan when she sees him through the window of the King's Arms, underlines for us the extent of Henchard's transformation. This gentleman's garb persists, pathetically, after his ruin, and the shabby, thread-bare suit, silk hat, and satin stock of his mayoral days in which he works for Farfrae and attempts to give his own welcome to the Royal Personage dramatise for the reader that past which Henchard cannot relinquish and which holds him trapped. When that past finally drops away and Henchard prepares to leave Casterbridge it is an earlier past which surfaces as he reassumes the clothes of his original trade. Even 'the regularly interchanging fustian folds, now in the left leg, now in the right, as he paced along', of the opening page return as Elizabeth-Jane, watching him disappear across the moor, notices 'the creases behind his knees coming and going alternately till she could no longer see them' (ch. 43). This use of repetition is managed without strain, occurring quietly as a distant echo in the reader's memory rather than as something we consciously mark in the process of reading. It is, for example, very different from George Moore's self-conscious, almost ostentatious use of a similar device in *Esther Waters*, where the opening paragraph of the novel is artfully repeated four chapters from the end when Esther returns to Woodview. The cumulative effect of all this on the reader is to produce a sense of seeing character through a screen of detail which registers shifts in consciousness and circumstance. Henchard's last change of clothes, the 'rough yet respectable coat and hat . . . new shirt and neck-cloth' (ch. 44) which he buys on his way back to Casterbridge for Elizabeth-Jane's wedding is painfully contrasted with the glimpse of the white-waistcoated Newson he gets through the half-open door at the wedding party. This contrast, deftly made, instantly compresses both the finality of Henchard's displacement and his renewed sense of dignity, both of which flow into the tragedy of his death in a crumbling eroded cottage on the edge of Egdon Heath.

Lucetta also carries her history with her, and is constantly seen by the reader in terms of her past. Her exclamation 'I won't be a slave to the past' (ch. 25) is deeply ironic. She has her own furmity woman figure in the person of Jopp, who knows of her past with Henchard. On one level Jopp isn't convincing. He is dragged in at various points to give impetus to the story, yet he is as important for Lucetta's future as the furmity woman is for Henchard's, and as his function in the novel's design becomes clear to the reader his staginess becomes less of a problem. The threads of Henchard's and Lucetta's past are pulled together in Peter's Finger when Jopp and the furmity woman meet and she persuades him to read Lucetta's letters to the crowded pub, which results in the skimmity ride and Lucetta's death.

It is only Farfrae who is not bound by any past. The 'insight, briskness, and rapidity of his nature' (ch. 42) partly accounts for this, but it is also that, unlike the other characters in the novel, he enters it 'clean'. We know nothing of his past; he brings no memory with which to engage the reader's own. Solomon Longways is essentially correct when he describes the Scotsman as having 'travelled a'most from the North Pole' (ch. 8). Whereas Henchard is constantly seen in prehistoric, Roman, and medieval settings, Farfrae inhabits a world free of such associations; the Ring, Mai Dun, the Franciscan Priory and mill have no part in his history.

Yet by the end of the novel Farfrae has begun to acquire a past, one which is recorded by the collective memory of Casterbridge—Christopher Coney, Solomon Longways, Buzzford, Billy Wills, Mother Cuxsom, Nance Mockridge, and their friends. As Farfrae becomes a prosperous merchant, and then Mayor, he loses much of the charm he originally had for this group. Lucetta is disliked; sympathy is felt for Elizabeth-Jane; slowly Farfrae's history is assimilated to this collective memory, which functions throughout the novel as yet another kind of past within which character and action are sited. It is worth considering the ways in which the reader's response to the novel is affected by the presence of this collective memory; how it feeds our memory as we read; the view out into history which this group opens up for the reader.

This group is more than simply a 'touch of local colour', and even to describe its function as choric is distancing and flattening. It certainly carries a 'folkloric' knowledge of Casterbridge, as Buzzford's reflections suggest;

> Casterbridge is a old, hoary place o'wickedness, by all account. 'Tis recorded in history that we rebelled against the King one or two hundred years ago, in the time of the Romans, and that lots of us was hanged on Gallows Hill, and quartered, and our different jints sent about the country like butcher's meat;
>
> (ch. 8)

Buzzford makes this speech looking at the grain of the table, as if the memory of Monmouth's rebellion, and Judge Jeffrey's 'Bloody Assize', is held there in the wood. Yet this is not simply picturesque. Farfrae, Susan, Elizabeth-Jane, and Lucetta are all newcomers to Casterbridge, and Henchard was not born there. The Three Mariners' crowd expresses a local memory which goes back well beyond the arrival of any of the main characters in Casterbridge. Their conversation as they gather outside the church on the morning of Henchard's and Susan's wedding recalls Henchard's early days in Casterbridge, and then pushes back more than forty-five years to memories of Mrs Cuxsom's mother, and Mellstock parties at old Dame Ledlow's, farmer Shiner's aunt (ch. 13). This conversation, with its references to the world of *Under the Greenwood Tree*, surrounds the wedding with a body of local memory and judgement which has a strong resonance for both the reader of this novel, and the general Hardy reader.

Although this group carries most of the novel's humour, behind the stock comic roles is a whole social history, one which the novel itself invites us to read through to. The social rank of these characters is a 'middling' one, between the King's Arms on one hand, and Peter's Finger on the other. Within the Three Mariners they form 'an inferior set at the unlighted end', distinct from the master tradesmen who occupy the seats in the bow window (ch. 8). Billy Wills is a glazier, Buzzford a general dealer, Smart a shoe-maker. This social group, its collective memory, and the past it speaks for,

is seen to be slowly disappearing. Some of these 'middling' sections of rural society—artisans, small life-holders and copyholders,
that class of 'stationary cottagers' whose disappearance Hardy de-
plored in his introduction to *Far From the Madding Crowd*—have
in *The Mayor of Casterbridge* been reduced to living in Mixen Lane
(ch. 36). The signboard of the Three Mariners with its fading painting 'but a half-visible film upon the reality of the grain, and knots,
and nails', can be seen as an image of their historical situation. The
neglected state of this signboard is no fault of the landlord. It is
because of 'the lack of a painter in Casterbridge who would under-
take to reproduce the features of men so traditional' (ch. 6). In
terms of the economy of Casterbridge and its surrounding villages
this group is shown to be increasingly marginal as large scale trad-
ing edges out the small independent dealer, and rural society is
more and more stratified into two main classes, the respectable
farmers and dealers we see leaving the market place in Casterbridge late on Saturday afternoon, and those who replace them,
the field labourers coming into town at the end of the day to do
their weekly shopping (ch. 24).

Attempts at reading history into this novel have been taken to
task. In his introduction to The New Wessex edition Ian Gregor
reproves Douglas Brown for placing the significance of the repeal
of the Corn Laws at the centre of the novel.[2] Brown's position here
is not a strong one, but it seems important not to dismiss that kind
of approach altogether. Ian Gregor's general conclusion that 'when
concentration is made too directly on the historical implications
of the novel, so that we see a precise agricultural crisis constituting
its centre, the move is further and further away from its imaginative life', is in danger of confusing one specific example of this
approach with the whole method itself.[3] This is no place to attempt to construct a methodology for moving between history and
text. However I do want to argue that the reading experience itself
directs our attention through *The Mayor of Casterbridge* out into
history, not specifically to the Corn Laws or the movement of prices,
but to something which goes on more quietly, page by page: that
sense of an actively changing social structure which we register as
we follow its effects on individuals and groups. This is felt most
strongly in the Three Mariners' group, but it is found throughout
the novel. Newly emerging class factors help define the relationships of all the main characters, from Henchard's embarrassment

119

at Elizabeth-Jane's lack of refinement, to Farfrae's transfer of affection from Elizabeth-Jane to Lucetta, and Lucetta's calculated preference of Farfrae to Henchard.

This view is not obtained by 'deducing' things from Hardy's novel, nor by 'reading in' from history (although a priori there seems no reason why such approaches should be ruled out), but rather by reading *through* the fiction into that view of history which the novel itself opens up. The reader who fails to register the significance of detail of this kind is, directly or indirectly, a victim of certain limiting assumptions about the novel.

One of the scenes which does seem to open out into history in this way is that of the old shepherd at the hiring fair which Ian Gregor discusses in his essay in this book.[4] His discussion seems to me to isolate the scene in a manner that tends to neglect the reason why the bow of the old shepherd's crook is polished to silver brightness, and shuts out that history which the novel invites the reader to consider. Hardy had written about the reduced state of the agricultural labourer in an essay, 'The Dorsetshire Labourer',[5] published shortly before *The Mayor of Casterbridge*, and it was from here that he took the scene of the old shepherd and incorporated it, almost word for word, in the novel. This vignette of the old shepherd standing in the market place, eyes lowered, heedless of the negotiations going on between his son and a prospective employer, expresses, in the larger context of this novel which marks other, roughly parallel experiences, the kind of marginality which changes in the economic and social structure of Victorian rural society were producing. We don't view the scene simply as one views the passage of the seasons or as an emblematic confrontation of Youth with Age. Rather, the novel invites the reader to place it within a specific historical context.

Farfrae's hiring of the young man and his father is an act of calculation rather than sentiment, the real purchase being credit in the eyes of Lucetta, and in its ironic way is perfectly consonant with the new values which are entering Casterbridge life. It is Farfrae's excited account of recent buying and selling transactions which has just stirred Lucetta's interest in him. Indeed Ian Gregor's account underplays the reverberations between High-Place Hall and the market place; by making the scene outside emblematic, its separation from events inside High-Place Hall is exaggerated. There is some irony in it being a hiring fair which forms the background to the early courtship of Farfrae and Lucetta. In a muted way it recalls the market place scene in *Madame Bovary*, where Rodolphe's love talk to Emma is punctuated with shouts from the Agricultural Show.[6]

There is nothing sudden or dramatic in this picture of a social structure in the process of transformation which the novel opens up to the reader, but the changes are there, within the society and encroaching on it. 'The railway had stretched out an arm towards Casterbridge at this time, but had not reached it by several miles as yet' (ch. 27); the clumsy construction gives an accurate rendering of the halting, uneven but unmistakable map of change.

As the map becomes more detailed and comprehensive Coney and his friends will be threatened. But this is in the future. Like the old shepherd they are significantly and vividly present for the reader, even as history is moving away from them. It is here that the novel is poised between two worlds, exploring and enacting continuity and dislocation through that familiar double movement between present and past.

3

My main interest in the previous section was with how history and the past, as themes within the novel, are conveyed to the reader. I want now to examine in less objective, more directly affective terms, the way in which time is experienced by the reader as he or she turns the pages.

The Mayor of Casterbridge is a novel written in the 1880s, about the 1840s, which begins in the 1820s. It looks further back to Casterbridge as it was before Henchard's arrival, and it ends with Elizabeth-Jane looking into the future, as Henchard already begins to recede into a vanishing past. The reader begins viewing the narrative—'One evening of late summer, before the nineteenth century had reached one-third of its span . . .'—from his or her own present, but becomes drawn into the careful construction of all its other time layers. This offers a distinctive kind of reading experience, and one which is peculiarly well suited to the novel's thematic preoccupation with time.

As we read the novel we are reminded that Hardy is looking back to Dorchester as he knew it in his childhood.[7] The description of the evening chimes of the local church is footnoted: 'These chimes, like those of other country churches, have been silenced for many years.' A description of the old timber houses in the High Street is similarly footnoted: 'Most of these old houses have now been pulled down'. This footnote is then dated (1912), having been inserted at the time of the 1912 Wessex edition of Hardy's novels, adding yet another layer of time to the novel's structure. Both these footnotes occur in Chapter 4, which marks the novel's entry into Casterbridge, and they help establish that complex relationship between fictional Casterbridge and historical Dorchester of which the novel is constantly reminding us. A later footnote to another detailed description of Casterbridge emphasises this: 'The reader will scarcely need to be reminded that time and progress have obliterated from the town that suggested these descriptions many or most of the old-fashioned features here enumerated' (ch. 9).

This sense of historical retrospection the reader experiences is not, of course, confined to Hardy's curious use of footnotes or his more formal set-piece descriptions of Casterbridge. It is a distinguishing feature of the narrative throughout. Consider, for example, the episode in which Henchard is shamed and angered by Elizabeth-Jane's inability to write 'ladies-hand' (ch. 20). This is how Hardy describes Elizabeth-Jane's writing.

> She started the pen in an elephantine march across the sheet. It was a splendid round, bold hand of her own conception, a style that would have stamped a woman as Minerva's own in more recent days. But other ideas reigned then:

As the contrast between past and present is inserted the perspective lengthens for the reader. Yet the effect is not so much one of distancing the scene or reducing its immediacy, as of lending depth and resonance to the narrative. Another example of this kind of effect is the description of the end of the fight between Henchard and Farfrae.

> He instantly delivered the younger man an annihilating turn by the left fore-hip, as it used to be expressed, and following up his advantage thrust him towards the door, never loosening his hold till Farfrae's fair head was hanging over the window-sill, and his arm dangling down outside the wall.
>
> (ch. 38)

What is particularly significant here is the parenthetical comment, 'as it used to be expressed', inserted into the culmination of one of

122

the novel's most dramatic and vividly rendered scenes. At precisely the moment Farfrae is beaten and apparently about to be killed, we are reminded that Hardy is describing an old mode of conduct, almost of a gladiatorial kind, which like so much else in the novel has now vanished. As if to reinforce this, Henchard relents and flings himself down in a corner of the loft, while Farfrae picks himself up and goes off to Weatherbury on business. Again the lengthening of the perspective doesn't detract from the power of the scene, but gives it that sense of depth which, in this case almost subliminally, is a central part of the reading experience of the novel.

Ian Gregor's remarks on the recent T.V. adaptation of *The Mayor of Casterbridge* are relevant here.[8] The unremitting gloom and claustrophobia he describes were in part a result of the inability to transfer on to the small screen the kind of depth the novel offers the reader.[9] In the episode of Elizabeth-Jane's handwriting the depth created by the inserted contrast between past and present offers a certain relieving irony, with also a suggestion that Elizabeth-Jane's time is still to come. In the second example the sudden change of focus in a scene we have been brought very close to momentarily softens the picture, and helps emphasize the contrast between Henchard and Farfrae which the fight and its aftermath underlines. This created depth within the novel can variously distance, soften, qualify, and focus, effects which disappeared in the T.V. adaptation when the viewer simply confronted a flat screen filled with characters, and watched the life and death of Michael Henchard.

The narrative itself therefore, which constantly reminds us we are looking back in time, is one of several 'presents' within the novel. The 1820s, the 1840s, the 1880s, 1912 (1979), all constitute separate layers of time which structure both the novel and the reader's experience of it. As readers, our involvement in this layering is not simply through an awareness of the author's intention, but also through memory. Within the novel it is memory which connects past and present, carrying one into the other, holding and retaining experience in a way which is analogous to the novel's overall design. In a sense the whole novel is structured around the reappearance of characters from the past and the memory they bring with them. This is true of Susan and Elizabeth-Jane, Lucetta, Jopp, Newson, and the furmity woman, all of whom are entangled in Henchard's past and carry memories which affect him. But the reader is also involved rather differently, through the way in which his or her own memory is exercised in the act of reading the novel. Indeed *The Mayor of Casterbridge* makes peculiar demands on our memory as readers.

On the most obvious level, our memory gives us privileged access to Henchard's past. We revisit Weydon-Priors fair eighteen years after Henchard's sale of Susan, and we are able to see that it is dying, so that when Mrs Goodenough, the furmity woman, complains to Susan, 'the world's no memory' (ch. 3), we as readers are exempt from the charge. It is because we do remember, that we are able to understand the significance of the decline of Weydon-Priors fair, both for Henchard and for Wessex. There are other, more detailed ways, in which the reader is involved, through memory, in the text. Like Henchard, we are given signs and clues to the past which memory can discover. At the beginning of the novel we are told that Elizabeth-Jane has black eyes (ch. 1). When she 'reappears' with Susan eighteen years later there is an uncharacteristic lack of detail in the several descriptions we are given of her, and this persits until her visit to Henchard the morning after her arrival in Casterbridge. As Elizabeth-Jane and Henchard face each other, the 'dark pupils' of Henchard's eyes are noted, and quickly followed by a description of tears rising to Elizabeth-Jane's 'aerial-grey eyes' (ch. 10). Immediately after Henchard and Susan have remarried we get another description of Elizabeth-Jane's 'grey, thoughtful eyes', and this is followed by Henchard's musing on the colour of Elizabeth-Jane's hair 'brown—rather light than dark', and his question to Susan: '. . . didn't you tell me that Elizabeth-Jane's hair promised to be black when she was a baby?' (ch. 14). All this is preparing us for Susan's posthumous disclosure of Elizabeth-Jane's true parentage, and Henchard's candlelight examination of Elizabeth-Jane's face, in search of a past which is confirmed as illusory. Eye colour is a peculiarly haunting yet palpable clue to the past. The signs of Susan's disclosure are there to read; our memory as readers is exercised in a manner which shadows Henchard's own.

Much of the later part of Henchard's tragedy rests on his inability to reconcile the memory of his original Elizabeth-Jane with the fact of Susan's second daughter. Yet although Henchard's tragedy dominates the novel, it does not override it. *The Mayor of Casterbridge* finishes with Elizabeth-Jane and the long view into her

future, so that although our memory remains engaged with Henchard and the past, our attention is directed, through Elizabeth-Jane,
to the future. And more generally, the use of different time perspectives and the depth these give to the novel creates for the
reader a sense of space within the novel which Henchard cannot
entirely fill, nor is intended to.

My use of the word 'space' should not be confused with Graham
Clarke's term 'bulk', although his remarks about spatial freedom
and temporal capacity are appropriate to my discussion.[10] By
Victorian standards *The Mayor of Casterbridge* is not a long novel.
It has one or two loose ends perhaps, but it is not a 'baggy monster'. What I mean by 'space' is something opened up within the
novel as we read it, and not dependent on length at all. It is the
cumulative product of factors I have considered in the course of
this essay: Hardy's selective use of expressive detail concerned
with history and the past; the function of memory both within
the novel and in terms of our reading experience; the construction
of its different layers and perspectives, and the reader's involvement
in this whole process.

From the moment we read the title of the novel, which emphasises the town and the office of mayor, our attention is directed towards the historical space which that town and that office occupy.
There are three Mayors of Casterbridge in the novel—Henchard,
Dr Chalkfield, and Farfrae—and we are encouraged to place them
within a much longer line of succession. Throughout the novel time
is continually stretched, and the effect of this is to help open up
those large spaces within which we view the events of the novel,
and which give us our full sense of its meaning. The clocks in
Casterbridge don't strike 8 p.m. at precisely the same minute. The
church clock is followed by the gaol clock, that of the alms-house,
and then by those inside the clock-maker's shop, so that some
'were appreciably on their way to the next hour before the whole
business of the old one was satisfactorily wound up' (ch. 4). The
stuttering effect this creates is a small example of the way in which
Hardy opens out time within the novel, giving it that sense of
depth and space which makes it so much more than its subtitle,
'A Story of a Man of Character', and helps account for the special
satisfactions it offers. This space allows the reader an imaginative
freedom, a sense of incompleteness which exists in contrast to the
completeness of Henchard's tragedy and surrounds it. It is within

125

this space that our total impression of the novel and our memory of it lives.

NOTES

1. Gregor, p. 90.
2. Gregor, *The Mayor of Casterbridge*, intro. The New Wessex Edition, pp. 26–8.
3. A much cruder example of this tendency occurs in Laurence Lerner's *Thomas Hardy's The Mayor of Casterbridge: Tragedy or Social History?* (1975). Lerner's approach is evident from the tired opposition of the title—tragedy or social history? and is laid bare in this passage:

   > To read through a book like *The Agricultural Revolution 1750– 1880* by Chambers and Mingay with Hardy in mind is to notice how little it has to tell us about the concerns of his novel. The upward and downward movement of prices; the relative prosperity of the labourer in corn-growing areas and in pasture; the increase in the size of farms—these are not the issues that appear in Hardy, and underlying economic forces of this kind could never be deduced from his fiction. (p. 83)

   The methodology used here—take a piece of history, apply it to a literary text, does it fit? no—is so crude that the rejection of this kind of significance for the novel follows inevitably from the attempt.
4. Gregor, p. 103.
5. 'The Dorsetshire Labourer', *Thomas Hardy; Personal Writings*, ed. Harold Orel, (London, 1967).
6. Flaubert, *Madame Bovary*, Part 2, Ch. 8.
7. Hardy's memory of Dorchester however is very different from the kind of authorial memory Robert Lee discusses in his essay on *The Mill on the Floss*. Casterbridge has an objectivity which makes Lee's distinction between Eliot's landscape of feeling and Hardy's myth of region a very useful one (Lee p. 81). There is no Wordsworthian sense of memory in Hardy's creation of Casterbridge. The following extract from the speech he made to the Mayor and Corporation of Dorchester on the occasion of being granted the freedom of the town in 1910 is characteristic, and could never have been made by George Eliot.

   > True, it might be urged that my Casterbridge (if I may mention seriously a name coined off-hand in a moment with no thought of its becoming established and localised) is not Dorchester—not even the Dorchester as it existed sixty years ago, but a dream-place that never was outside an irresponsible book. Nevertheless, when somebody said to me that 'Casterbridge' is a sort of essence of the town as it used to be, 'a place more Dorchester than Dorchester itself', I could not absolutely contradict him, though I could not quite perceive it.'
   > *The Life of Thomas Hardy 1840–1928* (London, 1973), p. 351.

8. Gregor, p. 101.
9. Apart from the obvious anachronism in the cliché about Hardy's 'cinematic technique' (see, for example, John Wain's introduction to *The Dynasts*, London, 1965), attempts at translating Hardy on to the screen have revealed how much more there is to his multi-perspective technique than the simple alternation of 'close-up' and 'long-shot'.
10. Clarke, pp. 54–5.

Interchapter 2

The last group of essays highlights a problem that we encountered repeatedly. The numerous hypotheses, explicit or implied, about reader response, reader involvement, reader resistance, beg a question that is vital to this book: Which reader are we talking about? Most of us, for various reasons, have chosen not to speculate about the Victorian reader. Even if we go much further, and for working purposes concentrate on the likely habits and reactions of our immediate contemporaries, the possible variations are innumerable.

We are concerned with a reading, an experiencing, of, say, *Great Expectations*. Is our 'reader' male or female, old or young, educated or uneducated? Has he (she) embarked on the novel purely for pleasure, or with a view to acquiring knowledge? Has he some ulterior motive—a school or university examination to pass, a thesis to write, a class to teach? Is he English? Does he know England? Is English his first language? Is he familiar with novels in general, with Victorian novels, with other novels by Dickens? Has he seen one of the filmed versions of *Great Expectations*? Is he coming to the book for the first time, the second, the third? When we speak of a reading, in fact, do we mean an *informed* reading, a re-reading, an informed re-reading?

Regularly our discussion was led outward in this way, and we were at any rate agreed that we weren't dealing in mere casuistry. An assumption as to what constitutes the typical or the ideal reading is implicit in virtually any book or article or seminar about fiction. We point our students towards 'the reading' (in general terms) that we think the informed and sensitive critic would experience. We theorise about the author's attempts to mystify or involve or cajole 'the reader'.

Yet on examination these concepts disintegrate. It is obvious, surely, that Dickens, in *Great Expectations*, like Jane Austen in *Emma*, is expending much creative energy in devising signals or clues that will mislead the first-time reader as to the development of the plot. But it is equally obvious that in both novels there are signals of a different kind that can only be recognised at a second encounter. Certainly the second reading can include—must include—the first; but that first reading is in itself irrecoverable. Perhaps no teacher of English can truly experience a first reading, a virgin reading, of *Great Expectations*. Even if he has contrived to postpone a direct encounter with the novel the main outlines of the plot will have reached him by hearsay.

The modern marketing of Victorian fiction certainly makes provision for distinct categories of reader. The New Wessex edition of Hardy's novels, for instance, available in paperback, features footnotes and scholarly introductions for the intending student. The Pan edition, on the other hand, though it offers literally the identical text, dispenses with all apparatus, leaving small gaps in place of the footnote numbers. Presumably it is aimed rather at the random buyer—the traveller or the holidaymaker.

Whether he chooses a 'scholarly' or a 'popular' edition the modern reader is likely to have his judgement influenced in advance. Almost invariably he will be offered an assisted passage. Footnotes, Forewords, Afterwords serve notice that a given text is intellectually taxing—that he is likely to need help. Such apparatus is likely to be a positive disincentive to casual reading. But a cheaper edition may offer interference of another kind. Reminders, in words or pictures, of Julie Christie's Bathsheba Everdene or Michael York's Pip can perhaps create a beguiling sense of accessibility. But they may also pre-empt the imaginative responses of the reader.

Victorian novels make large claims upon a reader's time and energy, claims that we may nowadays find impossible to meet. The modern reader may lack the opportunity or the capacity to read more than brief snatches at a sitting or to respond intently. He may be unable to find the time and the silences he needs. The television or the radio may be blaring; the telephone may ring. The intermittent reading that he can achieve is likely to cleave to the 'story' at the expense of the finer detail.

The popularity of the television serialisation of Victorian fiction implies perhaps that we find it harder today to sustain the individual and solitary relationship between reader and book. Such a serial does the work of reading and imagining for us, allowing us an easy progress through the narration. There is no encounter between word and eye, only between spectator and performer, spectator and scenery. Similarly with a dramatisation or even a reading on the radio. As we listen to 'A Book at Bedtime' the voice leads us comfortably away from the forbidding compilation of paper and print into the hospitable rhythms of a capacious, flowing story. We switch on and close our eyes.

Such considerations should make the critic cautious. It is easy to speak of pace, for example, as a controlling factor in a reader's response; and certainly style, story or voice may affect the speed at which he moves through the text. Yet the reading may in practice be affected far more by external factors quite outside the author's intention. We should be prepared to take account of a much more varied audience than academic criticism usually recognises—an audience that does not move into the world of the book but draws the book into its own world.

In Ray Bradbury's *Fahrenheit 451* characters fight against the destruction of books by, literally, becoming books themselves. An entire text is memorised word for word. One character *becomes* Plato's *Republic*, another *Gulliver's Travels*. While this posits an extreme, almost mechanical example of 're-reading' we can use it as a useful metaphor for the academic reading process. Arguably the more a critic seeks to *know* a text, the less he exists as a *reader*. The problem was aptly summed up by the experience of a colleague, a lecturer in English, who felt it impossible to 'teach' *Middlemarch*, since he 'knew' the text so intimately that the crucial imaginative space between reader and text was lost and any creative relationship had atrophied—the novel had 'fixed' itself in his mind. It might be argued that a degree of unfamiliarity with the details of a novel's patterned texture is crucial to any sense of its life, to any possibility of *active* encounter with it. The 'normal' reader, unlike Bradbury's characters, will make his own unfinished text that is at once shifting, ambiguous, partial and *magical*. We should never 'know' the text, for the more we know and 'fix', the less we read.

7

Jane Eyre and 'The Warped System of Things'

by DOREEN ROBERTS

The first unanalysed impression that most readers receive from *Jane Eyre* is that it has a very violent atmosphere. If this were simply the effect of the plot and the imagined events then sensation novels like Walpole's *The Castle of Otranto* or Mrs Radcliffe's *The Mystery of Udolpho* ought to produce it even more powerfully. But they do not. Nor do they even arouse particularly strong reader responses. Novelists like Charlotte Brontë or D. H. Lawrence, on the other hand, are able quite quickly to provoke marked reactions of sympathy or hostility from readers. The reason, apparently, is that the narrator's personality is communicating itself through the style with unusual directness. It is for reasons deriving from this one that I do not re-read middle and late Lawrence with pleasure, and find the opening of *The Rainbow* hard to get past. Those who do not admire the fifth paragraph for instance, can find its incantatory quality irritating, even faintly embarrassing.

A number of Charlotte Brontë's nineteenth-century readers, including Matthew Arnold, reacted to her work in a comparably personal (sometimes immoderate) way. And it does indeed offer a mixed and restless reading experience—on one page a striking psychological insight, on the next, a piece of fiercely self-righteous invective charged with an evidently real yet (in fictional terms) obscure emotion. We may be successively impressed by the conscious and penetrating registering of oddnesses or weaknesses in the heroine, and staggered by the apparent authorial obliviousness to others. We encounter a minutely analysed psyche moving through a world of shadowily adumbrated or else luridly postercoloured figures. Brontë is a writer who can be as irritating, even maddening, as she is interesting and often fascinating. The power of her work seems to depend on the way it bulldozes through our notions of decorum and stylistic restraint, our respect for balance and a sense of proportion and—at a quite radical level—our notions of fairness. The narrative method being, to my mind, the central issue, I would like to approach *Jane Eyre* initially by way of the style.[1] The dangers of generalising about a whole novel from a single extract are real ones and are often pointed out. But, the appropriate caveats accepted, looking at a passage in detail does seem to be one of the obvious ways of making the point that in this novel there is a particularly close connexion between the medium and the message, and again, that the tone of the book is an especially important influence on the reader's response. Apart from this, it is the case that less stylistic variation is felt in *Jane Eyre* than in, say, *Villette*. Indeed the strangeness that we frequently note about the dialogue is traceable to the relative constancy of the style, one peculiarly unadapted to conveying idiomatic conversation. The example chosen is a striking but representative passage that comes at the end of Chapter 26 and describes Jane's feelings just after the interrupted marriage ceremony and ensuing revelation of the existence of the first Mrs Rochester.

> I was in my own room as usual—just myself, without obvious change: nothing had smitten me, or scathed me, or maimed me. And yet where was the Jane Eyre of yesterday?—where was her life?—where were her prospects?
>
> Jane Eyre, who had been an ardent expectant woman—almost a bride—was a cold, solitary girl again: her life was pale; her prospects were desolate. A Christmas frost had come at midsummer; a white December storm had whirled over June; ice glazed the ripe apples, drifts crushed the blowing roses; on hayfield and cornfield lay a frozen shroud: lanes which last night blushed full of flowers, to-day were pathless with untrodden snow; and the woods, which twelve hours since waved leafy and fragrant as groves between the tropics, now spread, waste, wild, and white as pine-forests in wintry Norway. My hopes were all dead—struck with a subtle doom, such as, in one night, fell on all the first born in the land of Egypt. I looked on my cherished wishes, yesterday so blooming and glowing; they lay stark, chill, livid corpses that could never revive. I looked at my love: that feeling which was my master's—which he had created; it shivered in my heart, like a suffering child in a cold cradle: sickness and anguish had seized it; it could not seek Mr. Rochester's arms—it could not derive

warmth from his breast. Oh, never more could it turn to him; for faith was blighted—confidence destroyed! Mr. Rochester was not to me what he had been; for he was not what I had thought him. I would not ascribe vice to him; I would not say he had betrayed me; but the attribute of stainless truth was gone from his idea, and from his presence I must go: *that* I perceived well. When—how—whither, I could not yet discern; but he himself, I doubted not, would hurry me from Thornfield. Real affection, it seemed, he could not have for me; it had only been fitful passion: that was balked; he would want me no more. I should fear even to cross his path now: my view must be hateful to him. Oh, how blind had been my eyes! How weak my conduct!

My eyes were covered and closed: eddying darkness seemed to swim round me, and reflection came in as black and confused a flow. Self-abandoned, relaxed, and effortless, I seemed to have laid me down in the dried-up bed of a great river; I heard a flood loosened in remote mountains, and I felt the torrent come: to rise I had no will, to flee I had no strength. I lay faint, longing to be dead. One idea only still throbbed lifelike within me—a remembrance of God: it begot an unuttered prayer: these words went wandering up and down in my rayless mind, as something that should be whispered, but no energy was found to express them.

'Be not far from me, for trouble is near: there is none to help.' It was near; and as I had lifted no petition to Heaven to avert it—as I had neither joined my hands, nor bent my knees, nor moved my lips—it came: in full heavy swing the torrent poured over me. The whole consciousness of my life lorn, my love lost, my hope quenched, my faith death-struck, swayed full and mighty above me in one sullen mass. That bitter hour cannot be described: in truth, 'the waters came into my soul; I sank in deep mire: I felt no standing; I came into deep waters; the floods overflowed me.'

This is typical of many of the strange effects of Charlotte Brontë's style, an extremely uncolloquial and un-modern one beside that of, say, Mrs Gaskell in *Wives and Daughters*. It is highly literary and consciously rhetorical, yet at the same time vehement and perfervid. It keeps setting up formal, stylised sentence-patterns and then disrupting them with rhetorical questions, exclamations, exhortations, appended clauses and appositional phrases. It loves word-runs of two or three, like 'waste, wild, and white', 'stark, chill, livid', or 'self-abandoned, relaxed, and effortless', the linkage often reinforced by alliteration or assonance. It builds up structures of echoing serial phrases or clauses, again in twos or threes and often arranged with crescendo force, like 'nothing had smitten me, or scathed me, or maimed me. And yet where was the Jane Eyre of yesterday?—where was her life?—where were her prospects?' Here the harmony of the pattern is characteristically dissolved in the effect of staccato abruptness produced by the frequent and insistent pauses between sense-units and the heaviness of the punctuation. (Charlotte Brontë makes unusually lavish use of the dash, and often has a punctuation mark where a conjunction might have been expected, and in general, despite the apparent length and complexity of her sentences, tends to work in rather short sense-units and to like paratactic clausal or phrasal arrangements.) Such a style cannot possibly flow. Nor is there any of the effect of rising and falling emphasis normal in narrative prose. It is more like a sustained series of small explosions.

Again, the narrator has a marked fondness for balanced or antithetical clauses and various forms of isocolon: 'Mr Rochester was not to me what he had been; for he was not what I had thought him!' or (rather biblically) 'to rise I had no will, to flee I had no strength.' But the patterns are not repeated constantly enough to establish them as guiding syntactic principles (as they are in some eighteenth-century prose). Expectancy is defeated by the abrupt shifts and staccato sharpness.

In another respect the eighteenth-century mannerisms fail of an eighteenth-century effect. One important use of personification for the Augustans was to universalise individual crises, and statements of antitheses like Wit and Judgment, Fancy and Reason, Taste and Genius, the Beautiful and the Picturesque or Sense and Sensibility were current because they believed in universally recognisable categories. Through these, individual conflicts, dilemmas or problems of choice could be brought into the realm of public debate, where they could be analysed in a more general and objective context, according to received ethical principles. Thus they also became amenable to rhetorical treatment, and it is notable that Charlotte Brontë adopted the more rhetorical of those stylistic habits that we associate particularly with the century before her own. Most modern readers take *Jane Eyre* to be dramatising a psychological conflict between opposing impulses in the self, at a level which precedes (but may lead to) the moral. But apparently the book believes itself to be debating a general and familiar moral issue, in the received 'Sense and Sensibility' terms. The 'public' element in the style seems to be trying to distract attention from the personal and idiosyncratic element. It might be interesting, from this point of view, to examine the problems of terminology in the ambiguous 'temptation' scene of Chapter 27, where Jane seems unsure whether she is defending her God-commanded chastity, her status in Rochester's eyes, or her self-image.

Another almost obsessional stylistic device is syntactic inversion: the object, predicate or adverb of the sentence is often found in an abnormal place, as in the last two quotations above, or in 'from his presence I must go'. This is, of course, a device for isolation and emphasis. The style also leans towards archaistic or obsolescent words like 'smitten', 'scathed', and 'lorn'. A small sample of this vocabulary (much of it eighteenth-century Miltonese) elsewhere in the book would be ' 'ere', 'e'n', 'ire', 'ireful', 'front [forehead]', 'viewless', 'jetty [black]', 'ebon', 'trackless', 'shrilly', 'gore', 'drear' and 'curbless'. There are many Latinistic or Miltonic locutions like 'his idea [the idea of him]', 'my view [the sight of me]' and 'I doubted not'. Unusual, often double-barrelled, adjectives abound: 'rayless', 'self-abandoned', 'death-struck'. There are also many participial or gerundive adjectives, again sometimes used in a quasi-Miltonic way: 'the whole consciousness of my life lorn' (for 'of my life being lorn', plus 'of my forlorn life'), and this goes with a liking for the use of the ablative absolute construction.

Still more noticeable is the recurrent and weird use of passive constructions where one would have expected active ones: 'these words went wandering up and down in my rayless mind, as something that should be whispered; but no energy was found to express them' (for 'as something that I should whisper; but I found/ had no energy to express them'). This is only one of many dissociation techniques in the style. It gives the effect of someone behaving compulsively, or being acted upon by external forces. That is, the self is presented as object, not subject (I believe this is also common in the thinking of schizophrenics). Thus Jane does not *think* disconnected words—words go wandering up and down in her mind, as if it were a place, full of independent entities. Related to this is the trademark of personification or semi-personification, especially of the heroine's feelings. I have already mentioned a major traditional use of personification, but the more personal use is different in its effect. Jane visualises her emotions as separate agents, and the style sets them to work in very physical, indeed violent ways. She energises the old metaphor of dead hopes by describing them as 'struck dead' and sees her love as a suffering child in a cold cradle over which she is helplessly watching. Reflection and, by implication, tears, come in a black confused flow; Jane *hears* her own feelings approaching her. The black confused flow becomes a flood that threatens to drown her, and the stricken faith sways sullenly above her (like an avalanche threatening to fall?).

The consciousness is stretched and so hyperactive that it splits into parts and the observer-self sits in the middle, registering all this activity around it. The narrator tries to numb herself, and to regain objectivity, by describing herself in the third person, as if she were somebody else: 'Jane Eyre, who had been an ardent expectant woman—almost a bride—was a cold, solitary girl again: her life was pale; her prospects were desolate.' Or one part of the consciousness addresses another in the second person.

So sustained is the dissociation-projection technique, so strong the sense of a drama going on not just within but around the heroine, that it takes a second for the reader to register that the 'Christmas frost' which has 'come at midsummer' bringing the 'white December storm' is part of an inner landscape, not an external scene.

The stage on which the psychic struggle is enacted is progressively expanded in space and time till it reaches cosmic proportions. The metaphor extends outwards to the pine-forests of Norway and backwards in time to the plagues of Egypt. The naturalness of that allusion reveals how readily the heroine thinks of herself as an object specially marked out by divine providence. From here, after a brief echo of *Macbeth*, the passage moves into a series of overt biblical references: 'Self-abandoned, relaxed, and effortless, I seemed to have laid me down in the dried-up bed of a great river; I heard a flood loosened in remote mountains, and I felt the torrent come' unites an image of spiritual lassitude from the Book of Job (14: 11–12)[2] with a cry of panic from Lamentations (3:54)[3] and the end of the passage is a loose quotation of the opening of the sixty-ninth Psalm.[4] The heroine boldly identifies herself through, and finally with, the great paradigms of suffering.

The novel implies a reader very familiar with the Old Testament, and with Bunyan. But its use of the Bible is idiosyncratic. Unlike, say, George Eliot, Charlotte Brontë blurs the dividing line between a quotation and her heroine's 'own' words. She uses a close, or only close-ish, quotation and works it intimately into the text, on two occasions unannounced even by quotation marks. She uses the Bible less as the source of ideas about God or moral conduct than as a way of defining her own experience. Bunyan of course does the latter, but in a specifically religious context, whereas Charlotte Brontë's narrator projects herself dramatically into the situation of the Old Testament speaker and rapidly adapts it to fit her own (a reverse of the usual practice). The biblical situation is removed from its original context into an erotic one. It is used 'blasphemously' in that a comparison is being made between a soul cut off from its God and a woman cut off from her lover.

However we read it, the passage sounds febrile and highly charged. But taken on its own like this, of course, it seems a good deal wilder, even madder, than when it is encountered in context. Naturally this is partly because we then have the whole story to date to assist us in interpreting the passage and in judging whether the heroine's reactions are excessive. But equally importantly, what in isolation might be seen as a congeries of purely stylistic features (lurid ones at that) turn out not to be used at random. A lot of them, in fact, turn out to provide some of the book's recurrent images and motifs, a substantial part of the 'detail' of the fictional world, miniature versions of events in it, and a microcosmic reflection of its dialectical structure. The ice and fire contrast has already emerged as a pattern in the book at both the literal and the metaphoric level, the white December storm reminds us of the 'real' one that has blasted the Thornfield chestnut tree, the image of the suffering child relates both to the young Jane—and one of her recent dreams—and to Helen Burns, and the world of Jane's childhood reading provides the nordic imagery.

But still, everything in the passage, as in the book, has a tremendously centripetal, egocentric reference, though this is partly disguised by the concreteness of the imagery. The effect is of nervous intensity cutting weirdly through a formal, literary style and a syntax that has a marked tendency to the stilted and the pedantic. The style of the Age of Reason meets and clashes with the style of the romance and its assimilations from the Bible and Bunyan. There is a double effect of repression and violence. The style itself enacts the struggle which is the theme of the plot: between Id and Superego, reaction and quiescence, private and public.

In one way the style, with its intense and unremitting concentration on the heroine and her feelings, is a highly self-conscious one. But in its uninhibited honesty and its lack of detachment it is unself-conscious in a manner now impossible to the post-Jamesian, post-Freudian English novel, aware that the House of Fiction has many windows and that the most significant glimpses of the author are the ones that are not intended. Charlotte Brontë has paid the price of this in the amount of biographically or psychoanalytically slanted criticism that her writing has attracted.

The loudness of tone in *Jane Eyre* is undoubtedly effective in communicating tension and frustration, but the style does of course have its related limitations. It precludes the use of the small suggestive detail or the quiet but telling observation that Mrs Gaskell and George Eliot are so good at. In such a fortissimo performance as this, the pianissimo gets drowned out, or noted only as an incongruity (which helps to account for the book's moments of unintended comic bathos). Again, it makes the whole question of modulation of tone a difficult one,[5] and it is also hard to manage irony elegantly, as the Brocklehurst and Ingram portraits show. There is unconscious ambiguity but little deliberate irony in *Jane Eyre*. Hence the remarkable unity of critical interpretation of the book—the reader knows all too well what he is meant to think about the heroine and the subsidiary characters. The novel does not merely request our judicious sympathy for the heroine, it demands that we see with her eyes, think in her terms, and hate her enemies, not just intermittently (as in *David Copperfield*) but *in toto*. It was, incidentally, because James Joyce recognised the similar tendency of *Stephen Hero* that he reshaped his autobiographical material as *A Portrait of the Artist as a Young Man*, retaining the 'first-person effect' but building in stylistic and structural irony that would guard against the appearance of wholesale authorial endorsement of Stephen.

There is not much of the middle or neutral narrative style in *Jane Eyre*— the sort of unremarkable style whose function is simply to get the plot along or the characters established for the reader. That the lurid style is not reserved for maximising the impact of the most sensational narrative events is evidenced by the above passage, which is analysing Jane's feelings *after* such an event. In fact one of the novelties of the Brontë method is that she manages to cast a unique aura of excitement around even the most superficially ordinary or bread-and-butter events, like Jane's decision to apply for a job as a governess (ch. 10). This comes to us as a dramatic dialogue between the heroine and herself, with all the momentousness of the conversion of a St Paul on the road to Damascus; and apparently the same divine agency is involved. It is at points like this that the reader is most struck by the book's intensity of treatment because the event is intrinsically so much less sensational than, say, the locking in the red room, not to mention the doings at Thornfield, so that the air of drama here is more obviously a function of the personality of the narrator. The red room description, in fact, has its companion-piece in the description of Thornfield drawing-room (ch. 11), a lavish and arresting study in the 'blending of snow and fire'. But in this drawing-room there takes place nothing more (or less) *tressaillant* than Jane's first extended cross-examination by Rochester. On the other hand it is the events that are sensational enough in themselves not to need a lot of stylistic intensification that offer a few surprises in the way of downbeat, deliberately humorous treatment. There is, most notably, the episode in which Jane saves Rochester from the maniac's bonfire. I am not sure whether Charlotte Brontë intended this symbolically, but the image of Jane pouring cold water on her 'master's' fiery bed is pleasingly reminiscent of Jane's habit, in the courtship scenes, of damping him down (verbally) whenever his behaviour becomes too amorous.[6]

But it is the prevalent intensity of treatment that establishes the book's atmosphere. It is also responsible for the absence of perspective. Since the scale of values is supplied by the heroine's feelings, it is difficult to make any useful distinction between 'major' and 'minor' events. If feeling is involved at all it is stirred to its depths. If not, the treatment is, on examination, unmistakably perfunctory, as in the way the novel presents (or fails to present) Jane's relationships with Mrs Fairfax and Adèle. Here there is a thinness of detail, and the reader, subconsciously missing the dramatic style, senses that he can relax his attention.

This absolutism is the stylistic equivalent of the all-or-nothing approach that Jane admits apropos St John Rivers (ch. 34): 'I know no medium: I never in my life have known any medium in my dealings with positive, hard characters, antagonistic to my own, between absolute submission and determined revolt. I have always faithfully observed the one, up to the very moment of bursting, sometimes with volcanic vehemence, into the other.' And of course this dialectic between absolute and violently opposed polarities is the essence of the book. Even the two Reed sisters make such a pair—an ascetic one with a mania for order and a hatred of the flesh, and a flighty sensualist. The reason why Helen Burns cannot function for the reader as the pattern of true Christian resignation that the author evidently intended her to be is that this exaggerative imagination has created her instead as the image of morbid stoicism, whose answer to the problem of suffering is to cultivate an exterior indifference to pleasure or pain, and whose death is the logical culmination of her effort to detach herself from the world. Her natural anti-type is of course mad Mrs Rochester, the fictional vandal of all time, who would like to tear the world apart with her teeth and then burn up the remnants.

The strain of Calvinism in Charlotte Brontë'e writing curiously reinforces the Romanticism with which it competes. It can be seen doing so in the long passage already quoted. Just as the style lacks a middle ground, so there is no middle ground—such as a sense of society would provide—between the individual self and the cosmos at large. This self-absorption is characteristic of both tempers, and Charlotte Brontë offers an unmediated confrontation between the self and its world, or the soul and its God. By the same token the fortissimo tone and the lack of rising and falling emphasis is a feature not only of the style but of the book's whole rhythm. It lives on its nerves, from crisis to crisis, and the pauses in the plot are not moments of quiet but bursts of mental activity.

I think this lack of middle ground or middle-distance detail can be related to the all-or-nothing feeling towards most of the subsidiary characters in Jane Eyre (apart from the one or two like Mrs Fairfax, for whom Jane feels a tolerant contempt). Usually the heroine either loves people intensely or is instantly repelled by them, deeply admires them or scathingly scorns them. (One catches the idiolect as one discusses the book.) Occasionally the heroine does both; her feelings may be mixed but they are seldom moderate. The lack of casual acquaintanceships and ordinary daily contacts in the *Jane Eyre* world increases the reader's sense of the heroine's psychic isolation, her orphanhood.

A pertinent case to cite here would be the revisit by the adult

Jane to the Reed household. To be sure it corrects the child's sense of the phantasmagoric awe-fulness of her aunt. But Jane's claimed forgiveness of her does nothing to render her less unpleasant or more understandable and hence pitiable (though her instinctive, irrational hatred of Jane is convincingly rendered).[7] But the heroine's new-found patience and tolerance is the measure less of a deepening view of her old foe than of the distance Jane has travelled on the road to external self-command, and of her new superiority to rejection and insult, which is mostly Rochester's doing. Indeed, she relishes the new challenge to 'subdue' Mrs Reed 'in spite of her nature and her will'. And her forgiveness has, as it were, no fictional outcome as the woman dies horribly and her children all go to the dogs.

Mrs Reed will stand for the pattern of all the dislikable characters in the book. All the nasty characters dislike or despise the heroine (Miss Abbot, the Reeds, Mr Brocklehurst, the Ingrams and so on), while all the good and nice characters admire or respond to her (Bessie, Helen Burns, Miss Temple, Mr Rochester of course, the Rivers sisters—their brother is a special case).

This fits entirely with the way the minor figures in the book are presented; though 'minor' is perhaps a misleading term in the context of autobiographical narrative, and certainly in the context of this book. The narrator's response to them is visual-intuitive. She studies their appearance, their faces and figures and often their voices too, and then makes a leap into a reading of their inner selves. This method has affinities with Bunyanesque allegorical portraiture, reinforced by phrenology.[8] But since both allegory and phrenology have to assume that character is fixed and given, not contingent and developing, the implication is that people do not change. More important in *Jane Eyre* is that the heroine's *view* of them cannot change or deepen in any essential respects; though we find that she herself resents the way other characters jump to conclusions about her, on the mere external evidence of her small plain appearance and lowly status. Again, the persistence of the phrenological method reveals the very real continuity of the adult with the childhood sections of the book. The child's vision persists, and the qualities that were strengths in the child (her imagination, her fighting spirit, and her will to survive) remain in the adult Jane as mixed blessings. It is for this reason that I remain admiring but doubtful about Q. D. Leavis's energetic attempt to read *Jane Eyre* as a realistic novel and to discuss it in terms of what Jane learns.[9]

At all events, by the same token that it is non-developmental, the phrenological method precludes gradual revelation of character, because all the evidence is there from the outset. Because of this, and also because the effect is so concentratedly vivid, the part that the characters will play later on is quite unpredictable from the mode of their introduction. There is no gradation of detail to indicate the characters' 'rank' in the book, little sense of a scale as between a full portrait and a light sketch (such as we can find in most Victorian fiction apart from that of Dickens). The method of presenting John Reed, Mrs Reed, Miss Temple, Lady Ingram and her daughter, and Mr Mason is essentially the same. Here is Mr Mason (whose failure to reappear significantly in the book in a villain's role would be bound to surprise a child reader)—

> His manner was polite; his accent, in speaking, struck me as being somewhat unusual—not precisely foreign, but still not altogether English [always a bad sign in a Brontë novel]: his age might be about Mr. Rochester's—between thirty and forty; his complexion was singularly sallow: otherwise he was a fine-looking man, at first sight especially. On closer examination, you detected something in his face that displeased; or rather, that failed to please. His features were regular, but too relaxed: his eye was large and well cut, but the life looking out of it was a tame, vacant life—at least so I thought.
>
> The sound of the dressing-bell dispersed the party. It was not till after dinner that I saw him again: he then seemed quite at his ease. But I liked his physiognomy even less than before: it struck me as being at the same time unsettled and inanimate. His eye wandered, and had no meaning in its wandering: this gave him an odd look, such as I never remembered to have seen. For a handsome and not an unamiable-looking man, he repelled me exceedingly: there was no power in that smooth-skinned face of a full oval shape; no firmness in that aquiline nose and small cherry mouth; there was no thought on the low, even forehead; no command in that blank, brown eye.
>
> (ch. 18)

In a similar fashion Lady Ingram's features and deportment all bespeak patrician pride, fierceness, hardness, pomposity and dogmatism. She has not one redeeming feature. She is Mrs Reed writ even larger, just as Bertha Rochester is Blanche Ingram gone crazy, and the confrontation between Jane and Bertha in Chapter 26 is a kind of re-working in reverse of the 'look upon this picture and on this' episode in which Jane tortures herself by drawing and comparing the portraits of herself and her imagined rival (ch. 16). In their address to servants, the Ingrams actually say things like 'Cease that chatter, blockhead, and do my bidding' and the mother calls her daughter 'My queenly Blanche'.

By contrast, benignant light shines from the irids of Miss Temple, and her sensitivity cannot be mistaken in her 'fine pencilling of long lashes'. It is eminently in keeping that Jane Eyre likes to paint people. She tends to represent them in terms of flashing eagle glances, sea-blue eyes, ivory or 'jetty' brows, and carrion images. But the main point is that this kind of presentation suggests no scale. That Miss Ingram should elicit hostile reactions is understandable, given her lofty station and supposed position as rival. There is some reason for the book's attention to her effect on Jane. But the extraordinary floodlighting of a character so microscopic as Mr Mason is quite unnecessary to the plot, and makes its real contribution to the understanding of the heroine's preferences and needs. It also reveals how, in the end, she confuses people's temperamental characteristics with their moral qualities. As in the case of St John Rivers, an emotional reaction from the heroine is also a moral judgement.

Characters in Brontë's work respond to each other immediately, intuitively and demonstratively. If they dislike each other, they radiate vibrations of antipathy and contempt. If they attract each other, it is straight away. Even Jane's accidental meeting with Rochester, before she knows who he is, strangely excites her and at once revives her dormant discontent with her useful, easy, secure but drab existence at Thornfield. When the pair have their first social introduction they get straight to the point and establish a personal, intimate, self-consciously suggestive tone of exchange, with Rochester laying on thick his image of aggressive, gruff, pouncing abruptness and Jane counterpointing it with demure caginess.[10]

The method is dramatic and strange even in the context of quite natural encounters. St John Rivers does not introduce himself to Jane by walking straight up his own garden path and inviting her into his house: he lurks around in the darkness listening in on her plea to the servant for help, till he overhears her say to herself 'I can but die, and I believe in God. Let me try to wait his will in silence.' Whereupon his disembodied voice sepulchrally replies 'All men must die, but all are not condemned to meet a lingering and premature doom, such as yours would be if you perished here of want.' And Jane, naturally, is startled. But the reader is by this time so inured to the strange atmosphere that he hardly notices St John's behaviour is odd. At least, it is not one of the incidents in the book that gets pointed out. Again St John, who seems to have some kind of an ancestor in Angelo in *Measure for Measure*, before he launches into a very Jane-ish declaration of passion for Miss Oliver, takes out his watch and puts it on the table to ensure that he will not indulge himself for longer than fifteen minutes. The ensuing discussion makes it clear that he is very angry with Miss Oliver for attracting him when she is such an unsuitable mate for him.

The attitudes throughout the novel are not balanced or compromised, but polarised. Jane Eyre's own violence emerges equally as passionate love, bitter hate, masochistic self-mockery and (when turned on society) as moral censoriousness. Since there is, for instance, no means offered for seeing past the heroine's vision of the Ingram family, it is more useful to take it as evidence about the narrator rather than as the social criticism she imagines it to be. It is part of that unbuttoned confessional honesty—honesty because it so unblushingly includes crabbed bigotry—which is one of the reasons why this novel is so original. We get the heroine fully, warts and all. Her prejudices are plain to see. On five separate occasions Jane indicates that all the child Adèle's failings stem from her continental heritage. In the final chapter it is claimed that 'a sound English education corrected in great measure her French defects.' And of course the improvement is accelerated by the fact that Adèle is now removed from the influence of Rochester's mistresses, of whom all are foreigners: Bertha is a Creole, Céline is French, Clara German, Giacinta Italian and, as it were, Blanche is also Angrian.

All this is really part of the characterisation of the fiercely Protestant, chauvinistic and self-righteous heroine, with her need to feel justified even if she cannot feel happy or socially accepted. Even her erotic drives include an element of conflict and pain that no English novelist apart from Richardson had ever recognised before as part of the experience of love. We need only consider the house-party at Thornfield, during which Rochester, with character-istic sadism, torments Jane by studiously ignoring her and paying attentions to Miss Ingram. 'I looked, and had an acute pleasure in looking—a precious yet poignant pleasure; pure gold, with a steely point of agony: a pleasure like what the thirst-perishing man might feel who knows the well to which he has crept is poisoned, yet stoops and drinks divine draughts nevertheless' (ch. 17). But Jane gets her own back at Ferndean when, under pretence of rous-ing him out of his melancholy (as she claims), she prolongs as long as she can his painful suspense about her relationship to St John Rivers, just as she punishes him for his cruel teasing of her in Thornfield garden by allowing him to suppose that he has only imagined her back at his side. Charlotte Brontë cannot imagine a love that does not include a powerful strain of violence and aggression—best exemplified, of course, in mad Mrs Rochester with her lust to attack the man she once loved, and her unerring knack of identifying the new object of his affections.

We are always sure that the heroine is fiery and passionate, which is quite an achievement when the plot has had to keep her passive, inactive and loveless for long stretches. Up to the point when Jane's love declares itself, the novel establishes the passion largely by negatives—a method very prophetic of that of D. H. Lawrence, who was in many ways influenced by Charlotte Brontë. Before we see the heroine in love, we are persuaded that she is a good hater. But the hatred has to be used as an oblique way of measuring her capacity to love. So it has both a cathartic function and a function in suggesting the heroine's affirmative side. She usually claims to dislike characters like Mr Mason on account of their lack of a quality she holds dear. In Mason it is the lack of that decisiveness and fiery courage that Rochester (and she) so conspicu-ously possess. The heroine's capacity for love has no channel until the lover presents himself, so it emerges as its opposite and con-tinues to imply it. And meanwhile the characters she hates are magnified into pseudo-objective symbols of that which is hateful. It is a 'wound and bow' process, à la Edmund Wilson.

At this point I would like to return to the question of the plot movement and the different narrative levels of the book. David Lodge raises a crucial issue when he asks 'how Charlotte Brontë created a literary structure in which the domestic and the mythical, the realistic world of social behaviour and the romantic world of passionate self-consciousness, could co-exist with only occasional lapses into incongruity.'[11] As far as the plot and setting go, however, this states the question rather misleadingly, for in fact at Thornfield there begins a progressive plot movement from realism to fantasy. By 'realism' I do not mean the predominance of the every day and commonplace, or an authorial objectivity of treatment, but simply the use of material that the reader can accept as existing in the ordinary world as well, or of events of a kind that might happen in it without being viewed as extraordinary. That is, things that have a face-value currency of meaning prior to any concealed meaning they may hold or suggest. Thus while Gateshead and Lowood School fit neatly into, and contribute importantly to, the symbolic pattern of the book, they are perfectly believable places in their own right. Even the heavy-handed and obvious satire of Mr Brocklehurst and his family does not invalidate him as a credible conception. But with the beginning of the mystery of the Thornfield attic the plot starts moving away from this face-value actuality. The Ingrams belong to the Angrian world; there is the coincidence of Uncle Eyre in Madeira happening to know the Masons in Jamaica, and alerting them to the bigamous marriage; the still more remarkable coincidence that Jane, wandering aimlessly around England, should stumble first go on her unknown cousins; then come the handy legacy, the still more convenient conflagration (after umpteen abortive attempts by the culprit), and the final telepathic communication that rescues Jane from St John Rivers at the eleventh hour.

Why do not more readers notice this drastic and quite sudden shift in plotting? They certainly notice the changes of gear in Dickens, Melville or Twain. It must be because there is no marked change of atmosphere. Charlotte Brontë may have a divided consciousness but she has a remarkably unified sensibility and this holds the book together even when the 'story-line' starts shooting off in strange directions. The reason it does so is that it has become increasingly difficult to continue the plot in the realistic vein because this would necessitate a modification of Jane's characteristic sensibility and vision. On the other hand, once the actual childhood is past, the book has to produce concrete 'evidence' to justify this way of seeing and relating to the world. So increasingly these elements that were initially visible mainly in the style, and also in the world of Jane's reading and dreaming, become concretised as characters and plot events. It is the early stages of this process that we can see in the passage from Chapter 26, in the dramatisation of Jane's emotions. But meanwhile, starting with the child's magnified vision has established the dominant viewpoint and prepared the reader for the persistent distortion which is the essence of the book's method. This is really only a way of saying that the book moves increasingly closer to expressionism, and this can, in a way, be measured in the progression from Mrs Reed to Blanche Ingram to the first Mrs Rochester.

Reading Mrs Gaskell's *Life of Charlotte Brontë* after *Jane Eyre* is a curious experience. The subject of the biography is recognisably the same person who wrote the novel, but the effect of the two books is utterly different. The biography is indeed depressing and painful reading. It captures better, I believe, than any any subsequent biography the introverted and puritan pessimist side of Charlotte Brontë, and conveys the real dreariness of the world of privation, critical discouragement and limited opportunity that so often made her complain in her letters that she felt marked out for suffering.

Jane Eyre, on the other hand, is exhilarating reading, partly because the reader, far from simply pitying the heroine, is struck by her resilience, and partly because the novel achieves such an imaginative transmutation of the drab. Unlike that of Jane Austen's Fanny Price or Dickens's Arthur Clennam or John Harmon, Jane Eyre's response to suffering is never less than energetic. The reader is torn between exasperation at the way she mistakes her resentments and prejudices for fair moral judgements, and admiration at the way she fights back. Matthew Arnold, seeking 'sweetness and light' was repelled by the 'hunger, rebellion and rage' that he identified as the keynotes of the novel. One can see why, and yet feel that these have a more positive effect than his phrase allows. The heroine is trying to hold on to her sense of self in a world that gives it little encouragement, and the novel does put up a persuasive case for her arrogance and pugnacity as the healthier alternatives to patience and resignation. That the book has created a world in which the golden mean seems such a feeble solution is both its eccentricity and its strength.

NOTES

1. After writing this essay I encountered Margot Peters's interesting book *Charlotte Brontë, Style in the Novel* (Wisconsin, 1973), and found that some of the stylistic features which have struck me, such as the syntactic antithesis and adverbial displacement, had also engaged her attention. I have left my earlier paragraphs as they were, in the interests of an argument that takes a rather different direction. But it is significant that neither reader has experienced the medium as a perspicuous one or reacted to it *as* a medium; rather, it impinges directly as part of the message.

2. As the waters fail from the sea,
   And the river decayeth and drieth up.
   So man lieth down and riseth not;
   Till the heavens be no more, they shall not awake,
   Nor be roused out of their sleep.

3. Waters flowed over mine head; I said, I am cut off.

4. Save me, O God;
   For the waters are come in unto my soul.
   I sink in deep mire, where there is no standing;
   I am come into deep waters, where the floods overflow me.

5. There is a kind of parallel to this in the later style of Gerard Manley Hopkins. It revels in the more violent emotions but finds it hard to change key or accommodate the quieter emotions. Poems like 'That Nature is a Heraclitean Fire' have to be wrenched forcibly around to convey changes of mood. This poem starts in exuberant animal spirits, suddenly plummets to black despair, and then equally suddenly soars up in confident hope in the last section. The effect is rather manic-depressive.

6. A similar episode, which everyone remembers, involves Jane's naughty retort to the question about what she must do to save her soul. She replies that she must keep in good health and not die. Moments of humour like this mark the occasions when she is able to manifest her inner self-confidence.

7. Cf. the way Miss Scatcherd dislikes Helen Burns, and Miss Ingram dislikes Adèle.

8. Direct references to phrenology would include the following:

   'I suppose I have a considerable organ of veneration.' (ch. 5, p. 79)

   'And Helen obeyed, my organ of veneration expanding at every sounding line.' (ch. 8, p. 105)

   'He lifted up the sable waves of hair which lay horizontally over his brow, and showed a solid enough mass of intellectual organs, but an abrupt deficiency where the suave sign of benevolence should have risen.' (ch. 14, p. 163).

'Really your organs of wonder and credulity are easily excited.'
(ch. 18, p. 222)

'You who have an eye for natural beauties, and a great deal of the
organ of Adhesiveness?' (ch. 23, p. 278)

Serious uses of the concept that the whole character and inner life can be
deduced or 'read' in the 'physiognomy' are a vital part of the method of
characterisation throughout the novel.

After Jane's formal introduction to Rochester, she gives a portrait of him
based on a reading of his 'broad and jetty eyebrows, his square forehead, . . . his full nostrils, denoting . . . choler; his grim mouth, chin, and
jaw.' (ch. 13, p. 151). In ch. 14 Rochester achieves a lengthy divination of
Jane's character, all based on what he 'reads' in her 'eyes' having already
guessed her unspoken thoughts simply from her 'glance'. (pp. 166–7). He
follows this up, of course, with more of the same in the famous gypsy
scene. Jane says that he 'had sometimes read [her] unspoken thoughts with
an acumen to [her] incomprehensible.' (ch. 22, p. 273). This fits in with the
instinct he has developed which tells him when Jane is in the offing, without having to look. (ch. 23). Even Lady Ingram claims to be 'a judge of
physiognomy' who can read in Jane's 'all the faults of her class.' (ch. 17,
p. 206). St. John Rivers has the same powers: 'I trace lines of force in her
face which make me sceptical of her [Jane's] tractability.' (ch. 29, p. 366).
After reviewing only the barest sketch of Jane's history, he discerns that in
her nature is an alloy as detrimental to repose as his own. His evidence is
a leisurely reading of her face, 'as if its features and lines were characters
on a page.' (ch. 30, pp. 380–1). Jane intuits the characters of the Rivers
trio with the same immediacy, and has even less difficulty in understanding
Miss Oliver: 'I had learnt her whole character.' (ch. 32, p. 394). And St
John also has a Rochesterian 'instinct' which 'seemed to warn him of her
[Miss Oliver's] entrance, even when he did not see it.' (ch. 32, p. 393. All
references are to the Penguin Edition.)

I have not even given a complete list here of such phenomena.

9. In her Introduction to the Penguin edition of *Jane Eyre*.
10. Robert Heilman in 'Charlotte Brontë's "New" Gothic' is the first critic
    to have given a really thorough account of the pervasive sexiness of
    Charlotte Brontë's writing. It needs more than the specific history of
    Rochester to account for the strength of Victorian attacks on *Jane Eyre*
    as an immoral work.
11. 'Fire and Eyre: Charlotte Brontë's War of Earthly Elements', in *The
    Language of Fiction* (London, 1966). Both this essay and Heilman's
    appear in *The Brontës*, ed. Ian Gregor, in the Twentieth Century Views
    series.

8

Reading *David Copperfield*

by KEITH CARABINE

I first read *David Copperfield* in the autumn of 1977 over a period
of three weeks, instalment by instalment, with up to a day's wait
between each. I want in this essay to remain faithful to my initial
responses, and to my simultaneous attempt to record and understand my involvement, anticipations and queries. I am now in a
position of hindsight which Dickens only totally attained at the
end, as over a period of nineteen months, never more than one
instalment ahead, he had the courage and confidence in his creative
genius to share his shifting, developing sense of the meaning and
shape of David's life with his expectant readers.[1]

The opening note of interrogation which so unsettles the reader
—'Whether I shall turn out to be the hero of my own life, or
whether that station will be held by anyone else these pages must
show'—is, until the death of Dora, the keynote of the novel.
Immediately we are alerted to the startling possibility that the
autobiographer is not only unsure of the status of his own life *at
the time of writing*, but that it will be the very act of writing itself
which will enable him to discover the form and value of his life.
And, as a serial reading emphasises, the shape David's autobiography assumes is the shape Dickens discovers and the reader is
invited to anticipate and share. It is not surprising, therefore, that
the opening words should draw attention to the fiction as process,
exploration and discovery for the author, the autobiographer and
the reader.[2]

I want in this essay (1) to register the different kinds of reading
experiences the novel's shifting perspectives elicit: namely, our
absorption in David's recreation of his childhood years; the emblematic patterning which occurs 'post Dover' as we become aware
of the novel's themes; and our equivocal participation in David's
equivocal responses to such figures as Heep; (2) to show that the

form which *David Copperfield* traces on the reader's mind is, for
three quarters of its span, extraordinarily plural and unsettling,
as we follow a consciousness at once capable of triumphantly conveying the richness of its own experience, but finally being tested
(and found wanting) by that experience. Now whether that failure
is created in the book, or exists putatively—as through a glass
darkly—in the space between Dickens's writing self and his narrator,
is a puzzle we may never solve. It is however a puzzle which engages our reading selves in an analogous way so that we, too, are
involved in the sustained delight of re-creating youthful memories,
yet forced into a cautious, bemused scrutiny once David moves
from witness into judge.

Let me begin with the opening of Chapter 2 where child, autobiographer, author and reader 'observe in little pieces as it were;
but as to making a net of these pieces and catching anybody in it,
that was as yet, beyond me' (ch. 2).

> The first objects that assume a distinct presence before me, as
> I look far back, into the blank of my infancy, are my mother with
> her pretty hair and youthful shape, and Peggotty, with no shape
> at all, and eyes so dark that they seemed to darken their whole
> neighbourhood in her face, and cheeks and arms so hard and
> red that I wondered the birds didn't peck her in preference to
> apples.

> . . .

> This may be fancy, though I think the memory of most of us
> can go farther back into such times than many of us suppose;
> just as I believe the power of observation in numbers of very
> young children to be quite wonderful for its closeness and
> accuracy. Indeed, I think that most grown men who are remark-
> able in this respect, may with greater propriety be said not to
> have lost the faculty, than to have acquired it; the rather, as I
> generally observe such men to retain a certain freshness, and
> gentleness, and capacity of being pleased, which are also an in-
> heritance they have preserved from their childhood.

> . . .

> Looking back, as I was saying, into the blank of my infancy,
> the first objects I can remember as standing out by themselves

151

from a confusion of things, are my mother and Peggotty. What else do I remember? Let me see.

There comes out of the cloud, our house—not new to me, but quite familiar, in its earliest remembrance. On the ground-floor is Peggotty's kitchen, opening into a back yard; with a pigeon-house on a pole, in the centre, without any pigeons in it; a great dog kennel in a corner, without any dog; and a quantity of fowls that look terribly tall to me, walking about in a menacing and ferocious manner. . . . Of the geese outside the side-gate who come waddling after me with their long necks stretched out when I go that way, I dream at night; as a man environed by wild beasts might dream of lions.

Here is a long passage—what an enormous perspective I make of it!—leading from Peggoty's kitchen to the front-door. A dark store-room opens out of it, and that is a place to be run past at night; for I don't know what may be among those tubs and jars and old tea-chests, when there is nobody in there with a dimly-burning light, letting a mouldy air come out at the door, in which there is the smell of soap, pickles, pepper, candles, and coffee, all at one whiff. . . . There is something of a doleful air about that room [the parlour where we sit on Sunday] to me, for Peggotty has told me . . . about my father's funeral, and the company having their black cloaks put on. One Sunday night my mother reads to Peggotty and me in there, how Lazarus was raised up from the dead. And I am so frightened that they are afterwards obliged to take me out of bed, and show me the quiet churchyard out of the bedroom window, with the dead all lying in their graves at rest, below the solemn moon.

This passage anticipates James's observation nearly fifty years later in his preface to *What Maisie Knew* that 'small children have many more perceptions than they have terms to translate them; their vision is at any moment much richer, their apprehension even constantly stronger, than their prompt, their at all producable vocabulary.' Yet though we are aware of Dickens creating a language for the child's 'seeing', we do not feel as in *What Maisie Knew* that we have lost the perspective characteristic of the closeness and accuracy of the wonderful 'power of observation' that 'numbers of very young children' possess—particularly the young child who grew into the novelists Charles Dickens and David Copperfield.

'Let me see' is a deliberate attempt to invoke childhood memories which come involuntarily 'out of the cloud' with the dramatic immediacy of genies out of a magic lamp. When we read 'here is a long passage—what an enormous perspective I make of it' or later 'here is our pew in church. What a high backed pew!', we are sharing not only the experience firsthand of the child for whom all objects were 'enormous' and all events frightening, but too we are living through the recollecting novelist's attempt at once to fill the 'blank of my infancy' and 'blank' space of the page with words. Dickens has achieved 'an enormous perspective' which enables us simultaneously to share the painful immediacy of the child's experiences and the triumphant joy of Dickens/David who has conquered the blank void of childhood via the magic of his art. In this long passage we delight in the freshness of the child's responses and 'the capacity of being pleased' and in the exhilarating activity of remembering and composing so characteristic of the charm of the marvellous early chapters of *David Copperfield*.

Neither David's mother with 'her pretty hair and youthful shape' nor Peggotty's presence can, however, prevent the recreation of infancy taking the shape of bad dreams; fear, insecurity and loneliness are the notes struck even before the Murdstones appear to shatter the fragile peace of Blunderstone. And, of course, David's pre-adolescent experiences chronicle the exploitation of David's innocence and trusting good nature. It is not surprising, therefore, that in the midst of his agonised remembrance of his awful schooldays David should fixate on the handsome, dashing, powerful Steerforth, and should remember 'one other event in this half-year out of the daily school life that made an impression upon me which still survives . . . for many reasons.'

> One afternoon, when we were all harrassed into a state of dire confusion, and Mr. Creakle was laying about him dreadfully, Tungay came in, and called out in his usual strong way: 'Visitors for Copperfield!' . . .
>
> . . . and then I . . . quite faint with astonishment, was told to go by the back stairs and get a clean frill on . . . These orders I obeyed, in such a flutter and hurry of my young spirits as I had never known before; and when I got to the parlour door, and the thought came into my head that it might be my mother—I had only thought of Mr. or Miss Murdstone until then—I drew back my hand from the lock, and stopped to have a sob before I went in.

At first I saw nobody; but feeling a pressure against the door, I looked round it, and there, to my amazement, were Mr. Peggotty and Ham, ducking at me with their hats, and squeezing one another against the wall. I could not help laughing; but it was much more in the pleasure of seeing them, than at the appearance they made. We shook hands in a very cordial way; and I laughed and laughed, until I pulled out my pocket-handkerchief and wiped my eyes.

Mr. Peggotty (who never shut his mouth once, I remember, during the visit) showed great concern when he saw me do this, and nudged Ham to say something.

'Cheer up, Mas'r Davy bor'!' said Ham, in his simpering way. 'Why, how you have growed!'

'Am I grown?' I said, drying my eyes. 'I was not crying at anything in particular that I know of; but somehow it made me cry, to see old friends.'

'Growed, Mas'r Davy bor'? Ain't he growed!' said Ham.

'Ain't he growed!' said Mr. Peggotty.

They made me laugh again by laughing at each other, and then we all three laughed until I was in danger of crying again.

'Do you know how mama is, Mr. Peggotty?' I said. 'And how my dear, dear old Peggotty is?'

'Oncommon,' said Mr. Peggotty.

'And little Em'ly, and Mrs. Gummidge?'

'On-common,' said Mr. Peggotty.

There was a silence. Mr. Peggotty, to relieve it, took two prodigious lobsters, and an enormous crab, and a large canvas bag of shrimps, out of his pockets, and piled them up in Ham's arms.

'You see,' said Mr. Peggotty 'knowing as you was partial to a little relish with your wittles when you was along with us, we took the liberty. The old Mawther biled 'em, she did. Mrs. Gummidge biled 'em. Yes,' said Mr. Peggotty, slowly, who I thought appeared to stick to the subject on account of having no other subject ready, 'Mrs. Gummidge, I do assure you, she biled 'em.'

(ch. 7)

This isolated sponstaneous act of kindness to the weeping, neglected child, following so sharply upon the spectacle of the innocent child complicit in the sacking of the gentle Mr Mell, doubly vulnerable to the sadism of Creakle and the arrogance and mean-spiritedness of Steerforth, so tugged my own sympathies that when I first read this sequence I found myself crying. The final wrench for me was David's observation that Mr Peggotty spoke to 'relieve' a silence (how different to Tungay's ferocious cry of 'Silence' at the beginning of the chapter which struck all the boys 'speechless and motionless!') and that he spoke slowly and repeated 'Mrs Gummidge, I do assure you, she biled 'em' 'on account of having no other subject ready'. How marvellously true to experience this distancing remark of David's is. Peggotty and Ham have sailed over a hundred miles to be kind to a little boy; they find themselves in a strange school and feel embarrassed; David's tears unnerve them further, and they can only mutter awkward commonplaces. Peggotty, unlike Steerforth for example, does not have 'charm'; he feels, and his feelings redeem the true meaning of such words and values as 'duty', 'earnestness' and 'humbly' (which the novel goes on to scrutinise via all the relationships, but particularly Agnes to her father, Heep to the world, and Mrs Steerforth to her son). The artless kindness of the pair serves effortlessly to illuminate the empty class pride and callowness of Steerforth (writ large we learn later in Rosa Dartle, one of Steerforth's mirror characters). The subsequent entrance of Steerforth increases our unease because we realise that Peggotty's immense good nature and earnestness go hand in glove with an alarming ignorance about human behaviour and manners. As we know from Dickens's notes for this third instalment he first intended the visit to the school to be made by Peggotty herself, but then realised that this would be an ideal moment for her brother to meet Steerforth and thus prepare for the latter's visit to Yarmouth and his eventual seduction of, and elopement with, David's childhood sweetheart, Little Em'ly.[3] Thus this is a key moment in the narrative patterning of the book and is, in fact, the first indication that the novel will be patterned (in part) around recurrences of the various characters. But though the scene is introduced retrospectively as an event which 'made an impression upon me which still survives for many reasons' the reader is left to deduce the reasons for himself. David the elder is true both to the emotions of his younger self which we share with delight and foreboding and to his elegiac recognition during the actual writing that he 'still believes in', and succumbs to, Steerforth's 'spell . . . to which it was a natural weakness to yield'; especially to the sensitive, isolated child whom he protected and inadvertently prepared for authorship by insisting on playing the Sultan to David's Scheherazade.

David's arrival at Dover, even on a first read, is clearly a watershed in the novel, and follows upon perhaps the most dramatic 'wait' Dickens imposed upon his original readers. I certainly had no sense that the young boy I had left at the end of the fourth instalment in a characteristically exploited position—alone in the middle of London, 'panting and crying' after being robbed by the 'long legged carter' (ch. 12)—would by the end of the new number not only have arrived safely at Dover on foot, but that the redoubtable Aunt Betsey of the opening chapter would turn out to be a fairy godmother, who after vanquishing the Murdstones, would adopt him and generously provide him with a place in a select public school where he is, immediately, set fair to 'make another beginning.'[4]

David at Dover has reached that point James noted of Maisie in the preface to *What Maisie Knew*: Maisie 'wonders . . . to the end' which is also 'the death of her childhood, properly speaking, after which (with the inevitable shift, sooner or later, of her point of view) her situation will change and become another affair subject to other measurements and with a new centre altogether . . . there will be another scale, another perspective, another horizon'. Unlike James however or Dickens's early novels *Oliver Twist* and *The Old Curiosity Shop*, which end with 'the death of childhood', Dickens faces the challenge of finding a point of view flexible enough to handle David's changed situation and new 'affairs'. In order to do so Dickens has David bid farewell to his childhood.[5]

> Thus I began my new life, in a new name, and with everything new about me. Now that the state of doubt was over, I felt, for many days, like one in a dream. . . . I never thought of anything about myself, distinctly. The two things clearest in my mind were, that a remoteness had come upon the old Blunderstone life—which seemed to lie in the haze of an immeasurable distance; and that a curtain had for ever fallen on my life at Murdstone and Grinby's. No one has ever raised that curtain since. I have lifted it for a moment, even in this narrative, with a reluctant hand, and dropped it gladly. The remembrance of that life is fraught with so much pain to me, with so much mental suffering and want of hope, that I have never had the courage even to examine how long I was doomed to lead it. Whether it lasted for a year, or more, or less, I do not know. I only know that it was, and ceased to be; and that I have written, and there I leave it.
>
> (ch. 14)

And 'there' indeed David tries to leave it. (Even the solicitous Heep in Chapter 18 fails to pump 'Murdstone and Grinby . . . and my journey' out of him.) In the first fourteen chapters David had been most definitely 'the hero of (his) own life' and the 'centre' of the reader's experience. Furthermore the reader has felt that the very activity of remembering and recording 'so much pain' 'even in the narrative' is typical of the courage and resilience of the child who walked to Dover. One problem for the reader subsequently is that we seem to remember the 'mental suffering and want of hope' more acutely than David himself. There is a seeming want of psychological and experiential continuity between David the child, the adolescent and the adult, which he himself recognises in the first 'Retrospect' of the novel when, from the double perspective of head boy and autobiographer, he thinks of his younger self 'as something left behind upon the road of life—as something I have passed rather than actually been—and almost think of him as somebody else' (ch. 18). The reader however remembers the 'actual road' which lies behind the fond metaphor.

One feature of the first fourteen chapters which no commentator, to my knowledge, has noticed is that the pattern of David's childhood provides the paradigm for all the subsequent 'plots' in *David Copperfield*. The remaining three quarters of the novel repeat the curve of David's childhood: and the reader gradually realises that Dickens is charting and interweaving the growth and increasing dominance and subsequent removal of the threats of Jack Maldon to the Strongs (ch. 45); of Aunt Betsey's shadowy husband (ch. 49); of Steerforth to Em'ly and Peggotty (ch. 50); of Heep to the Wickfields and David (ch. 52); of Dora to David (ch. 53); of impecunity and Heep to the Micawbers (ch. 54); and of Sophy's mother to Traddles (ch. 59). At the end of the novel all disturbing influences have been banished and all the main 'good' characters have made successful 'new beginnings': the Strongs as a happily married couple; Peggotty, Em'ly, Mrs Gummidge, Martha, the Micawbers and Mr Mell in Australia; Mr Dick as a copyist; Traddles as judge and family man, and of course David as blissfully happy husband of Agnes, father of a thriving brood and a respected and successful author.

The fairy story ending to David's awful childhood may provide the 'horizon' of all the other 'affairs' of the book, which therefore parallel David's own career, but 'the perspective and the measure' of the initial paradigm has been drastically shifted. This is not merely because David as an adolescent and young man has views, hopes and passions (e.g. that to be a proctor is an admirable vocation, or that Dora is everything he wants in a woman) which inevitably involve him in several different 'centres', nor is it merely because David must become more passive and colourless in order to record such vibrant colourful individuals as Heep, Miss Mowcher, Littimer *et al*: rather it is that the imperative need he discovers in the writing to let 'the curtain' fall forever on his life at Murdstone and Grinby's necessitates he begin 'life' anew with 'a perspective and measure' which will ensure he need never raise it again.

Not surprisingly the figure whose role and task it is to ensure this compulsive wish be granted is introduced the moment David makes 'another beginning.'

> We accordingly went up a wonderful old staircase; with a balustrade so broad that we might have gone up that, almost as easily; and into a shady old drawing-room, lighted by some three or four of the quaint windows I had looked up at from the street: . . . It was a prettily furnished room, with a piano and some lively furniture in red and green, and some flowers. It seemed to be all old nooks and corners; . . . On everything there was the same air of retirement and cleanliness that marked the house outside.
>
> Mr. Wickfield tapped at a door in a corner of the panelled wall, and a girl of about my own age came quickly out and kissed him. On her face I saw immediately the placid and sweet expression of the lady whose picture had looked at me down-stairs. It seemed to my imagination as if the portrait had grown womanly, and the original remained a child. Although her face was quite bright and happy, there was a tranquillity about it, and about her—a quiet, good, calm spirit—that I never have forgotten; that I shall never forget.
>
> This was his little housekeeper, his daughter Agnes, Mr. Wickfield said. . . .
>
> She had a little basket-trifle hanging at her side, with keys in it; and she looked as staid and as discreet a housekeeper as the old house could have. She . . . proposed to my aunt that we should go upstairs and see my room. . . . A glorious old room it was, with more oak beams, and diamond panes; . . .
>
> I cannot call to mind where or when, in my childhood, I had seen a stained glass window in a church. Nor do I recollect its

subject. But I know that when I saw her turn round, in the grave light of the old staircase, and wait for us, above, I thought of that window, and I associated something of its tranquil brightness with Agnes Wickfield ever afterwards.

(ch. 15)

Agnes is both amalgam and apex of all the 'good' characters we have encountered in the book. She has the gentleness of David's mother and Mr Mell, and the goodness and devotion of the Peggottys, Ham and Aunt Betsey. Similarly her house, like Peggotty's boat and Aunt Betsey's cottage is a 'retreat', neat, clean and old-fashioned. One crucial feature of this passage is that we are conscious for the first time in the novel that David is *not always*, as he claims, 'a child of close observation'. Nothing in the above passage is individuated. Whereas 'quaint', 'old', 'pretty', 'some lively furniture . . . some flowers' are unspecific and tired phrases, Peggotty's boat which has 'a nosegay of seaweed in a blue mug on the table' (ch. 3), and Aunt Betsey's cottage where even 'the tall press has an expectant air' are idiosyncratic and precise, and richly illustrative of their owner's personalities.

Clearly to remember Agnes is neither (as with Peggotty) to dramatise her, nor is it to allow the reader to share either the immediacy of the youth's experience of her, or the joy of creating her and filling the blank space on the page; nor is it as with the remembrance of the bottle factory to face 'without any invocation . . . a ghost' which 'haunted happier times': rather to remember Agnes is to suggest that David *immediately* wishes to render her as beyond change as 'a stained glass window in a church'. Her 'quiet, good, calm spirit' her 'tranquillity' from this point on permeates and finally determines the ostensible shape and meaning of David's life and of his narrative. As Agnes says, and all the plots prove, 'real love and faith are stronger in the end than any evil or misfortune in the world' (ch. 35). David learns to 'discipline his heart' and cleanse it of 'the alloy of self' in order to earn the right to share and enjoy 'the tranquil brightness' she has always had: and which to extol is (fictionally) to embalm her.

Agnes serves as the emblem and source of an accepted and desired piety, involving self-abnegation, passive endurance and Christian hope; but, fortunately, her influence only gradually pervades David's consciousness and forms his narrative. David does not seem to realise that the values, meanings and the vision she embodies are at odds both with those of the first fourteen chapters, in which the 'source' of Dickens/David's creative energies are to be found, and with the equivocal, subterranean energies his narrative releases. Thus David the child survives because he has the will and animosity to bite Murdstone and the tenacity both to endure 'the secret agony of my soul' and to ensure that his ambition to become 'a learned and distinguished man' (ch. 11) should not perish among the dirty bottles in Murdstone and Grinby's warehouse. David's walk to Dover is as irrepressible an assertion of individuality and of the will to succeed as Heep's faith in his father's words, 'be 'umble Uriah . . . and you'll get on' (ch. 39), or Littimer's persistent worship of the god of 'respectability'. Moreover the child survives not because of the intermittent love and protection he receives from his mother and the Peggottys and Mr Mell, but because, though 'an innocent romantic boy', his active curiosity and close observation enable him, as it enabled his creator, 'to make his imaginative world out of such strange experiences and sordid things'.[6]

Henry James noted in his Preface to *The Ambassadors* that in *David Copperfield* the hero is equipped with 'the double privilege of subject and object' which 'single mouthful of method' risks 'the terrible fluidity of self revelation'. James felt confident he had used and placed his protagonist because Strether had 'exhibited conditions to meet'. The 'fluidity' of *David Copperfield* is such that one cannot be certain of either David's relation to his own narrative or of Dickens's relationship to his narrative or his protagonist. One great bonus however in reading *David Copperfield* which James with his emphasis on 'the large ease of autobiography' misses, is that the reader is aware of mysterious, ambivalent and disturbing forces at work in the fiction; and, as ever in Dickens, that the strange experiences and sordid things are embodied in the eccentrics (Heep, Micawber, Barkis, Miss Mowcher, Mr Dick *et al*). As we follow their careers we see that they promote rival centres and perspectives to those of both Agnes and David. They are more compelling refractions of David's attempt to discover his identity and they sponsor equivocal reactions in David and the Reader. They promote such powerfully suggestive, insidious images that one soon suspects that the initial icon of Agnes reflects David's (Dickens's) need to try and anchor his wishful positives, because he is aware of the subterranean depths he wants to ignore but which he has plumbed and must ineluctably canvass.

The middle chapters (15–44) of *David Copperfield* chart the clash between David's initial recognition and movement towards 'the tranquil brightness' of Agnes and the patterns she sponsors, and his ambivalent, fascinated involvement with such figures as Dora, Mr Dick, Heep and Miss Mowcher who provide irresistible opportunities for 'volatility', proliferation and self-assertion.[7] I do not have room to explore this argument, but I would like to extract two 'threads' in the novel, namely Heep's place in David's life and narrative and Dora's death, in order to capture how elusive, uncertain and surprising these middle chapters are, and how intimately connected the ramifications of the former are with the central decision the latter involved.[8]

Heep and Agnes appear for the first time in Chapter 15 and are immediately presented as opposites: Heep is like 'a face on the beam end', gargoyle as against 'stained glass window'. Heep's 'cadaverous face' is the first occupant of the Wickfield home David espies and he is immediately entranced by him: 'I caught a glimpse . . . of Uriah Heep breathing into the pony's nostrils, and immediately covering them with his hand as if he were putting some spell upon him'. Heep's 'spell' on David, as the single image testifies, sponsors more fictional life and suggests more imaginative involvement than the reams of 'uplift'[9] embodied in Agnes's rival 'quiet, good, calm spirit'. Heep becomes for the reader one of the most haunting and richly suggestive of all Dickens's characters because David's spellbound state, his fear and loathing (which he never analyses) are turned back on himself.[10] Following upon what Micawber inappropriately calls 'the final pulverisation' of Heep we learn from Traddles that Mr Wickfield 'relieved of the incubus that had fastened upon him . . . is hardly the same person' (ch. 54).[11] Heep is an incubus in both the literal and figurative senses of the word, namely, 'a demon supposed to mate with sleeping women' and an 'obsessive anxiety or nightmare'. To see Heep as an incubus is clearly to mitigate and deflect criticism of Mr Wickfield's culpability; similarly, but more significantly, Heep embodies and deflects those elements of David which the new 'perspective' demands he deny—namely his ambition and his sexuality. Heep thus channels the guilt which as Hillis Miller has observed always hovers for Dickens 'over the man who takes matters into his own hands'.[12] Heep, who like David is fatherless, is 'brought up at a foundation school', fed ' 'umbleness' as the key to worldly success, and who embezzles, is one potential fate David knows he has avoided: . . . 'I might easily have been a little robber or vagabond' (ch. 11).

Heep as incubus threatens Agnes's purity and the Wickfield home which constitutes a hallowed, unchanging spot in David's memory. In a revealing juxtaposition David's 'fall into captivity' with Dora (ch. 26) occurs in the ninth instalment following upon Heep's confession (and warning) that 'the image of Miss Agnes had been in my breast for years. Oh, Master Copperfield with a pure affection do I love the ground my Agnes walks on!' David's reaction is extremely strange:

> I believe I had a delirious idea of seizing the red-hot poker out of the fire, and running him through with it. It went from me with a shock, like a ball fired from a rifle: but the image of Agnes, outraged by so much as a thought of this red-handed animal's, remained in my mind . . . and made me giddy. He seemed to swell and grow before my eyes . . . and the strange feeling . . . that all this had occurred before at some indefinite time, and that I would know what he was going to say next, took possession of me.
>
> . . .
>
> . . . 'I call her mine, you see, Master Copperfield. There's a song that says, "I'd crowns resign, to call her mine!" I hope to do it, one of these days.'
> Dear Agnes! So much too loving and too good for anyone that I could think of, was it possible that she was reserved to be the wife of such a wretch as this!
>
> ch. 25)

Heep knows ('I'd crowns resign') what David has to learn, and even on a first read we anticipate David will marry Agnes and see Heep as a dark parody of David's own desires; hidden from him by *his* Agnes, whom he has anxiously encompassed and fixed, but denied sexuality by his images of 'sister' and 'good angel'. Heep here registers (as Steerforth did earlier) the sexual feelings David ('Daisy') fails to recognise in himself because of his commitment to the values of childhood innocence which he ostensibly embraces at the end with Agnes who has kept 'everything as it used to be when we were children' (ch. 60). Heep at the height of his influence supplants David and sleeps in his room in the Wickfield home (ch. 35). Heep is a rival and 'double' David cannot and will not recognise; and his presence suggests that David's images of Agnes may be implausible, and that his values embody an unconscious regression.

The 'wretch' Heep as a potential husband and polluter of the Wickfield home affects David 'like a walking nightmare' later that night when the Wickfield's 'arose before me with appealing faces and filled me with vague terrors'. David however falls into captivity with Dora and thus betrays 'the appealing faces' (and his true self as he would later have us believe), leaving Agnes increasingly vulnerable to Heep's blackmail.

Though we may feel that Dickens has used Heep to provide a perspective on David that the latter does not share, we cannot know of course what was in Dickens's mind when he wrote 'was it possible that she was to be reserved to be the wife of such a wretch as this!' but once again we note as in the opening sentence of the novel how Dickens seemingly is intent on keeping his options open. The Heep/Agnes and David/Dora 'courtships' run in tandem throughout chapters 25 to 47 and one curious spin-off is that despite David's protestations to the contrary we realise Dora is as big a threat to his integrity as Heep to Agnes's and to his own. During these middle chapters the reader is continually unsettled as the 'threads' of David's fear that Heep will supplant him, tangle with his movement towards marriage (particularly in the thirteenth instalment (ch. 38) when Mr Spenlow is unceremoniously killed off thus facilitating the marriage), and with the thread of the Dora and Agnes opposition (mainly to the latter's disadvantage of course) and with David's persistent tributes to the 'precepts' he owes to Agnes (as late as Chapter 42) which precede his marriage to Dora.

It came as no surprise when I read Forster that Dickens's 'principal hesitation occurred with the childwife Dora who had become a great favourite as he went on'; that as late as 7 May 1850 (that is before the fourteenth instalment which ends with the wedding in Chapter 43) he was 'still undecided about Dora, but MUST decide today'.[13] I agree with Butt and Tillotson that Dickens must be referring to Dora's death and not her wedding, but what an extra-ordinary situation! The wedding chapter ends:

> 'Are you happy now you foolish boy?' says Dora, 'and sure you don't repent?'

> 'I have stood aside to see the phantoms of those days go by me. They are gone, and I resume the journey of my story.'

The gap in the text emphasises that David's austere reflection is not the only answer he could have given had she lived, when 'yes I do repent' would have been the inevitable answer. David as with Steerforth ('think of me at my best, if circumstances should ever part us') can be true to Dora's request that she be remembered as 'a childwife' (ch. 48), and tenderly remember his love for her and honour her incapacities because for Dickens she 'died' before she was married. Dora may have become a great favourite of Dickens (and thus he overdid his enjoyment of 'comic love' and his fond remembrance of Maria Beadnell) but Dickens discovered he had to kill her in order that the faith of Agnes could inform the paradigm of fulfilment, which his imaginative commitment to 'such strange experiences and sordid things' as Heep and Dora was threatening to subvert. David would like to believe post-Dover 'that I began my new life . . . with everything new about me', but from the moment Heep appears he confronts an 'incubus' which has no need (as with Mr Wickfield) to 'fasten' upon him because in Heep David inadvertently confronts disturbing forces in himself.

Not surprisingly Heep appears more honest than David. Thus, in the scene when Micawber, implausibly inspired by 'the appealing monitor' of Agnes, exposes him as a stage villain, Heep rounds on David: ' "Copperfield I have always hated you. You've always been an upstart, and you've always been against me." ' David's reply, however, lacks that 'disinterested indignation' we share (say) in his strictures on Mr Creakle: ' "As I think I told you once before," said I, "it is you who have been in your greed and cunning, against all the world. It may be profitable to you to reflect, in future, that there never were greed and cunning in the world yet that . . . did not overreach themselves. It is as certain as death" ' (ch. 52). At least Heep recognises the rivalry, whereas David's pompous moralising is felt to be a downright evasion.

Dora's death ensures that the remaining quarter of the novel is, unfortunately, no longer as unsettling or surprising an experience for Dickens, David or the reader. David and Agnes will now marry (Dickens even has Dora endorse his design—and her death!—by anticipating and blessing the match) and all other threatening shadows are successively removed. Together at the close David and Agnes 'thank [ed] our GOD for having guided us to this tranquillity' (ch. 62). The reader, however, substitutes David/Dickens for 'GOD' and feels that all the characters deserve a more complex fate than the various 'tranquillities' which are imposed upon them; thus, Emily and Martha become pale copies of Agnes; Traddles, Micawber and Doctor Mell implausibly achieve worldly success; Mrs Steerforth is rendered senile; Miss Dartle is left to eat her heart away; Ham and Steerforth are killed off together.

David's success at the end is allegedly all-encompassing. Like all the good characters he is financially secure, and he is also happily married like Traddles and, unlike Micawber, a successful and serious author. Yet the reader is embarrassed by and sceptical of these multiple fulfilments which David/Dickens has imposed *and* which David enjoys. The shadows may be removed in the closing instalments of the narrative but as ever in 'the terrible fluidity' of a Dickens novel, they continue to haunt the reader.

'King Charles I' so greatly agitated Mr Dick's mind that his 'Memorial about his own history' can never become 'perfectly clear' (ch. 14). Mr Dick's state at the close—King Charles banished, pathetically copying the work of other men—provides an irresistible analogy to David's, who is convinced that 'he holds the centre of myself, the circle of my life, my own very wife' (ch. 62) whose 'tranquil brightness' renders *his* long 'Memorial' 'perfectly clear'. Such clarity has however only been gained by ousting 'King Charles I' from his own mind and thus denying, even betraying, the plurality and richness of his own experiences and his imaginative involvement in and the reconstruction of them. Fortunately we have his *whole* 'Memorial' to constantly remind us that David, like his creator, was no more capable of banishing the 'strange experiences and sordid things' which haunt and feed his imagination than he was of pinning down the curtain 'forever' on 'the young outlaw', the stranger self of his childhood.

NOTES

1. I am not suggesting of course that Dickens never *planned* ahead: as early as Chapter 3 he remarks that it might 'have been better for little Em'ly to have had the waters close above her head'—an aside which is recognised to be 'premature'. Incidentally Butt and Tillotson show that the above passage, beginning ' "You're quite a sailor I suppose?" I said to Em'ly' and ending ' "This may be premature" ', was interpolated after the draft of the first number was completed. *Dickens at Work* (1957; rpt. London), ch. 6, p. 115. All references to *David Copperfield* are to the Oxford Illustrated Edition.

2. Though the novel is told retrospectively we do not sense from the beginning, as say in *The Mill on the Floss*, that the story we are about to hear was shaped and finished 'many years ago' (ch. 1). Robert E. Loughy, 'Remembrances of Death Past and Future: A Reading of *David Copperfield* (*Dickens Studies Annual*, 6, pp. 72–101), is an existentialist interpretation which is forced and overwrought; but his comments on how in *David Copperfield* 'the narrator travels forward into a past he is trying to redeem and to make whole' (p. 74) are provocative and suggestive.

3. John Butt and Kathleen Tillotson, *Dickens at Work*, p. 123.

4. Having read *Oliver Twist* and *The Old Curiosity Shop* one anticipates that David may be surrounded with 'grotesque and wild but impossible companions' (Preface to the latter) for several instalments.

5. Reams have been written about Dickens's experience in Warren's Blacking Factory which constitutes the basis of the autobiographical fragment printed in Forster's *Life of Charles Dickens* (1872–74) Vol. I, ch. 2. For Edmund Wilson ('Dickens: The Two Scrooges', *The Wound and the Bow*, 1941: rpt. London, 1961) 'These experiences produced in Charles Dickens a trauma from which he suffered all his life' (p. 5): a trauma which explains his obsession with 'the prisoner and the rebel' (p. 15) and his sense 'that to the English governing classes the people they govern are not real' (p. 23). Q. D. Leavis takes an opposite view: 'Dickens felt his whole life to be a miracle'. ('Dickens and Tolstoy: The case for the Serious View of *David Copperfield*' in F. R. and Q. D. Leavis's *Dickens the Novelist*, London, 1970, p. 92). For a summary of the various critical positions see Albert D. Hutter, 'Reconstructive Autobiography: The Experience at Warren's Blacking', *Dickens Studies Annual*, 6, pp. 1–14. Hutter provides an Eriksonian reading of Dickens's childhood—namely that 'adolescence, not only in spite of, but rather because of, its emotional turmoil, often affords spontaneous recovery from debilitating childhood influences, and offers the individual an opportunity to modify or rectify childhood exigencies which threaten to impede his progressive development' (p. 9). Basically I agree with Erikson and with Hutter's sensible comment that by the time 'we learn anything directly about Warren's Dickens has grown up and, in the process, learned to use the experience as part of his growth. . . . Dickens

portrays himself as he wishes to be seen, and as he needs to see himself, so that the values of innocence and the non-aggressive childhood emerge as a significant part of his adult and creative vision' (p. 11). As my article shows however I think that 'David's' autobiography is more self-assertive than Hutter would allow and that his commitment to the values of innocence and self-denial pose a threat to his 'creative vision'. Incidentally Dickens ends his autobiographical fragment by confessing: 'I have never, until I now impart to this paper, in any burst of confidence with anyone, my own wife not excepted, raised the curtain I then dropped, thank God' (Forster I, ii, 26). As I go on to argue, 'thank God' he was mistaken.

6. *See* Roger Gard, 'David Copperfield', *Essays in Criticism*, 15 (1965), pp. 313–25, who argues: 'It is not only . . . that he is wonderfully successful with children when working from their viewpoint: but that, when his vision of the *whole of his world* is at its best, it is analogous to that of the child' (p. 325, Gard's emphasis).

7. Miss Mowcher's catchphrase in Chapter 22 of the novel is 'Ain't I volatile'.

8. 'Thread' is Dickens's habitual term in his notes for *David Copperfield*. See Butt and Tillotson, *Dickens at Work*.

9. The phrase is Mrs Leavis's, p. 71.

10. 'Unlike Dr. Strong or Martha, who are *only* emblems of, in Dickens's words, "the good old doctor" and "the girl already lost".' Butt and Tillotson, *Dickens at Work*, pp. 132, 141.

11. 'Inappropriate' because, as so often in Dickens, his lack of faith in the institution of law and his need to protect the father of 'the real heroine' from its consequences, means that, as Traddles recognises, their proceedings against Heep are 'perfectly lawless'. Agnes is dreaming when she anticipates 'papa once free with honour'. Similarly, Traddles' belief that 'money would never keep that man [Heep] out of mischief' is pure piety (ch. 54). As Dickens recognises, even to put Heep in gaol is merely to prepare him for another career in hypocrisy.

12. *Charles Dickens: The World of His Novels*, (1958; rpt. Bloomington & London, 1961), p. 159.

13. Forster, Book VI, Ch. 7. Some measure of Dickens's commitment to the icon of 'the childwife' can be seen in the name he gave to his third daughter, born 16 August 1850 (as he was 'killing' Dora in the serial) namely Dora Annie!

9

The Voicing of Fictions

by MARK KINKEAD-WEEKES

Novels begin and end with, consist of, and indeed in one sense are nothing but voices. So reading is learning to listen sensitively, and to tune in accurately, to varying frequencies and a developing programme. From the opening words a narrative voice begins to create its own characteristic personality and sensibility, whether it belongs to an 'author' or a 'character'. At the same time a reader is being created, persuaded to become the particular kind of reader the book requires. A relationship develops, which becomes the essential basis of the experience. In the modulation of the fictive voice, finally, through the creation of 'author' and 'reader' and their relationship, there is a definition of the nature and status of the experience, which will always imply a particular idea of ordering the world.

So much is perhaps familiar enough, and a useful rhetoric of 'voice' has developed. Yet I notice in my students and myself, when its vocabulary is in play, a tendency to become rather too abstract or technical, and above all too spatial and static. Perhaps we need to remind ourselves what it can be like to listen to close friends, talking animatedly and seriously in everyday experience, in order to make sure that a vocabulary which often points only to broad strategies does not tempt us to underplay the extraordinary resourcefulness, variety and fluctuation of the novelist's voice. For our friends communicate by choosing to be 'reliable' and 'unreliable' from moment to moment or in different ways at the same time; they run through gamuts of selves in a conversation, and articulate tonal relations with us that would take a barograph to record—yet we are able to respond with a good deal of precision, spotting the interplay between role and direct communication, and changing our own roles accordingly. And the trouble with concentrating on 'technique', indeed, I rather suspect, the trouble with a number of modern critical attitudes, is their implication that a literary work is a patterned and crafted object whose parts relate to one another and the whole across space; whereas the actual experience of reading a novel, especially a Victorian novel, is of a fluctuating human relationship in time, a constantly changing process.

Several implications follow. In spatial criticism, one extrapolates directly from detail (some chosen passage) to form and judgement; but a more lively sense of voicing, aware of fiction as essentially process rather than state, calls in question any assumption that isolating a still can enable one straightforwardly to judge the quality of the movie. And even though a voice can have an identifiable 'print' through all modulation, it seems a positive advantage to have, in 'voicing', a critical term which insists also on mobility and connection: on having to do with characterisation, with the narrative arc, with the relation of reader author and text, with shifting perspective and final vision. Here, too, there come together both the conscious articulation of a speaker, and an auditor's sense of effects of scale, time and implication, which can only be arrived at, not preconceived.

'Whether I shall turn out to be the hero of my own life . . .', the voice that begins *David Copperfield* is that of an 'author' who will only learn how to read and evaluate his life by the process of voicing his story. From the start, also, the voice is oddly both inside itself and aware of itself from the outside, announcing a personal life, but with a very public tone. So the process of discovery, which the reader will share, must also involve an adjustment of private and public perspective. The original readers who bought the novel in monthly instalments hardly needed to be reminded to read it as an unresolved process in time; but it is only when we think that way, that the implication of those changing nicknames dawns: — Davy, Daisy, Doady, and only then David. For each points to a phase of reading: a *different* relation of author and hero, of inner and outer, and of author and reader. The changing voice requires different kinds of listening.

The childhood of 'Davy' is the part everyone remembers and loves and is surprised to find, on coming back to the book, is only a quarter of the whole. The voice moves first to involvement and indeed, at its most memorable, towards a vivid re-embodiment of the adult within the child. It not only insists romantically that children are observant and sensitive and innocently visionary in ways that grown-ups lose; it annihilates time in order to re-experience the child's energies of perception and feeling. Each of the first five Numbers has such moments unforgettably, diffusing their influence over the whole.[1] So when, elsewhere, the older 'I' lends the resources of his voice to mediate the child's experience, that experience is still kept primary, and the adult hardly ever interferes or judges.[2] Even when we know more than Davy, the essential medium is one of feeling through the child's innocent affection and sensitivity. Davy is precisely not 'Brooks of Sheffield'; but he is a touchstone which brings out the essential nature of everyone he meets. Nearly always the reader knows exactly what, not to think, but to feel; the voice does not dissect or judge, but our responses to the child's experience are movements of the heart which seem, simply, irrefutable. 'A loving heart' does indeed seem 'better and stronger than wisdom' (ch. 9), and the reader's overall sense of 'Davy' by the fifth Number is compounded of loving pity and genuine admiration. On a first reading, only his response to Steerforth and Mr Mell, and that vision relocating himself as a baby in his dead mother's arms, might pinpoint the beginnings of unease and the need for a more adult perspective.

When the story reaches Canterbury, however, there is a sense of change, of discontinuity, and for many readers if not for David Copperfield, of loss. Partly this has to do with an apparent loss of energy: that tranquil interlude while Davy lapses back into boyhood; and those new apparently tranquil characters who are praised for virtue while Uriah Heep has all the life. Yet the story soon picks up again, and to read the novel as process is soon to see that the 'tranquillity' of Dr Strong and of Agnes is there to be investigated rather than merely taken as 'spatial' patterning. Mostly, however, the sense of loss comes from a marked change of attitude to Davy and his world. Suddenly there are questions everywhere which the young Copperfield cannot and the older Copperfield blandly will not answer. The 'Retrospect' of Number 6 is the opposite of the earlier 'Let me remember', for the voice confirms a new ironic distance. There can be little confidence now that the loving heart suffices alone; (suddenly one remembers that Dickens christened his newborn son Henry Fielding as though to acknowledge the influence of *Tom Jones* on his new book.)[3] A newly widespread suspiciousness is everywhere: Wickfield looks for motive, Uriah's eyes peer like red suns, Rosa asks 'Is it really, though?', Miss Mowcher is volatile, even Davy's 'sanctuary' is desecrated by seeing a look on Annie's face that needs seven nouns to describe, for nothing is simple any more. Because he clearly does not know or see enough, now, there can be no more trusting his feelings to guide the reader's response; he is too obviously blind to whole areas of disturbing evidence, to the real feelings of others, and to the significance of his own. A new kind of reader is being called for. On important occasions there are overt signals over the character's head, and on a second reading it is remarkable how much double meaning is covertly conveyed. For 'Davy' has become 'Daisy', to be regarded with affection still for his old loyalty and 'amiable innocence', but with the distance of comedy and with more than a litttle impatience, if not with Steerforth's touch of contempt. (Moreover the new reader is now likely to become more critical of the other amiable innocents too: Dr Strong, the Micawbers, even that 'babby in the form of a great sea porkypine'. Looking back, weren't all the lovable characters of the first phase 'children', and didn't our pleasure in them have something 'maternal', like the Genuine Stunning landlady?) The tenth Number closes with the elopement of Emily and Steerforth, and Daisy weeping over the desolation his innocence had brought in its train.

Yet Number 11 begins by recalling an even stronger impulse of the heart to Steerforth, despite the new bitter judgement of knowledge (ch. 32); and this voice signals the keynote of the new phase. It will be highly emotional: the characters keep defining themselves again, in strong reassertions of feeling (Mr Peggotty, Ham, the Strongs), or in re-defining outbursts (Mrs Gummidge; Rosa Dartle, going clean counter to her own critique of Steerforth as she abandons herself to jealous rage; Mr Wickfield; the open hatred and violence between David and Uriah). But there is, also, even sharper awareness now of the chasm that is liable to open still more widely than before, between the impulsive heart and wisdom. The older Copperfield begins to analyse and to judge his younger self more openly; but there may also be more covert 'unreliability' when the voice is apparently taken over by the 'young' emotional pitch. For 'Daisy' has turned to 'Doady', whose doting is specifically related to his 'disappointment and distress' over

Steerforth, as well as to other tugs at his childhood heartstrings. When he not only dotes on Dora but idealises and sanctifies Agnes and Mr Peggotty, he responds with his old 'pliant disposition' and 'earnestness of affection' to what he perceives, but is also 'blind, blind, blind!' to much that is becoming ever clearer to the reader. To Agnes we will return—but when Doady himself begins to recognise the egotism entwined with his love for Dora and for his Aunt; when Mr Wickfield bursts out in bitter knowledge of how his love became 'infected'; the new reader may begin to wonder (for example) whether there is not some admixture of egotism even in Mr Peggotty's devotion, as the voice mediates Doady's simple reverence.[4] After he has committed himself to Dora—as told in 'Another Retrospect' which adds to distance a quality of dream—the implicit questioning becomes explicit as Annie's words re-echo in David's voice: 'the mistaken impulse of an undisciplined heart'. Yet it was an impulsive heart that brought the Strongs together when the wise could not. . . .

This has been an oversimplified account—yet I hope it at least gestures towards the sense of process a reader needs in responding to David's feelings for Dora and Agnes, at the centre of the novel's concern with love. For it is very important, I believe, if we are to respond with the necessary complexity, that we should experience the moments created by the fictive voice both within the peculiar time-warp of young David, and with a sharp sense of how the relations of 'author', 'hero', and 'reader' have shifted. (The one thing we must not do, is to isolate some moment from the flux and make it representative of the whole.) And only a sufficient sense of the novel-as-process, it seems to me, will tell us why David, even after his significantly violent reaction when Uriah flaunts his intentions towards Agnes, should not only remain blind to that significance, but be immediately bowled over by Dora in the next chapter; and why, as the reader should then come to see, he has always got the tranquillity of Agnes wrong.

David's feeling for Dora actually began in Chapter 2, dancing with his mother ('I watch her winding her bright curls'); and in the fancies he wove in Chapter 3 around that 'baby', that 'blue-eyed mite' little Emily; and in Chapter 10 shortly after his mother's death, when Emily looked 'so extraordinarily earnest and pretty' as she glanced up through her curls 'that I stopped in a sort of wonder'. So, when Dora is carefully not described as they meet in Chapter 26, it is the reader's sense of inevitable process that must fill the space behind the voice—'anything that no one ever saw, and everything that everybody ever wanted'—with the particular sense of what Davy would want: a fusion of his mother and little Emily. The reader is no more surprised to see Miss Murdstone beside her than David is; nor when, for the first time in a long while, time vanishes:

> The scent of a geranium leaf, at this day, strikes me with a half comical, half serious wonder as to what change has come over me in a moment; and then I see a straw hat and blue ribbons, and a quantity of curls, and a little black dog being held up, in two slender arms, against a bank of blossoms and bright leaves.

Then the voice which opens Chapter 32, Doady's phase, makes sure we understand how the feeling for Dora is intensified by the loss of Steerforth and Emily. So the reader, himself aware of having been Davy's reader, and Daisy's, is able to know how the child, and the longing for childhood, are still compulsively alive within the young man, and to respond with some of the old tenderness. Yet Doady's reader is aware of his foolishness too, in comedy. And the greater the distance, the sharper has been the realisation that 'love' in the book has always been a feeling for the child-like, a paternalism with some disquieting features, in all the loving relations: between the author and his characters, among them, and in our responses too.[5] Yet how charged with tenderness 'little' is, in several languages beside David Copperfield's; how pleasantly protective; and when the diminutive is also vivacious and child-playful, how 'graceful, variable, enchanting'. Dora almost persuaded Dickens to change his plan.[6] Yet to marry a child-wife—how foolish and insubstantial! The response the voice wants at this time ('there is none that in retrospection I can smile at half so much, and think of half so tenderly') is a sympathy and a comic criticism equally strong, but impossible to tune into one across the gap— 'Davy' and 'Doady' held together.

Only now at the end of the third phase, and in terms of the voice-as-process again, can one realise the full extent to which Davy/Daisy/Doady has seen Agnes wrong. He cannot recognise what he feels for her as 'love', for that feeling belongs to the vivacious child-woman, and even as a child Agnes impressed him as womanly and tranquil. What strikes me moreover, on re-reading their meeting in Chapter 15, is less the inadequacy of the description of the house than the sheer oddity of 'seeing' Agnes in terms of a house and a stained-glass window at all. Responding to the tranquil look on the girl's face, and recognising 'a quiet, good, calm spirit', Davy has no idea of any inner dimension behind the expression; instead he 'associates' his own feelings externally with the house and the memory of the light through the window. He sees, not Agnes the person, but his own feelings aureoling her. He weaves fancy about her, idealising, just as he had done with little Em'ly, but to express other needs: for peaceful order; for the endurance and security of the 'old' which becomes a key-word as emotive as 'little';[7] for an otherworldly light which softens and brightens everyday reality. But a reader aware of the voice-as-process should be taking this as 'Davy'. 'I love little Em'ly, and I don't love Agnes—no, not at all in that way—but I feel that there are goodness, peace, and truth . . .' (ch. 16). Much of the vitriol that critics throw at Agnes comes from not listening to the voice in its phase, and so not being prepared for the shifts in perspective.

The first evidence that Agnes is in love with David comes as early as Chapter 19, though Daisy of course doesn't see it. The first evidence of what has always lain behind that so externally observed tranquillity—the stress of responsibility which Agnes intensely and self-denyingly accepts—becomes visible in Chapter 25 as she breaks down for a moment, before recovering her 'beautiful calm manner' again. The degree to which Doady takes Agnes for granted as a 'home' for his own feelings, rather than a person, becomes very clear as he writes to her about Dora:

> cherishing a general fancy as if Agnes were one of the elements of my natural home. As if, in the retirement of the house made almost sacred to me by her presence, Dora and I must be happier than anywhere.
>
> (ch. 34)

The fusion of egotism with idealisation is remarkable—but so is the revelation of unacknowledged feeling as he is 'soothed to tears' by the thought of Agnes; or when he suddenly comes across her in the London street; or in his rage with Uriah; or the two experiences of déja vu which suggest something in his mind that he has 'known before' but never recognised. But it is the revelation of how, in David's blind ignorance, he says something to hurt and humiliate Agnes every time he meets her, that allows Doady's reader finally to see what Agnes's tranquillity means. (The art here is surprisingly like Jane Austen's in the Box Hill episode of *Emma*, where re-reading brings up, entirely between the lines, the ignorant torturing of Jane Fairfax.) When Agnes laughs in the street in Chapter 35; when she looks up 'with such a heavenly face' in Chapter 39 before comforting David and speaking tenderly for Dora; and above all when she thinks for an astonishing second, after the Uriah episode, that she has heard what she longs above all to hear, but is not in David's mind, the reader aware of what can lie behind words will catch a glimpse of real suffering—but also of what a 'disciplined' heart is, almost instantaneously pushing egotism aside and thinking of others rather than herself. It is no accident that Faulkner caught a cadence for endurance from this:

> Oh! long, long afterwards, I saw that face rise up before me, with its momentary look, not wondering, not accusing, not regretting. Oh, long, long afterwards, I saw that look subside, as it did now, into the lovely smile, with which she told me she had no fear for herself . . .
>
> (ch. 39)

Of course there are problems with Agnes. Because David must be blind to her, we can only get glimpses past him. And because it is her essential strength to overcome conflict arising from the self, her inner life is anti-dramatic; while, outwardly, she isn't given enough to do. Nevertheless she has been imagined more interestingly that critics can realise, if they take Davy's first impression as Dickensian pattern, static iconography, and miss the whole process of seeing the suffering person behind Daisy and Doady's 'angel'.

In the last phase, as Doady grows into David, the voice seeks to harmonise feeling and wisdom, inner and outer vision, 'author', 'character' and 'reader' in final concord. Like *Tom Jones* again, the heart turns out to be 'disciplined' not by loving more prudently, but by loving more—in terms of the reality of others, unselfishly. Already in Doady's phase Mr Dick had shown a kind of wisdom *in* feeling, 'which leaves the highest intellect behind. To this mind of the heart . . . some bright ray of the truth shot straight'. Dr Strong and Ham earn a new respect in similar terms, not by forgiving so much as by becoming aware through the mind of the heart of needing forgiveness themselves, for the selfishness twined into their love. (It is a pity that there is never the same clarity for Mr Peggotty.) On the other hand, Doady had also begun what the voice reckons a hardly less important 'Progress . . . to a working state';[8] the child born at midnight has to become Saturday's child as well as Friday's, the vision to become outer workaday and social as well as inner. The attempt at overall resolution, however, may cause strain. One may not always agree that the adult voice has grown enough, or feel in tune with all its Victorian intonations. Because final concord is demanded, one may be aware of one's own voice dissenting here and there. But if this be so, I would contend all the more that the richness of the experience lies in the journeying rather than the arrival or the pattern of the map spread out afterwards. In *David Copperfield*—for all the Dickensian splendours of character and scene—the journeying and the disciplining is done essentially within the fictive voice itself, and hence within the process of reading-response, as an experience of varying tensions, change, and growth, through time.

Where that voice aimed eventually at unison, however, of 'personal' and public, of author character and reader, the voice of *Villette* seems intensely private and divided. Once again the peculiar life and form of the book will be bound up with the process of the voice; but here the reader experiences not so much a 'growth' as a penetration deeper into its own divided and separate selfhood. *Jane Eyre* still preserved a sense of journeying, though the outer stages were really a pilgrim's progress within the self; but in *Villette*, the crossing of the channel only serves to hold the same self and the same condition as before, under a more powerful microscope. Before Lucy Snowe arrives at Villette, a primary rhythm has been voiced; and essentially the same story is then told again, and again, until the reader can hear its full depth of implication, its final sense of division.

The voice that speaks first seems only half-like the one Doreen Roberts describes;[9] it has the late-'Augustan' formality without the Romantic feeling and the intensely personal idiosyncrasy. It cherishes peace, order, old-fashioned calm; resists stimulus or disturbance; pleads not guilty to imagination or enthusiasm; finds intense feeling oppressive; takes pride in its own cool temperance. Miss Snowe's voice keeps the child Polly at a distance, registering the comic discrepancy between the diminutive size and the aspiration to be grown-up; and apparently untouched by the intensity, the loneliness, the grief. Yet by the moment in the third chapter when 'I, Lucy Snowe, was calm' might have indicated an inhuman refrigeration, the reader will have seen through the protective façade. The voice protests too much, and so obviously fears emotion and involvement that its coldness suggests repression rather than insensibility. (On a second reading we know about the collapsing home and the insecurity of the fourteen-year-old.) She cannot help registering, while she fears, the attraction of Paulina's emotional depth and delicacy, as well as of her struggle for self-control; cannot help betraying how much, although wise people and books and reason suggest caution in being more than coolly friendly to 'Celtic' young men, she is moved by the self-forgetfulness and wholehearted commitment to Graham, vulnerable though it may make the child to hurt and to loss. As she comforts Paulina in her bed, the snow-maiden is far less cold towards both the child and the lad than she had seemed.

After the eight-year gap, and the brusque refusal to talk about the domestic tragedy which leaves her quite alone, another quality of voice begins to emerge. Self-reliance and exertion are forced on her, but the relationship with Miss Marchmont leaves her 'shaken in nerves'. The old woman's story of the mutilation of her love, and her sudden death, seem to bear out the omen of the wild wind, and the foreboding that attachment must lead to suffering. The new voice is plangent, turbulent, careless of temperance or decorum:

> I must be goaded, driven, stung, forced to energy. My little morsel of human affection, which I prized as if it were a solid pearl, must melt in my fingers and slip thence like a dissolving hailstone.
>
> (ch. 4)

Here again, as in the 'purple' of *Jane Eyre*, are the rhetorical amplifications, the emphatically concretised metaphors of inner experience, which may strike a reader as idiosyncratic or excessive, and yet have a kind of personal integrity in their very lack of embarrassment or reticence, their carelessness as to what that reader might think. And then, as Lucy looks at the lucent Aurora Borealis, or boards the 'Vivid', there is also a new animation, an energy, a readiness to gamble the self. So as 'Lucy Snowe' knocks at the door of Madame Beck's, the reader has become aware of the implications of divided modalities within a single voice: its capacity both for rigid control and self-possession, and for emotional abandonment and self-risk. The prelude has set up a rhythm of thaw and relationship, of disaster, and of recovery, which will happen again, and again, at a deeper level each time.

At the pensionnat, the reader hears how Lucy Snowe made an existence for herself, but collapsed into breakdown when left alone; was rescued and restored by the Brettons and dared to hope for love; only to see hope die, and to bury belief in love and happiness beneath the old 'convent-tree' in the garden. (The appearance of the 'nun'—malignant in the grenier as Lucy rejoices in her letter; able to be faced in the garden beside the 'grave' of hope for human love—is gothick on the first reading but ominous in quite a different way on the second; when it is not the explanation of the phenomenon but the attitude of Lucy that matters, and when we can see the 'spectre' as a projection of Lucy, though not in the way Dr John suggested.) This time, however, the reader must attend to a new kind of focus: the contrast of a number of types of Woman, with the voice of Lucy herself.

In the wholly cool and self-interested, unscrupulous manœuvring of Madame Beck, and the blonde jeune-fille 'charm' of Ginevra, it is almost as though Becky Sharp had been divided in two, the better to anatomise getting on in a man's world. Madame Beck (who is no mere type but a splendid character) earns at this stage a wry respect as a 'little woman' who has won success in the men's world, though without hope of male susceptibility. The spell cast by Ginevra over Dr John, on the other hand, produces from Lucy a clear-eyed feminine exposure of the reality behind the 'jeune fille', and of the sentimental protectiveness of the male attitude, when she transposes it to apply to de Hamal. Puritan, protestant, English, she has only scorn for the grossly physical conception of the sensual in Rubens' 'Cleopatra'; or for the mawkish 'spirituality' of 'La Vie d'une Femme'; to which M Paul hustles her in yet another protective male misconception of woman. Yet again, in contrast with the 'expressionless calm' and 'passionless peace' of the real snow-women of the Low Countries, Vashti is abandoned to passion, heroically rebellious against suffering, yet to Lucy an image of demonic self-destruction. It is against these conceptions of woman that her voice now proceeds to define itself, in breakdown and recovery.

She has won a new place in the world, but the reader hears again, only tuned to far higher pitch, the deep division not merely between outward appearance and inner life, but between 'Lucy' and 'Snowe' inside: the passionate aspiration and the fearful stoic repression. But as the girl revels in the thunderstorm, or looks peacefully at the moon, the 'author' also shows a new consciousness of inadequacy and excess in language and image.

> I could not go in: too resistless was the delight of staying with the wild hour, black and full of thunder, pealing out such an ode as language never delivered to man—too terribly glorious, the spectacle of clouds, split and pierced by white and blinding bolts.
>
> I did long, achingly, then and for four-and-twenty hours afterwards, for something to fetch me out of my present existence, and lead me upwards and onwards. This longing, and all of a similar kind, it was necessary to knock on the head; which I did, figuratively, after the manner of Jael to Sisera, driving a nail through their temples. Unlike Sisera, they did not die: they were but transiently stunned, and at intervals would turn on the nail with a rebellious wrench: then did the temples bleed, and the brain thrill to its core.
>
> To-night, I was not so mutinous, nor so miserable. My Sisera lay quiet in the tent, slumbering; and if his pain ached through his slumbers, something like an angel—the idea!—knelt near, dropping balm on the soothed temples . . . By which words I mean that the cool peace and dewy sweetness of the night filled me with a mood of hope . . .
>
> (ch. 12)

The reader listening to this voice, knows that such brutal 'catalepsy' cannot be maintained against the 'quick' of her nature, nor such balmy hope. When she is left alone during the vacation, facing life without relationship, she reveals that just like the little Paulina years before, she cannot live so. Her breakdown takes two significant forms: a despairing conviction that God (whom she doesn't question) has doomed her to suffer; and an even more dreadful nightmare that she can be loved neither now nor hereafter. In her dreams, even the 'well-loved dead . . . met me elsewhere, alienated' (ch. 15). It is from this despair that the Brettons rescue her, and give her confidence to trust their relationship and

179

a less agonising self-discipline. She warms almost to hope of love; but she has been so firm in moderating expectation, and in pitting reason against imagination and feeling, that when hope dies in the seven weeks' silence and the recognition of Graham's attraction to the rediscovered Paulina, she can bury it herself, and feel an access of new strength—as when she had watched the Aurora Borealis after Miss Marchmont died. The reader marks the cyclic parallel: deeper disaster, but also stronger recovery.

From this new start she can learn to be just, and even loving, toward her successful rival—the little woman who is 'Dora' to her 'Agnes'—and come to terms also with her own sense of fate. Watching the injured girl after the accident without knowing who she was, Lucy Snowe's voice registered the delicate beauty, but instinctively reacted against the possibility of a spoiled child—before, amusingly, notice taken of herself changed her tone. But as she rediscovers Paulina now, she admires and is moved. It it one thing to voice, not unsardonically, the kittenish charm bringing out so surely the fascination, protectiveness, and flirtation that the child-woman seems to command as of right from the male; or to measure the gap between that Paulina and the little Countess. But once again, even more so than in childhood, a self-control and moral delicacy, an intelligence, and above all a depth of feeling and capacity for commitment reveal a fine womanliness, which Lucy cannot but respect and take to her heart. Indeed, her feeling for Paulina's kind of beauty and deserving becomes the ground of a new, as it were, 'Calvinist', belief in 'election'. This was first voiced as a realisation that 'a great many men, and more women, hold their span of life on conditions of denial and privation. I find no reason why I should be of the few favoured' (ch. 31). It proceeds, blessing Paulina's love for Graham, to insist that 'Some lives *are* thus blessed; it is God's will . . . Other lives run from the first another course' (ch. 32). It issues, at the end of Chapter 37, with a vision of the lovers in the Bois as the 'elect' of Nature and of God; and at the beginning of Chapter 38 with an apostrophe to all the others who, like herself, belong to the pilgrims and mourners—whose sufferings in this world are yet necessary, as 'proof of a life to come'.

Part of the equanimity, however, has come from the new relation with M Paul; and what is interesting about the voicing of this is, firstly, how his character is related to the nature of Lucy's own voice, and secondly, how her response to the 'little man' and to the child-woman compare. Respecting only his intellect and energy at the beginning, she rather tiresomely played winsome little woman to the tyrant, while she inwardly laughed at the child: the showing-off, the unconscious self-exposure, the vanity, the volatile moods. But once again the voice changes, for the total exposure acts in the same way as Lucy's own voice, proclaiming a certain integrity of being just as it is, scorning to stand on dignity or put on disguise. So no sooner has Lucy come to terms with the attractiveness to men of the 'little woman' in Paulina, than she begins to feel a very similar tenderness for the 'little man' herself. (There is even another little dog among flowers!) And as his inner qualities come out—the power of feeling, the generosity and self-sacrifice which appear when his insecurity is soothed by affection, and can make even Dr Bretton appear relatively shallow and worldly in Lucy's eyes—the tenderness deepens into love.

Suddenly hope is cruelly dashed again, as M Paul is manœuvred into exile; as Lucy is prevented from bidding good-bye; as in her drugged state she sees her enemies triumphant in the Park, and M Paul and the young Justine Marie in their midst.

> I *would* not look; I had fixed my resolve, but I would not violate my nature. And then—something tore me so cruelly under my shawl, something so dug into my side, a vulture so strong in beak and talon, I must be alone to grapple with it.
>
> (ch. 39)

Outraged by jealousy, the voice becomes Promethean, punished for stealing from the gods. The whole pattern of her life seems confirmed—the 'nun' on her bed so sardonic a comment that she falls on it in fury. And then the miraculous surprise: the school of her own, the full confirmation of Paul's goodness and love.

> Magnificent-minded, grand-hearted, dear, faulty little man . . . I was full of faults: he took them and me all home. For the moment of utmost mutiny, he reserved the one deep spell of peace.
>
> (ch. 41)

M Paul had said it too: 'Il est doux, le repos! Il est précieux, le calme bonheur!' (ch 38).

The third time round, the story seems to have a happy ending: the suffering ones united, the Calvinist determinism disproved, tranquillity achieved. At the last moment however, with M Paul

returning after three years, in a vivid present tense, the Banshee
wind rises again and the *reader* is invited to end the book.

> Peace, be still! Oh! a thousand weepers, praying in agony on
> waiting shores, listened for that voice, but it was not uttered—
> not uttered till, when the hush came, some could not feel it: till,
> when the sun returned, his light was night to some!
>
> Here pause: pause at once. There is enough said. Trouble no
> quiet, kind heart; leave sunny imaginations hope. Let it be theirs
> to conceive the delight of joy born again fresh out of great terror,
> the rapture of rescue from peril, the wondrous reprieve from
> dread, the fruition of return. Let them picture union and a happy
> succeeding life ...

It is an extraordinary gesture, but not a modernist one like *The
French Lieutenant's Woman*. For if the book seems willing to divide
its readers as much as it had divided its heroine, I think it has
already voiced the reader it wants, and will do without the others.
What militates against the 'sunny imagination' and would make
its ending sentimental, is not only the meticulously repeated pattern, or the regrettable give-away that the years of absence were
Lucy's happiest, but the conviction in the voice itself, from first
to last, that the meaning of life lay in the strength to overcome
disaster and accept black fate as providence. Conversely, the reader
who took 'Peace, be still!' (or the juxtaposing of the cry of faith
at the start of Chapter 38, with the announcement that 'the master'
will not return) as mutinously ironic, anti-Christian, would be
choosing a perfectly possible reading, but one that must sever him
from the voice. For the full sense of the voice-as-process must include the response of the older Lucy to the *writing* of the book.
As the older Lucy projects herself into the state of mind appropriate to the younger, the reader hears her re-experiencing the
growth from superstition to faith and acceptance, in spite of
the worst.[10] The voice that speaks so plangently towards the end is
clearly 'the author' coming through young Lucy Snowe. The very
last sentences are a challenge to get the tone right. Though ironic, I
do not think them bitter. For, in creating that author, the voice
overcomes pain in another way. She starts, crusty, Diogenes, Timon,
as though she hardly cared to have a reader: he is told to think his
own sentimental thoughts at the start of Chapter 4, warned not
to expect a description of London, ticked off for the oversimplifi-

cations of several reading 'selves'. But gradually the tone warms, the reader is brought in more often, becomes 'dear reader'. It is not too fanciful to say that the book seems written to secure (as after each disaster) a new friend to keep the heart alive: the reader. The voice-in-process, confirming the 'author' and creating the reader, is again a decisive element in one's sense of the book's form.

Vanity Fair might seem much more 'authorial' than the others, told not in the first person but with a third-person omniscience like Fielding's. Actually the voice might almost be said to impersonate as many 'authors' here as characters in *David Copperfield*. As one listens, the paradoxes mount steadily, and it is when the voice is most charming and confidential that it may turn out to be most sly. The tone is comic, but the frame is melancholy, and the laughter tends to be dark-edged. At some points the author seems all-knowing, or even a puppeteer commanding the wires; at others he pleads ignorance of significant facts in a pieced-together history. The voice is that of a man of feeling; of a cynical clubman and man-of-the-world; of someone jostling on the pavement to catch a glimpse of high life; of a worldly roué who has seen it all; of a man nearly sixty, or in his forties, or his mid-thirties. The more attentively we listen, the more the suspicion mounts that the author behind these 'authors' is evasive—or out to unsettle us.

Uncertainty about the voice inevitably leads to division within the reader or between readers. How are we supposed to respond to the characters and the story?

It seems plain sailing at first. Amelia 'had such a kindly, smiling, tender, gentle, generous heart of her own, as won the love of everybody who came near her' and is clearly a 'dear little creature' is she not? Whereas Becky's demure mask rapidly peels off to reveal first 'an almost livid look of hatred' and then 'a smile that perhaps was scarcely more agreeable'; clearly not 'in the least kind or placable', and 'a little artful creature' is she not? As early as Chapter 2 'the author' preaches a small sermon (especially perhaps to his young readers) as Fielding had done:

> we may be pretty certain that persons whom all the world treats ill, deserve entirely the treatment they get. The world is a look-

183

ing-glass, and gives back to every man the reflection of his own
face . . . and so let all young persons take their choice.

(ch. 2)

And the first instalment seems also, as Amelia's friends bid farewell, to requisition its true reader: *not* like Mr Jones at his club,
'rather flushed with his joint of mutton and half-pint of wine',
scorning the motions of the heart as 'foolish, trivial, twaddling, and
ultra-sentimental'.

But from the beginning the voice is blandly treacherous. To continue the sentence about Amelia ('. . . everybody who came near
her, from Minerva herself down to the poor girl in the scullery,
and the one-eyed tart-woman's daughter') is to become uneasy
about one's company, for Miss Pinkerton is no Minerva but a silly
owl, and the other points of view seem also a little defective and
hidden from the light. And to listen back to the beginning of the
sentence is suddenly to hear another and much more cynical way
of voicing the nature of Amelia's accomplishments and the order
of their importance.[11] As for the world of feeling, its quantity is
vouched for by twelve bosom friends out of twenty-four young
ladies, but what about quality and discrimination? Yet if Amelia
weeps over the stupid and the mawkish . . . it gets her special
treatment! Whereas Becky is altogether more lively, intelligent,
and 'capital fun'. The daughter of an artist, she has a gift for acting, and for languages, both literally, and figuratively as in that
splendid vision of Miss P., a grotesque Ophelia, floating down the
Thames 'turban and all, with her train streaming after her, and
her nose like the beak of a wherry'. Though Becky can play the
ingenue, her upbringing has made her an adult where Amelia remains a child. She is used to adult conversation, and has the
maturity to be able to laugh at herself. And as for the sermon,
why, it is Becky who follows the author's advice!—what cynical
advice it was, really—manipulating the world of Russell Square
by presenting to it a face modelled on Amelia's. And doesn't that
begin to suggest a cynical question about the special treatment
Amelia gets? Perhaps there was, after all, something to be said
for Mr Jones, insofar as he warned against too sentimental a
reading? Who are we to side with? The author as man of feeling?
Or the cynic murmuring 'vanitas vanitatum . . .'? Or the creator
who is drawn to Becky's plotting, characterisation, comic drama,
and vivid turn of phrase? The original title-page showed the jester

in front of a mirror, rather than on his showman's podium, gazing somewhat ruefully at his own face. Almost from the beginning of *Vanity Fair*, the reader should be doing the same.

Or rather, all his faces—for 'authors' and 'readers' proliferate. (There is a notable foregathering in Chapter 8, beginning the third Number.) Indeed the experience tends to become as much concerned with this, especially on re-reading, as with the characters and scenes. It is a novel without a hero partly because it is difficult to maintin heroic posture when mirrored from so many angles, but mostly because the central concern is with the writing, reading and judging process, dramatised in the voicing. 'Every reader of a sentimental turn (and we desire no other) must have been pleased . . .' 'Faithless, Hopeless, Charityless; let us have at them, dear friends, with might and main . . .' 'The observant reader, who has marked . . . and has preserved our report . . . has possibly come to certain conclusions . . . Some cynical Frenchman has said . . .' 'I throw out these queries for intelligent readers to answer, who know, at once, how credulous we are, and how sceptical . . .'[12] For every reading temperament there is an author, teasing, or flattering, or both— and there is another one who is perfectly aware of being mercenary and helping his sales by widening his appeal. Yet the book is also subversive. Hiding behind masks is useful for probing and undermining stereotypes, expectations, and stock-responses, in society, and in the acts of reading and writing. And all the characters and situations are seen from many sides, in dense complexity. But the experience is more and more discomforting, because, as one listens, every attitude seems undermined. Indeed one might almost wonder whether there is any face behind all the masks; whether the author is all things to all men because he hasn't found himself?

Perhaps the 'kind, fresh, smiling, artless, tender little domestic goddess, whom men are inclined to worship', and the 'artful little minx' her rival, might help to focus this question, if we took a stance at, say, the beginning of Chapter 64, when the wheel of fortune has made one complete revolution for each, and Becky has just turned up again in the little Rhineland town. It does seem by then that the novel has found a unifying voice, proportioning contradictions into judgement. The author seems at last to have decided to place himself, beside his friend Major Dobbin; and though he recognises very clearly the hypocrisy in Victorian mor-

ality, he seems also to have created his reader: the true gentleman (or lady) who, like the Major, has just thoughts, fairly good
brains, an honest and pure life, and a warm and humble heart
(ch. 62)—or values these.

To such a reader, the more Becky climbed the wheel, the more
clearly the siren's scaly tail appeared below the charm, no matter
how effectively voiced. One may have been delighted by her ingenuity, intelligence, energy. Nothing has become her more than
her courage, and her merry laughter at her own discomfitures—or
the moment of sheer sexual admiration when Rawdon strikes down
Lord Steyne. Perhaps, with a better husband and £5000 a year she
could have played the perfectly respectable lady in society; and
the cynical and satiric voices have left little room for delusion
about the moral worth of nearly all who judge her. Moreover the
link with the artist has strengthened, as she has created situations
and roles with enormous vitality and elan. The life seems to go out
of the fiction whenever she is off-stage. But that *true* reader (you,
of course, and I) cannot forgive her carelessness about the suffering she causes, her heartless egotism, her malice and treachery: the
sheer spite at the ball, the treatment of her child, the betrayal of
the husband whom we have watched become more feeling as she
has become more coldly treacherous. Whether or not she is tech-
nically 'innocent' of sleeping with Steyne, she has willed the act
and its consequences, for payment. (It is because Steyne is no Tufto
to be fleeced that we glimpsed her 'haggard, weary and terrible'.) She
is not finally or wilfully vicious, perhaps, as such a reader sums up
the voices, but she is predatory, destructive, wholly selfish.

Can there be equal confidence about Amelia? The cynical,
worldly and realist voices have kept 'sharply' aware of her foolishness, her timidity, her self-deception, her eternal tears. She is a
constant invitation to sentimentality, and there is often a voice
to supply it. She knew in her heart what George Osborne was, but
would never admit it even to herself. Having made an idol of his
spoilt father, she proceeded to spoil her son likewise. Of the three
books, this has by far the clearest diagnosis of the 'little woman's'
appeal to men, and why

> wherever she went she touched and charmed every one of the male
> sex, as invariably as she awakened the scorn and incredulity of
> her own sisterhood. I think it was her weakness which was her

principal charm:—a kind of sweet submission and softness, which seemed to appeal to each man she met for his sympathy and protection.

(ch. 38)

The reader has heard in the voice how her tears both caught George Osborne, and won him back, and how little difference a knowledge of her weakness makes to the image in Dobbin's mind. In spite of all this, however, the voice seems to settle for the loving heart in the end. Amelia's care for her broken-down parents, her long-suffering kindness and gentleness, her essentially loving soul, seem to come through the mockery unscathed and tip the balance. The voice seems fairly sure of the 'true lady' also:

> She busied herself in gentle offices and quiet duties; if she never said brilliant things, she never spoke or thought unkind ones; guileless and artless, loving and pure, indeed how could our poor little Amelia be other than a real gentlewoman!
>
> (ch. 56)

Some condescension remains, but the sense of value predominates . . .

What a fool one is! For the voice is of course still in process, and in a trice it is Becky who is behaving good-heartedly, and Amelia who is self-centred, artful, and if not predatory, parasitic. Becky plays astutely on the theme of her lost child and the voice praises Emmy's capacity for forgiveness; but her rage when Dobbin refers to that old injury shows that it is either *not* forgiven, or that she had 'private reasons of her own, and was bent on being angry with him', or both. In fact, the voice of Chapter 59 had hinted that Amelia is determined to keep Dobbin, but also to keep him firmly in his place. She cannot bring herself to the 'sacrifice' of loving him. So she seizes her chance to free herself from the sense of obligation, by putting him in the wrong. Had one wondered whether Amelia didn't manipulate her world, in her own way, as much as Becky?—only it seemed unconscious? It is naked selfish strategy now. Moreover it misfires, and the scales seem to fall from Dobbin's eyes, as he tells her she is unworthy of his love, and that he has had enough.

> Amelia stood scared and silent as William thus suddenly broke the chain by which she held him, and declared his independence and superiority. He had placed himself at her feet so long that the

187

poor little woman had been accustomed to trample upon him. She didn't wish to marry him, but she wished to keep him. She wished to give him nothing, but that he should give her all. It is a bargain not unfrequently levied in love.

(ch. 66)

It is Becky who, wholly free from rancour, is able to value her enemy at his true worth. Quite selflessly for once, she tries to help him, and by forcing Amelia to face up at last to the truth about George Osborne, she eventually does. It is true that Amelia had already written a letter, after being scared by Loder and Rook, but there can be no doubt which is the more unselfish action of the two. There are of course strict limits to Becky's good-nature, but it has been audible before, and we can see now that the irony which often voiced it has its limits too. Conversely, we cannot see Amelia without irony again. Though the happy ending is a 'sentimental scene', it would be difficult not to hear the cutting edge to the voice as 'Dobbin' gets his 'prize', and the soft appeal of weakness works again:

> The bird has come in at last. There it is with its head on his shoulder, billing and cooing close up to his heart, with soft out-stretched fluttering wings. This is what he has asked for every day and hour for eighteen years. This is what he pined after. Here it is—the summit, the end—the last page of the third volume. Good-bye, Colonel.—God bless you, honest William!—Farewell, dear Amelia. – Grow green again, tender little parasite, round the rugged old oak to which you cling!
>
> (ch. 67)

Reading expectations are also mocked, of course; and it isn't the final page yet, or the final voice. Here is the end, though, as Becky is discovered in a booth, at the Fair.

> She cast down her eyes demurely and smiled as they started away from her; Emmy skurrying off on the arm of George (now grown a dashing young gentleman), and the Colonel seizing up his little Janey, of whom he is fonder than of anything in the world—fonder even than of his 'History of the Punjaub'.
>
> 'Fonder than he is of me,' Emmy thinks, with a sigh. But he never said a word to Amelia that was not kind and gentle; or thought of a want of hers that he did not try to gratify.
>
> Ah! *Vanitas Vanitatum!* which of us is happy in this world? Which of us has his desire? or, having it, is satisfied?—Come,

children, let us shut up the box and the puppets, for our play is
played out.

The reader seems freer even than at the end of *Villette* to choose,
not a denouement, but a final voice. The first is the voice of Morality and of protective feeling—and there is new cause for regarding
Becky as suspect, over Jos. Yet the flight is ignominious, and the
voice has an air of making excuses. (One reader may feel that
Becky deserves the last smile, at these Pharisees.) The second voice
is the melancholy cynic. Nobody is satisfied: not Dob nor Emmy,
poor fools, with each other; nor the showman weary of his puppets and his audience of children, of the game, and of the world.
(Another reader, mindful of the Fool on the cover, might insist
that he, for one, is not a child and the novel has been quite unlike
a Punch and Judy show.)

I think here is double irony here, where two false positions imply
a third which can resolve and rectify. The fair is a *Charity* Fair.
Are there not hints of something greater than 'fondness', never
looking to its own satisfaction, going beyond the 'heart and brains
too', freely forgiving, and without which the world is vanity
'Though I speak with the tongues of men and of angels'? I think
there has always been the suggestion of a Voice behind the voices
in the novel, valuing unselfish love above all, but also valuing probing intelligence and fearful of cant, by no means certain of itself
or of its audience, yet seeking a wholeness of view by finding its
way *through* sentimentality and cynical 'sharpness'.[13] In doing so
(I believe) the voicing challenges the reader to do likewise, tuning
in the final voice, as it were, in the space between the others—
but *Vanity Fair* leaves its readers free to decide how to listen, in
the end.

Simple as these outlines have had to be, I hope they suggest
how important the process of voicing is to our sense of form; and
how sensitive a reader must be, within that process, to variations
fluctuations and divisions of the voice that are unique to each book
and essential to the nature of the experience it offers. *David
Copperfield* is a 'progress' through four kinds of voicing, *Villette*
pits two modalities of the narrative voice against each other,
Vanity Fair multiplies 'voices'—in no case can one assume that a

sample 'frozen' out of the whole complex process will do to diag-
nose the nature of the voicing, the form, or the vitality. To 'tune'
with any fineness, also, we have to become different kinds of
readers for each book, and, sometimes, within each book. Each
voicing signals a different sense of the relation between private
and public vision—a different mode of being 'Victorian'.

The 'first person' stance of two, and the 'omniscient author'
stance of the other, only place us at the garden gate of the fictive
estate. Yet these 'Victorian' fictions do also give us a powerful sense
of a 'person' behind the voicing, and also of a reaching-out towards
the reader, albeit in different ways. In modernist fiction the author
and the reader relate only to the book, which has a high degree
of autonomy. In these novels we have a sense of encounter *through*
the book. Yet one must be careful. Of course we are aware of, not
only a Voice behind the voices, but of Dickens, Thackeray,
Brontë: of Dickens's childhood traumas and strained marriage,
the feelings for Mary and Georgie Hogarth and the susceptibility
towards the child-woman; of Thackeray's financial crash, his mistress and the less 'respectable' side of his life, the recent tragedy
of his marriage; of Charlotte Brontë's traumatic loss of her family,
and her hopeless feeling for M Heger. Yet all fictive voices are characterised; only 'some part of myself into the Shadowy World' as
Dickens put it.[14] The awareness of private pressures does not help
us to hear *how* they are voiced; while unless we do hear that, we
cannot truly estimate either their effect or their true nature. Similarly with the writer's 'Victorian' attitudes: only a sensitive grasp
of the whole process of voicing will tell us what the attitude is.
(The gentle reader may have noticed that I have not allowed myself to use the writers' names until now.)

Finally, these are not 'end-directed' fictions, in the modernist
sense where the ending is the ultimate key to shape and pattern.[15]
Here, it is the process of reaching it that matters.

NOTES

1. See Keith Carabine on such a moment (above pp. 151–53).
2. An apparent exception, like the question in Chapter 3 of whether it
   might have been better for little Emily to have drowned, is instantly
   felt to be an intrusion by author and reader alike.

3. J. Forster, *The Life of Charles Dickens* (London, 1872–74), VI, **vi**.

4. The repetition of 'I' and 'my' thirteen times in a single speech in Chapter 40 could hardly (given Dickens's ear) be fortuitous. Mr Peggotty himself begins fleetingly to worry about self in Chapter 51— though he is swiftly reassured by Aunt Betsy—when he records a pain very different from the satisfaction the earlier speech anticipated. I find fault, however, with the last view of Mr Peggotty and Emily.

5. This was picked up, vividly, by the first reader of *Copperfield*, 'Phiz'. Steve Lutman remarks (below p. 208) how Browne exaggerated Davy's littleness. The maternal or paternal feeling is strongly appealed to in the illustrations throughout the 'Davy' section, but particularly perhaps in that fine matched pair 'My magnificent order at the public house' (the landlady's view, as in the text) and 'I make myself known to my Aunt'; and in 'Steerforth and Mr Mell'. When we find Dora hiding behind the door, we suddenly recognise the paternal element in our feeling for Mr Peggotty and Ham at Salem House. The most 'disquieting', to modern readers, is probably Dr Strong and Annie.

6. 'Still undecided about Dora,' he wrote on 7 May 1850, 'but MUST decide today'; and Forster remarks that 'his principal hesitation occurred in connection with the child-wife Dora, who had become a great favourite as he went on' (VI, vi).

7. Sylvère Monod, *Dickens the Novelist* (Norman, Oklahoma, 1968) pp. 335 *ff.* first indicated the prominence in the vocabulary of 'little' and 'old'.

8. *See* the memoranda to number 12, April 1950, *in* John Butt and Kathleen Tillotson, *Dickens at Work* (London 1957, repr. 1968) p. 150; and Chapter 36 *ff.* Friday's child is loving and giving; Saturday's child works hard for a living.

9. Above pp. 133–34.

10. I agree with David Blair (above pp. 49–50, note 18) that the exclamatory questions in the first episode with the 'nun'—'Are there wicked things, not human . . ?' etc—strike one on second reading as cheating; but I think the explanation is not merely a desire for gothick suspense, but also the need to suggest the 'older' Lucy re-experiencing a state of mind still over-intense (as in the 'sweet insanity' of keeping the letter, and the vision of Dr John as heroic) and hence liable to melodrama and gothick superstition. There would be no problem if the paragraph had been transposed with the next.

11. One is here, as with the last sentences of *Villette,* talking of the decisions one would have to make before reading aloud. Thackeray, like Dickens, seems to cry out to be read aloud, and to have conceived his 'voices' as talking. Charlotte Brontë's, on the other hand, is a special 'writing' voice, and her dialogue can sometimes be terrible.

12. Chapter 15, Chapter 8, Chapter 13, and Chapter 23.

13. 'What I want is to make a set of people living without God in the world (only that is a cant phrase) . . . perfectly satisfied for the most part and at ease about their superior virtue. Dobbin & poor Briggs are the only 2 people with real humanity as yet. Amelia's is to come. . .

READING THE VICTORIAN NOVEL

But she has at present a quality above most people whizz: LOVE— by wh. she shall be saved . . . / I wasn't going to write in this way when I began. But these thoughts pursue me plentifully. Will they ever come to a good end? I should doubt God who gave them if I doubted that.' 2 July 1807, *see* Gordon N. Ray (ed) *The Letters . . . of William Makepeace Thackeray* (London, 1945), p. 309.

14. 21 October 1850 to Forster, VI. vii.
15. *Cf.* Frank Kermode, *The Sense of an Ending* (London, 1967).

Interchapter 3

Is there perhaps not so much a 'debate' here—in which one might eventually be called upon to vote—as a dramatisation of stances? Would one wish finally to choose between seeing the novel as a process evolving in time and as a state contemplated spatially? Discussion of *Jane Eyre* could presumably go on to discover how the consciousness that Doreen Roberts analyses, as it were in cross-section, varies in response to Gateshead, Lowood, Thornfield, Whitcross, Moor End, Ferndean. Discussion of *Villette* could try to cut further into the underlying grain, at any stage, than Mark Kinkead-Weekes manages. Keith Carabine's essay shows a sense of process turning into a diagnosis of overall state. Isn't all criticism ideally a dialogue between these approaches, in which each needs constantly to be asserted against the other?

Or rather, a dialectic perhaps . . . for they do seem opposed. Is it possible to be a 'process' and a 'state' critic simultaneously? The latter has to hold the novel still, to stop, analyse, detach himself; the former to keep moving, provisional, involved. The dialectic will also have different proportions at different times in a first reading, and with every re-reading. Process will dominate near the beginning of a first reading, state near the end, and at every stage in between when a reader pauses, process intersects with state-so-far, experience with memory. A re-reading begins with some sense of state carried over from before, and each re-reading will solidify that sense. It will be the overall view that is hard to come by subtly and complexly enough after the first reading, since we tend to formulate starkly in order to gain some control. With greater confidence, we allow re-reading to modify our formulations, but the consciousness of process becomes all the more difficult to retain as the book becomes more and more familiar. One might conduct an interesting seminar on the 'rhetoric' of critical response. This critic might strike us as needing to read the book again, and that one as already having read it too often. Are we not in danger of teaching all 'state' when our students are all 'process'? Do we not need to become more aware of the implications of these two different stances?

Other basic differences in stance may also reveal themselves in implicit criteria of value. Does plurality imply plentitude? Or may it be loss of power and order? Is *Villette* a better novel than *Jane Eyre* to the extent that its heroine may be visible from more points of view (Ginevra, Madam Beck, M Paul etc.), and voiced more plurally (Lucy in youth, the older Lucy, Charlotte Brontë)? Or is the single point of view, indeed the 'warping' of *Jane Eyre*, not only intrinsic to its power but productive of greater power and unity than *Villette*? It has always been more popular. . . . Do we put the higher value on proliferation, or on comprehensive ordering and understanding? Do we charge Thackeray with sponsoring superficially contrasting voices in order to conceal his own irresolution, or argue that a resolving voice must have been less inclusive and challenging than the consort? And how do we judge between volatile energy and tranquil order not only in *David Copperfield*, but throughout fiction? A novel cannot be endless volatility or plurality. These qualities are only defined against order, while order is inevitably revealed as limited by what is left out. The point at which a novelist applies order and begins to close a novel down —is the introduction of Agnes such a point?—will indeed be a crucial one, which may signal a loss of energy or will, but it is so as part of a rhetoric of reading as well as of writing novels. One reader may be conscious of loss in the very fact of a demand for order, stasis, conclusion, rather than creativity, process, proliferation; another reader of gain and clarification through the same demand. Either response may begin before there is any question of how well the closing down is done. In *David Copperfield* it is arguable that the single first-person voice was incapable of being sufficiently 'comprehensive'—how could one voice contain so much?—but in *Bleak House*, where the narrator's 'prolific' and satiric voice counters and is countered by Esther's tranquillity, charity and order, the problem of basic reading response may occur even more sharply, when it is directed to half the novel's narration as well as to its closing down. Moreover our own criticism, too, can cope with plurality only so far, before we need to seize on some point of stasis to close down our own volatile response, and construct our idea of order, or of failure. And even the latter may partly be conditioned by our stance. The 'process' critic will tend to see 'flaws' as inadequacies of development which may or may not be resolved in the end; the 'state' critic will tend to see the flaw as fissuring the whole spread out before him. To get the partial failures of an important work into just perspective, may require conscious awareness of these tendencies, and a proportion gained by seeing from both angles.

And if, at the end of the day, critics still divide in emphasis, it may be owing to deep-lying differences of temperament, persisting below critical sophistication. One reader may be genuinely more responsive to process, more anxious to be involved, finding the life of fiction in energy driving forward, praising the exploration of the author who plunges further than he knew. Another may be genuinely more responsive to state and resolution, more detached, finding the essence of fiction in order contemplated from the end, praising the craftsmanship of the author who builds the comprehensive 'labyrinth'.

10

Reading Illustrations:
Pictures in *David Copperfield*

by STEPHEN LUTMAN

1

To the modern reader the central paradox of the illustrated novel is the combination of a static picture with a dynamic narrative form. In terms of reading experience the reader must stop and consider an illustration, even for a moment, before the page is flicked on and the flow of reading continued. There are moments like this in any prose narrative—the pause at the end of the chapter or book, the end of an episode, or a passage where the prose itself slows down and reflects on what has passed before. The illustrated novel is different because the mixture of visual and verbal forms suggests that the reader pauses to pursue a different kind of reading in the illustration from that of the text. This in turn raises questions of how the reader 'visualises' a novel and 'reads' an illustration, and of the relationship between these processes in a single work. Henry James objected to illustrations in the Preface to *The Golden Bowl*[1] on the grounds that they must be either decoratively superfluous to the text, or trespassers on meanings which should be carried by it, but this may not be a real objection. As A. J. Portas has pointed out, the relationship between reading a novel and 'reading' its illustrations can be one of complementary interaction, and 'The justification of the presence of these disparate forms lies in the positive contribution that can be made by their interaction but not by either on its own,'[2] so that for example, 'the illustrations will not cut across the reader's imaginative visualisation of pictorial passages.'[3] The nature of this complementary interaction between the pictures and the text can however be seen to be part of a much larger and related inter-

196

action of forms in the Victorian period which helps to condition it, and which provides a common area of reference for both writer and artist.

Dickens and Browne's collaboration as novelist and illustrator had important connections with other kinds of collaboration in the period which created a network of related visual and literary forms. Most prominently the narrative tradition in nineteenth-century painting and engraving which derived from Hogarth created a literary taste in art, and as Christopher Wood has indicated of the artists of the 1830s and 1840s. 'The artist became story-teller, novelist, as well as painter.'[4] At its most developed, this aesthetic used the picture sequence to tell a story[5] and is related to, though different from, the illustration sequence of a novel.[6] Another relevant relationship is that between melodrama and painting. Melodrama is an important influence on Dickens, and it uses pictorial techniques derived in some cases directly from contemporary paintings and engravings, re-creating their pictures in tableau form on the stage, and in turn provides the 'language' of gesture and sometimes the subjects for paintings.[7] Melodrama has a unique relationship to music in that this forms the background to dramatic speech and gesture, while music is also a significant motif in painting and fiction in the period.[8] Forms as disparate as photography and poetry have important connections with drama and narrative art.[9]

Dickens's novels can be seen to be at the centre of these related forms, not simply in having illustrations, but in the way the illustrations conspire with the text. It is by no means irrelevant that Dickens's novels inspire popular songs and music, even political cartoons,[10] and that the many melodramas based on his novels are careful to present re-creations of the illustrations on the stage.[11] But what is immediately noticeable about these connections is that they create a syndrome of related visual and literary forms of which the novel is a part, rather than the historical oddity of a single collaboration between illustration and fiction. Evidence that the novels and their illustrations inhabit this popular world of related forms can even be gleaned from the monthly numbers in which most of the novels were first published. Advertisements for popular music, melodramas, and prints, flourish along with those for patent medicines and mourning outfitters.[12] This interaction between fiction, illustration, drama, painting, and music, is important because as a phenomenon of early and mid-Victorian culture it can be generalised into something resembling a Victorian sensibility, but one in which differentiated and specific moments can be discerned. *David Copperfield* is clearly such a moment, in that the novel and its illustrations are peculiarly important in the development of Dickens and Browne as collaborators, and the novel itself creates an effect unique in their partnership.

The general point, that their collaboration is conditioned by a wider sensibility, is important because it acts as part of the framework within which Dickens and Browne developed a complementary interaction in their work. J. R. Harvey has indicated how the decline of Browne's importance to Dickens's work can be related to changes in the mode of illustration which separate the art from the popular aesthetic it had grown with previously; '*Bleak House* (1852–53) had in fact been the last novel in which Browne could feel that his style of illustration was the style of the time, for 1853 is generally acknowledged as the year in which a new mode of illustration, represented pre-eminently by Millais, began its rapid and victorious invasion of the whole field of book-illustration.'[13] Represented in Dickens's work by Marcus Stone, Luke Fildes, and the 'Household' edition artists like Fred Barnard, what Harvey calls the 'academic' style took over from the popular visual tradition of Cruikshank, Leech, and Browne, and 'the concentration on accurate drawing left no place for the subtleties of allegorical and allusive by-play that occur in the corners of the earlier illustrations.'[14] In other words the illustration becomes separated from its popular aesthetic milieu and—in Henry James's phrase—becomes 'the "grafted" image'.[15] Clearly this change is related to others in painting and drama, and in fiction presaged a divorce from illustration such that for the modern reader the illustrated novel may seem an anachronism. The modern novel is not illustrated, and is perhaps not illustratable.[16]

To discuss the 'interaction' of the two forms in Dickens's novels is not necessarily to make the assumption that they are really discrete elements in the Jamesian sense. The illustrations were developed during the course of writing the novels, and having grown with the text can be described as having an organic relationship to it, rather than the more mechanical relationship of illustrations added to a finished work.[17] The difference can be conveniently demonstrated by comparing the extra plates which Browne designed at a later stage, after the novels were completed, with the original illustrations. Both *Dombey and Son* and *The Old Curiosity Shop* were used by Browne for extra plates based on characters in the novels.[18] They are very different from the illustrations, being mostly portrait pieces, and the treatment is distant from the text. The Marchioness from *The Old Curiosity Shop* is completely changed from a grotesque midget in the novel to a conventionally pretty girl. Browne's independent work adds nothing at all to an understanding of the novels, and remains a mechanical spin-off. The illustrations are quite different, and relate to the text in a way which assumes a readership and an audience who were at home with this kind of mixed aesthetic and enjoyed it. Partly because of the tendency of modern editions to reproduce the illustrations poorly, incompletely, or in the wrong place in the text the modern reader is often experiencing a novel rather less than the one Dickens wrote, and this may account for the comparative lack of attention the illustrations have received critically. The question of how accessible the illustrations are in terms of their aesthetic to the modern reader is a more open question. But the survival of melodrama in film and television, the development of the picture sequence in comics, and the continuing popular interest in Victorian art, suggest that the ordinary modern reader is not completely cut off from his Victorian predecessors.

2

'Pictures' are crucial to both detail and form in *David Copperfield* because David as narrator and actor 'pictures' scenes from his life in his mind's eye. These scenes or pictures may or may not give cues for illustrations, as J. R. Harvey noticed:

> The chief feature of the *Copperfield* illustrations is the greatly extended use of the 'tableau'. In this novel Dickens will momentarily arrest his characters in a significant grouping which he describes as a 'picture' and which is evidently conceived with an illustration in mind. This pictorial technique had not occurred to Dickens at the start of the novel: in the first number a significant moment of this kind comes, and Dickens explicitly asserts its pictorial qualities, but there is no illustration.[19]

The example Harvey is referring to is that of Emily running along the timber over the sea, which for David 'is so impressed on my remembrance, that if I were a draughtsman I could draw its form here, I dare say, accurately as it was that day' (ch. 3). But Dickens uses a 'pictorial' technique where there is no corresponding illustration right through the novel, not just at the beginning of the book. It is clear that Dickens uses 'pictorial' effects in the text not simply to cue illustrations, but as a central aspect of the narrative method. Looked at in one way, the number of illustrations in the novel could easily be doubled. But the point is that Dickens is also using the word 'picture' in a complex way. The word refers to the graphic arts as the Emily episode indicates, but it also refers to the technical term in melodrama[20] for a tableau or group pose which may act as a climax or re-statement of themes during, or at the end of a scene. 'Close to picture' is a familiar stage direction which indicates the freezing of a scene into an emotional moment. It is important in melodrama that the picture is created without dialogue, focussed emotionally, and static in contrast to the typically athletic and swift action of a preceding scene. The tableau or 'picture' is like a form of static mime, and as well as being an important component of melodrama, has an independent existence as a form of entertainment in the period.[21] Its relationship to painting and photography is more obvious than that to the novel. The final scene of A. Halliday's version of David Copperfield, Little Emily, gives some idea of how a scene can be built in relation to a tableau or picture:

> Act V Scene III Ship at Wharf in 5th grooves. Discover on ship, Peggotty, Mrs Gummidge, Barkis, Martha, Em'ly, grouped picturesquely, Sailors, Officers, Passengers, Mr and Mrs Micawber. In row-boat, which is worked R. to L. Copperfield, Agnes, and a Boatman, who lays on his oars. Music 'Rule Britannia', 'The Girl I left behind me' etc. Ship is worked to R. Picture. All cheer and wave hats and handkerchiefs.

CURTAIN (slow)[22]

The picture opposite, framed by the bustle and action before and after, is used to point the emotional meaning of the scene through contrast, as when Dickens in the novel stops the scene for a moment, 'with all the life on board her crowded at the bulwarks,

'We arrive unexpectedly at Mr Peggotty's fireside'

and there clustering, for a moment, bare headed and silent, . . .'
(ch. 57) to prepare for David's last sight of Emily. Dickens's use
of the tableau or picture is related to dramatic effect in the text as
well as to the illustrations.

Dickens can make both dramatic and pictorial sense out of a
scene in this way, and this can be shown in the illustration in
David Copperfield, 'We arrive unexpectedly at Mr Peggotty's
fireside', and the text parallel to it.

Dickens describes the scene as follows:

> We said no more as we approached the light, but made softly for
> the door. I laid my hand upon the latch; and whispering Steerforth
> to keep close to me, went in.
>
> A murmur of voices had been audible on the outside, and, at
> the moment of our entrance, a clapping of hands: which latter
> noise, I was surprised to see, proceeded from the generally dis-
> consolate Mrs Gummidge. But Mrs Gummidge was not the only
> person there who was unusually excited. Mr Peggotty, his face
> lighted up with uncommon satisfaction, and laughing with all his
> might, held his rough arms wide open, as if for little Em'ly to
> run into them; Ham, with a mixed expression in his face of
> admiration, exultation, and a lumbering sort of bashfulness that
> sat upon him very well, held little Em'ly by the hand, as if he
> were presenting her to Mr Peggotty; little Em'ly herself, blushing
> and shy, but delighted with Mr Peggotty's delight, as her joyous
> eyes expressed, was stopped by our entrance (for she saw us first)
> in the very act of springing from Ham to nestle in Mr Peggotty's
> embrace. In the first glimpse we had of them all, and at the
> moment of our passing from the dark cold night into the warm
> light room, this was the way in which they were all employed: Mrs
> Gummidge in the background, clapping her hands like a mad-
> woman.
>
> The little picture was so instantaneously dissolved by our go-
> ing in, that one might have doubted whether it had ever been.
>
> (ch. 21)[23]

The tableau is created by David and Steerforth surprising the
group. The 'fireside' in the illustration title is important because
of the verbal associations of warmth and light with the emotions
of the characters in the 'warm light room'. Mr Peggotty's face is
'lighted up', Little Em'ly 'blushing and shy', Ham bashful, and
Mrs Gummidge excited. This is contrasted with the 'dark cold
night' from which Steerforth and David enter, and which 'stops'

the action of Em'ly springing towards Peggotty. Dickens uses the tableau to suggest the chilly consequences for the group of Steerforth and David's arrival, a motif picked up later in the snow scene where David meets Peggotty as 'The Wanderer'. Steerforth will later 'stop' Emily's relationship with Ham and Peggotty. Dickens's 'picture' in the text, as in melodrama, focusses and presents emotion by holding a crucial moment without dialogue, while at the same time pointing a theme.

The illustration reinforces this tableau by making the moment permanent in the illustration. As J. R. Harvey points out 'the illustration allows Dickens both to erase it in the text, and to leave us with an indelible picture of it.'[24] The illustration does more than this, because it also presents David and Steerforth to our view, whereas the text gives a viewpoint from David. Here David's gesture with his right hand, which is to keep Steerforth close for the surprise, combines with his left hand 'presenting' the scene. But the gestures are ambiguous. David is unconsciously 'pointing out' Steerforth with one hand, and indicating that he will come between Peggotty and Em'ly with the other. The 'picture' in the illustration combines that of the text with a view of David and Steerforth's place within it, so that the 'little picture' in the text and the illustration use complementary viewpoints.

If we return to moments in the text which are not illustrated, another important aspect of 'pictures' in *David Copperfield* emerges. David has a habit of mind as narrator and hero of picturing certain moments, and other characters, to himself independently of the illustrations. There is a 'pictorial' method in the novel which is not confined to moments when Dickens has an illustration in view. David's visual perceptions are very keen, as when he suggests 'that I was a child of close observation' (ch. 2) and this perception makes him respond particularly quickly to real pictures on the walls. David arrives at the Wickfield house for the first time:

> Opposite to the tall old chimney-piece were two portraits: one of a gentleman with grey hair (though not by any means an old man) and black eyebrows, who was looking over some papers tied together with red tape; the other of a lady, with a very placid and sweet expression of face, who was looking at me.
>
> I believe I was turning about in search of Uriah's picture, when, a door at the further end of the room opening, a gentleman entered, at sight of whom I turned to the first mentioned portrait

again, to make quite sure that it had not come out of its frame. But it was stationary; and as the gentleman advanced into the light, I saw that he was some years older than when he had had his picture painted.

(ch. 15)

Dickens is stressing changes in Mr Wickfield through the 'stationary' portrait, and at the same time suggesting David's interest in real pictures and paintings which is to be used as a motif in the novel. David even makes a casual reference to Dutch seventeenth-century painting in his later description of the emigrant ship.[25] But perhaps more important is the relationship of the mental images which David constructs imaginatively of other characters in the novel, to stationary pictures or portraits. Apart from little Em'ly who is pictured at a significant moment early in the novel, as we have seen, David also constructs 'stationary' mental pictures of his mother Clara, Dora, Steerforth, Agnes, and of himself. Steerforth for example is significantly 'lying easily, with his head upon his arm, as I had often seen him lie at school . . . let me think of him so again . . .' (ch. 29). This vision of Steerforth has both visual and moral consequences for David's attitude towards him. Steerforth's 'best' moments are when he is asleep—at least that is how David sees him in memory, and in his actual death. Dora too, is stopped as a mental image by David:

> The scent of a geranium leaf, at this day, strikes me with a half comical, half serious wonder as to what change has come over me in a moment; and then I see a straw hat and blue ribbons, and a quantity of curls, and a little black dog being held up, in two slender arms, against a bank of blossoms and bright leaves.
>
> (ch. 26)

These mental pictures, which freeze the characters in time in David's memory, are intense emotional visions which have significance for David's future in the novel as well as his past.

David as narrator uses pictures on the wall as a kind of comment on a scene, rather like the paintings on the walls in the illustrations. But his mental 'pictorial' ability is also a part of his imagination, as his pictures of the Murdstones show:

> While I sat thus, looking at the fire, and seeing pictures in the red-hot coals, I almost believed that I had never been away; that Mr and Miss Murdstone were such pictures, and would vanish

204

when the fire got low; and that there was nothing real in all that
I remembered, save my mother, Peggotty, and I.

(ch. 8)

Dickens can use this quality in his narrator with great skill. When
David first visits Steerforth's home and finds in his bedroom 'a
likeness of Miss Dartle looking eagerly at me from above the chim-
ney piece,' he uses the portrait imaginatively:

> It was a startling likeness, and necessarily had a startling look.
> The artist hadn't made the scar, but I made it; and there it was,
> coming and going: now confined to the upper lip as I had seen it
> at dinner, and now showing the whole extent of the wound in-
> flicted by the hammer, as I had seen it when she was passionate.
>
> (ch. 20)

David has to extinguish his light 'To get rid of her'. This eerie
little scene suggests David's imaginative look into passion through
the picture, a look which links his sensitivity to pictures to his
imaginative dreaminess as his dream following this passage in-
dictates. This is one reason why there are so many actual pictures
in the novel, and in the illustrations. The important effect is that
Dickens can create a context which will reinforce David's dreamy
and imaginative way of perceiving, because through this he can
control the narrative. The illustrations play a significant part in
this aspect of the novel.

3

A dimension to the illustrations to *David Copperfield* which is
so obvious that it eludes notice, is that they present the reader
with the only objective view of David, and indeed of the other
characters in the novel. As all the information in the novel is fil-
tered through David's perceptions and narrated by him, the illustrations begin to take on an important role in giving the reader
views of David. To an extent the illustrations offer a reading of
the novel quite different from the text, and *David Copperfield* is
unique in this.[26]

David as narrator can hide the significance of events in the novel
from his younger self by entering imaginatively into his younger
persona, as Mark Kinkead-Weekes suggests in this book in terms
of voice. David himself as narrator states this curious principle:

> I set down this remembrance here, because it is an instance to myself of the manner in which I fitted my old books to my altered life, and made stories for myself, out of the streets, and out of men and women; and how some main points in the character I shall unconsciously develop, I suppose, in writing my life, were gradually forming all this while.
>
> (ch. 11)

David as narrator connects his imagination with the character he will 'unconsciously' create for himself, and one aspect of his imagination which has been already touched on, is to freeze pictorially and morally, other characters in the novel who will become significant to his own unconscious character. In terms of narrative control this is crucial because if David knows himself too well, or realises consciously the wider significance of the other characters, he can no longer discover himself and develop. The reader is invited to make sense of patterns in the novel which are veiled from David, and this interpretive relationship is set up early in the novel in episodes like 'Brooks of Sheffield' and 'The friendly waiter' where the reader interprets the situations as having more meaning for David than he knows. Of course David can seal up a character or an episode in his mind—as Keith Carabine suggests in this book when David drops a mental curtain on his life at Murdstone and Grinby's—but Dickens can bring these elements into play through the plot. A good example is Miss Murdstone turning up as Dora's companion, a startling re-entry into the novel which David hardly notices: 'I had none but passing thoughts for any subject save Dora, . . .' (ch. 26), but which creates for the reader an important skein of connections with David's mother and his childhood which are to be pursued later in the novel.

The illustrations are important because they offer significant visual comments on David, and act in some sense as a reading of the novel outside David's viewpoint. Of course, there are views of David stated in the novel or implied, but we get a lot of objective information about him from the illustrations. As well as responding to specific scenes, Browne develops certain motifs which are only hinted at in the novel, in addition to others more clearly stated. As A. J. Portas has indicated, in relation to *Dombey and Son*, there is a cumulative and changing effect in the repetition and development of visual motifs similar to the verbal patterning which repetition can create in the text.[27]

The most general effect which Browne creates in images of David is that he is pretty as a boy, and both handsome and 'young' as a young man. In this he is responding to aspects of the text— David as 'Daisy' for Steerforth; 'Face like a peach,' for Miss Mowcher; and 'young' with Littimer—but he also adds a dimension of sympathy and compassion for David in placing him visually, which reinforces the sense that David 'was such a child and so little . . .' (ch. 11). Browne, however, uses this 'little' figure very tellingly in a more general way, especially in relation to chairs. With only two exceptions David is perched or uneasily seated on his various chairs. As a child his legs usually fail to reach the floor, and as a man he is never quite comfortable. If we look at a sequence of images of David seated we can see the progression.

David's 'first fall in life' is when he is removed from the coveted Box seat of the coach to London in favour of the 'shabby man with the squint' (ch. 19) and Browne pursues this theme through a long sequence. The only two illustrations where he seems at ease are dining with the Micawbers, and more importantly, the last illustration 'A Stranger Calls to see me', when David is finally settled in his ordered home.[28] This uneasiness in David—what he calls 'A distrust of myself . . .' (ch. 19)—is communicated by Browne's use of his uneasy seats, similar to Hogarth's use of the table in 'A Harlot's Progress', as a motif. This is by no means as extensive an allegory as Hogarth's, but constitutes part of the visual tone of David's image in the sequence of illustrations, confirming and extending suggestions in the text. Browne can also confirm and develop other characters through a contrast with this image of David, as when in 'Somebody turns up' David's feet can only just touch the rail of the table, while Heep's thighs squeeze the corkscrew table leg opposite in a very unpleasant manner.

Browne develops perspectives on David which help the reader to place important events for David's unconscious character, and he does this through shorter thematic sequences and contrasts. 'Steerforth and Mr Mell' in confrontation at the school is flanked in the previous monthly number by 'My musical breakfast', and in the same number by the following 'Changes at Home'.

The first of the three shows David asleep, but shows that his 'dream' is real, as Mr Mell's mother raises her hand to give Mr Mell 'an affectionate squeeze'. David has betrayed Mr Mell to Steerforth in the next illustration.

'My musical breakfast'

Here Browne is careful to organise the chaos of the scene around Steerforth with eddies of the sea of boys around Mr Mell and David. Behind Steerforth to the right of the picture Tungay and Creakle make their entrance, their joint personality rendered in the single bodied monster graffiti of them on the door. Behind them the barometer registers 'Stormy'. Mr Mell is threatened by this storm of which Steerforth (in heroic pose) is the centre, and by the implication of Mr Mell's hand on his head so is David. The narrative comment in the text on David's reactions is complex because it is contradictory—'a glow at this gallant speech', but later 'a flush upon my face and remorse in my heart' (ch. 7). The quarrel concerns Mr Mell's mother, of whom we are reminded by the graffiti on the desk just by David's face. Browne has a difficult task in presenting David's contradictory reactions of pride and shame, and solves the problem by showing David from behind where we cannot clearly see his face, and which allows for the ambiguity of response in David developed in the text. The thematic importance of the illustration to the theme of mother and son does not depend on the minute detail of the graffiti, but on the illustrations before and after which 'frame' it in the sequence.

Just as the first illustration of the three confirmed David's 'dream' when he was in a state 'between waking and sleeping', so the third confirms a picture of David's own mother which comes from a previous unconscious memory of David's. 'She was singing in a low tone. I think I must have lain in her arms and heard her singing so to me when I was but a baby' (ch. 8). This prepares for his later imaginative transposition of himself into his baby brother as he reconstructs 'the earlier image in my mind' of Clara after death. The illustration just holds the moment as memory is made real and David sees 'himself', an image to which he later returns:

> The mother who lay in her grave, was the mother of my infancy; the little creature in her arms, was myself, as I had once been, hushed for ever on her bosom.
>
> (ch. 9)

Steerforth's attack on Mr Mell separates the two illustrations which centre the theme of home and happiness through dream and memory, by a contrast of violence with tranquillity; and at the same time organises the sequence thematically. Browne's discretion

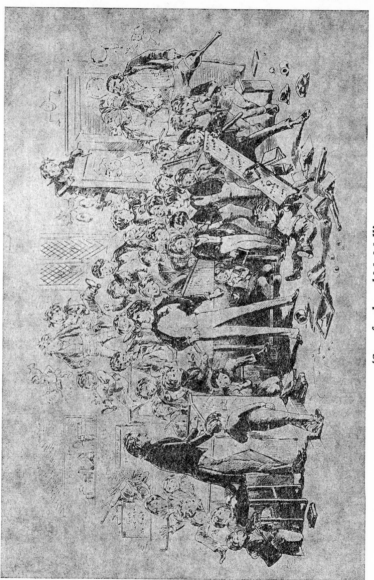

'Steerforth and Mr Mell'

in not showing David's face is crucial if he is not to cut across the textual treatment of the scene.

The deft relationship of text and illustration, and the way this connects to David's habits of mind as narrator, can be seen also in the illustrations which follow David's visions of himself. David as narrator sometimes sees himself very clearly as a third party in the novel, as in his visit to the public house and the accompanying illustration 'My Magnificent Order at the Public House'.

> The Landlord looked at me in return over the bar, from head to foot, with a strange smile on his face; and instead of drawing the beer, looked round the screen and said something to his wife. She came out from behind it, with her work in her hand, and joined him in surveying me. Here we stand, all three, before me now. The landlord in his shirt sleeves, leaning against the bar window-frame; his wife looking over the little half-door; and I, in some confusion, loking up at them from outside the partition.
>
> (ch. 11)

This view by David of himself is used as the basis for the illustration.

David the narrator is looking at himself in his mind's eye much as the reader looks at him in the illustration, and the moment suggests a collaborative gaze of reader and writer at the picture of one of David's happier moments.

In contrast, the illustrations can add to the reader's understanding of David, by giving a context of which David is unaware. The clearest example of many is in the early illustration, 'Our pew at church'. Here before we meet Murdstone in the text is a visual connection between him and Clara.

Locked in a pew on the left Murdstone is gazing very wide awake across a generally somnolent congregation at a modest Clara, her widow's veil to one side. David is also looking at his mother, and doesn't see Murdstone, nor does Peggotty who is busy making sure the Rookery is not on fire. Murdstone is identified by a boy pointing to the sleeping Beadle, but the gesture also 'points up' Murdstone. The identification is further completed by the hint on the upper pulpit on the left of the picture of Eve tempted by the serpent, and the strong vertical composition as those awake look up to the clergyman while Murdstone's steady horizontal gaze takes in Clara. In the text David later drops off his seat, perhaps

'Changes at Home'

disturbed by the falling hymn book in the background. At this point, the reader is unaware as David is of Murdstone's presence, as this is indicated later in the text: 'a gentleman with beautiful black hair and whiskers, who had walked home with us from church last Sunday' (ch. 2). The illustration is signalling an important feature of plot well before the text, and it is the first hint of the sexual and emotional events in the plot which are 'over' David's head, in this case literally. This effect assumes some conventions—not least that church presents romantic possibilities—but the illustration also depends on a keen visual awareness by the viewer unless the significance is to operate in retrospect. With a strong background in narrative and allegorical art we might assume that this significance would not be lost on a contemporary reader. The illustration, by re-organising the time scheme of the narrative, converts the picture from illustrating only a particular scene into a summary of later themes which can only be developed in a linear way in the text. This quality of instantaneous summary in the illustrations is used strategically to suggest direction in the novel, rather like the more formal summary of themes which the wrapper designs for the novels suggest.

4

Visual awareness is a learnt skill, and it is clear that Browne's illustrations require a sensitivity to both detail and composition in the reader, and an informed aesthetic eye. One assumption made in the illustrations is that the viewer is familiar with melodramatic conventions.[29] In more specific terms this is communicated by a shared language of gesture which both Browne and Dickens use, and which is related to dramatically conventional ways of expressing emotion. Annie Strong is, for example, never off her knees in the illustrations, and this is because 'supplication' is expressed in melodramatic terms by kneeling and raising the hands to a person. In an otherwise weak illustration, 'Mr Wickfield and his partner wait upon my Aunt', David and Uriah's common suspicion is communicated by their extraordinary left-handed handshake, itself a reminder of David's handshake with Murdstone. But this language of gesture and the aesthetic to which it refers, depends on a kind of double response; on the one hand a sense of composition, and on the other a response to detail. In part these

'My Magnificent Order at the Public House'

two aspects of visual response are connected by a kind of solidity in the scenes as well as by careful composition and placing of details. For example, the reader need not have noticed the rat in the bottom right-hand corner of 'The River' illustration, because Martha's situation is well expressed in compositional terms. The 'cavernous shadow of the iron bridge' (ch. 47) is simply suggested in the oppressive curve of the frame, and the dark and slimy impression of the river. But the centre background skeleton of a boat is well placed to suggest the discarded death which Martha is contemplating. The cumulative effect of the details can give an illustration density, solidity, and context.

Browne often suggests connections between these 'two readings' of the illustrations through the pictures on the walls. Though they are themselves details they can suggest compositional interpretations of the scene in which they appear, and these in turn can give moral point to the illustration as a whole. J. R. Harvey has pointed out the significance in the illustration 'Martha' of the picture above the mantelpiece of the woman washing Christ's feet, to the composition and moral theme of the illustration as a whole in suggesting Emily's movement away from Martha towards the half-open door behind which is a hint of her future in another picture of Eve tempted.[30]

A further element in the reading experience of the illustrations is that they can vary the tone from the sombre and tragic, to the lightly fantastic, and the broadly comic. This alternation of tone in the illustrations corresponds to similar variations in the text which have their origin in Dickens's melodramatic mode, summarised by Dickens with some humour in *Oliver Twist*:

> It is the custom on the stage: in all good, murderous melodramas: to present the tragic and the comic scenes, in as regular alternation, as the layers of red and white in a side of streaky, well-cured bacon. The hero sinks upon his straw bed, weighed down by fetters and misfortunes; and, in the next scene his faithful but unconscious squire regales the audience with a comic song.[31]

Dickens is much more complex than this in his use of the comic, but the principle of this contrast remains, as it does in the illustrations. Browne's treatment of comedy is good, and he can even suggest elements of verbal comedy which are extremely difficult to treat visually. In 'Traddles and I in conference with the Misses

'Our pew at church'

Spenlow' he leads the eye to the details through the composition, thus precipitating a second reading required by the details themselves.

Traddles and David face the Aunts on the left, and mediating the two groups in the centre are a pair of goldfish in a bowl. David's head is 'starred' in a halo-like effect by the pleats in the silk screen of the piano behind him, and labelled by the music on it open at a song entitled 'Will you love me?' David's halo can be seen to focus the books above, 'Loves and Angels', 'Paradise Regained', and 'Music', with a Dora-like statue above. Connected with these and above them is the picture 'The Last Appeal'. The compositional suggestion is that all these objects are really David's thoughts, focussed into his head by his halo. The companion picture to 'The Last Appeal'—'The Momentous Suggestion'—expresses the Aunts' views and between, over the door behind which Dora and Jip are hiding, is 'Arcadia'. This is well done. But the comic tone of the illustration has a purpose because it reinforces the comedy of the interview and the romantic themes of the Aunts, which in the text have more serious consequences.

> 'Affection' said Miss Lavinia, glancing at her sister for corroboration, which she gave in the form of a little nod to every clause, 'mature affection, homage, devotion, does not easily express itself. Its voice is low. It is modest and retiring; it lies in ambush, waits and waits. Such is the mature fruit. Sometimes a life glides away, and finds it still ripening in the shade.'
>
> (ch. 41)

The Aunts give a comic view of romantic love and Miss Lavinia's love of 'the stricken Pidger' in particular. But there is a more strategic suggestion here, in that Agnes is to be David's 'mature affection' and it is to be her fate to wait and wait 'ripening in the shade'. Dora as 'Little Blossom' never comes to fruit. Dickens is using the device of allowing an 'unreliable' character to spell out what will be the truth, and to hide this truth in the comedy, and the comedy of the illustration.

Without the comedy in the novel and in the illustrations, the novel would be one long and agonised wail, as exemplified by Mrs Gummidge's cry that she is 'a lone lorn creetur' myself, and everythink that reminds me of creeturs that ain't lone and lorn, goes contrairy with me' (ch. 10) which speaks for the real situation of

'Traddles and I in conference with the Misses Spenlow'

nearly all the characters in the novel. The illustrations help to mediate the comic and tragic aspects of the narrative, to create what J. R. Kincaid calls 'the most reluctant farewell to comedy'[32] in Dickens's work.

5

The illustrations operate sequentially and therefore create visual repetitions and cues which can become significant for the reader in both the development of character and in giving direction to the novel. They can also suggest parallels and complementary comparisons which may only be latent, or even suppressed in the text. In terms of the developing plot of *David Copperfield* it is important that some characters are kept apart. Dora and Emily never meet, nor Heep and Steerforth. The connecting links must be developed through David of course, but there are reasons why some characters must be kept apart in the text, but can be relevantly, if tactfully compared in the illustrations. Aunt Betsey and Mrs Steerforth never meet, and yet Browne suggests very strong resemblances between the two through the consecutive illustrations 'Peggotty and Mrs Steerforth' and 'My Aunt astonishes me'. Both are visually angular, stern, upright figures each with a cat and usually a footstool, and they each have an attendant who hovers behind their chair in the characters of Rosa Dartle and Mr Dick. This draws attention to their relationship in the novel, and the reader realises that their views on the sexes are almost equally in opposition. A meeting between these two pairs would be fascinating, but destructive to the shape of the novel because it would take over the centre from David. Safely locked into their respective illustrations, the comparison can be made without involving complexities of plotting.

The novel works through parallels and comparisons of characters who are separated, and these pairings and comparisons act as a kind of grading of personalities within which the reader locates the character of David. Browne can add to and develop these hints through the illustrations and in so doing suggest longer term patterns in the novel. This can be seen in the images of Emily, Dora, Agnes, and David's mother Clara, all four of whom turn up in one way or another in the last illustration of the book. Like Emily, Dora is usually shy and pictured with downcast eyes, except in her portraits. This connects her visually with Clara who is pictured in

'My child wife's old companion'

'A Stranger calls to see me'

the same way.[33] By contrast, as Dora peeps, Agnes looks steadily. Browne suggests the comparison of Dora and Agnes well in the illustration for Dora's death, 'My child wife's old companion'.

Dora is there in her portrait looking down at David and the dying Jip, the portrait allows Browne to have Dora of the scene, but not in it. Shaded by the door, Agnes enters gripping her right wrist with her left hand as if to control herself. Dora's portrait has almost the same gesture—the left hand laid on the right wrist. Browne avoids the 'solemn hand upraised towards Heaven'! (ch. 53) and concentrates on giving a sense of calmness in Agnes's pose, and tension in her hands.

The last illustration co-ordinates these patternings.[34] The central portrait is Dora looking down on the domestic scene, flanked by the picture of the Rookery on the left with its memories of David's first home and his mother, and Peggotty's boat on the right where an attentive viewer will see a tiny spot representing Emily, this picture being a miniature version of the vignette for the title page by Browne. These pictures in their symmetry suggest an ordered past in the upper part of the illustration. The next level suggests the present domesticity of David and Agnes, with the future below in the children and their games. Dora, Emily, and by implication Clara, remain as 'pictures' in the illustration, in David's memory, and in the reader's remembrance of the novel.

NOTES

1. *The Golden Bowl* (London, 1966.) James's objections are discussed by J. R. Harvey in *Victorian Novelists and their Illustrators* (London, 1970), pp. 166–67.
2. A. J. Portas, *The Style of Charles Dickens* (D.Phil. Oxford, 1974), p. 150.
3. *Ibid.*, pp. 141–42.
4. *Victorian Panorama: Paintings of Victorian Life* (London, 1976), p. 110.
5. G. Cruikshank, 'The Bottle' (1847), a series of eight engravings; Augustus Egg, 'Past and Present' (1858), a series of three paintings; and W. P. Frith, 'The Road to Ruin' (1877), a series of five paintings; are examples of sequences. Paired narrative paintings such as A. Solomon, 'Second Class—the parting', and 'First Class—the meeting' (1854) were popular, and single paintings with narrative themes common. *See* also: S. Sitwell, *Narrative Pictures* (London, 1937), J. Maas, *Victorian Painting* (London, 1976).

6. The taste for narrative art can be seen in the pictures on the walls in Browne's illustrations, in *David Copperfield* these are mostly of biblical subjects.

7. D. Jerrold in *The Rent Day* (1832) dramatised D. Wilkie's paired paintings 'The Rent Day' (1812) and 'Distraining for Rent' (1815); T. P. Taylor in *The Bottle* (1847) dramatised Cruikshank's sequence; and C. H. Hazlewood's *Waiting for the Verdict* (1859) was advertised as 'Founded on and embodying the celebrated Picture of that name, by A. Solomon Esq. in the Royal Academy'. There are numerous paintings and prints with dramatic or fictional themes.

8. There are many popular songs based on *David Copperfield*, mainly inspired by Dora. 'Good Night, Little Blossom', M. Keller and G. W. Birdseye (Musical Bouquet No. 4294, London: 1874) is an example. The title pages of the songs were often illustrated with a portrait or scene from the novel. Musical themes are important in the novel as Mr Mell's flute, Dora's guitar, and Rosa Dartle's harp indicate, and contemporary paintings use similar musical motifs, usually associated with emotion—Holman Hunt, 'The Awakening Conscience' (1854) and William Morris, 'Guinivere' (1858), using piano and harp respectively, are examples.

9. O. G. Rejlander and Mrs J. M. Cameron frequently treat dramatic and narrative scenes in their photographs. See also H. Gernsheim's discussion in *Creative Photography* (London, 1962) especially Chapters VII and VIII. Tennyson's *Maud: A Monodrama* (1855) and Browning's dramatic monologues are examples of the dramatic in poetry.

10. Browne's illustration 'I make the acquaintance of Miss Mowcher' for the December 1849 number of *David Copperfield* was used as the basis for a political cartoon on Lord Brougham in *Punch* (London, 1850), vol. XVIII, p. 135.

11. J. Brougham's version of *David Copperfield* (London, 1851) sets the first scene 'in Miss Trotwood's Apartment, (as in Picture).'

12. The facsimile reprint of *Nicholas Nickleby* in serial form (Menston, 1972) reveals advertisements for 'Webster's Acting National Drama', for engravings from 'Finden's Royal Gallery of British Art'; and for various publishers of popular music.

13. *The Victorian Novelists and their Illustrators* (London, 1970), pp. 160–61.

14. *Ibid.*, p. 162.

15. James, *op. cit.*, p. 13.

16. Modern childrens' fiction is an interesting exception. Dickens's readership had a greater proportion of child readers than the modern novel, and his novels were for family reading as his editorship of *Household Words* makes plain.

17. The details of the collaboration between Dickens and Browne are too complex to examine here. Dickens would give Browne the subject and suggest its treatment often checking the preliminary sketches, while Browne had considerable autonomy in the treatment of detail and of course the execution of the plates. See M. Steig, 'Dickens,

Hablot Browne and the Tradition of English Caricature', *Criticism*, XI (1969), pp. 219–33.

18. The extra plates were published in 1848 and reprinted in the National Edition of *Dombey and Son* and *The Old Curiosity Shop* (London, 1907).

19. Harvey, *op. cit.*, p. 142.

20. I am using the term melodrama here in its historical sense, as Dickens and his contemporaries would have understood the term in describing drama acted with a musical background having certain conventions of character, plot, staging, and acting styles, rather than the modern vernacular sense of the word. *Cf.* Michael Irwin's discussion in this book, above, pp. 15–17.

21. Tableaux and poses plastiques were popular. Gwendolen Harleth poses in a tableau as Hermione in George Eliot's *Daniel Deronda* (London, 1967), Chapter 6; and Walter mentions of a prostitute that she put 'the savings she had made by letting out her cunt, to open a Casino with *poses plastiques*, singing, dancing, etc.' *My Secret Life* (New York, 1966), Vol. 4, p. 660. *See* also Richard D. Altick, *The Shows of London* (London, 1978), especially Chapter 24, 'The Waxen and the Fleshly', pp. 350–62.

22. A. Halliday, *Little Emily* (New York, 1869), p. 42.

23. All references to *David Copperfield* are to the Oxford Illustrated edition, first published 1947.

24. Harvey, *op. cit.*, p. 144.

25. A reference to either Adrian or Isaac Ostade. *See David Copperfield*, Chapter 57.

26. Of the other novels using a first person narrative, *Great Expectations* was not originally illustrated, and Esther in *Bleak House* is a special case. *See* M. Steig, 'The Iconography of the Hidden Face in *Bleak House*', *Dickens Studies* IV, March 1968, pp. 19–22.

27. Portas, *op. cit.*, p. 142.

28. In the illustration 'Our Housekeeping', David should be seated to carve the joint, but the toughness of the meat forces him to his feet.

29. *See* also J. Hillis Miller's discussion of the use of melodrama in 'The Fiction of Realism: *Sketches by Boz, Oliver Twist*, and Cruikshank's Illustrations', *Dickens Centennial Essays*, ed. A. Nisbet and B. Nevius (London, 1971), pp. 85–153.

30. Harvey, *op. cit.*, p. 147.

31. *Oliver Twist*, ed. K. Tillotson (Oxford, 1966), p. 105.

32. *Dickens and the Rhetoric of Laughter* (Oxford University Press, 1971), p. 162.

33. There are three pictures of Clara if 'The Rookery' is included, as she is just discernible behind the lattice window through which Aunt Betsey is peering.

34. M. Steig in *Dickens and Phiz* (London, 1978) also discusses this sequence (pp. 129–30).

11

The Portrayal of Death and 'Substance of Life': Aspects of the Modern Reader's Response to 'Victorianism'

by W. L. G. JAMES

> '. . . you
> Contract my heart by looking out of date.' Philip Larkin

And now the bell—the bell she had so often heard by night and day, and listened to with solemn pleasure almost as a living voice—rung its remorseless toll for her, so young, so beautiful, so good. Decrepit age, and vigorous life, and blooming youth, and helpless infancy, poured forth—on crutches, in the pride of strength and health, and in full blush of promise, in the mere dawn of life—together round her tomb. Old men were there, whose eyes were dim and senses failing—grandmothers, who might have died ten years ago, and still been old—the deaf, the blind, the lame, the palsied, the living dead in many shapes and forms, to see the closing of that early grave. What was the death it would shut in, to that which still could crawl and creep above it!

Along the crowded path they bore her now; pure as the newly-fallen snow that covered it; whose day on earth had been as fleeting. Under that porch, where she had sat when Heaven in its mercy brought her to that peaceful spot, she passed again, and the old church received her in its quiet shade.

Charles Dickens *The Old Curiosity Shop*, ch. LXXII

Confronted with such a passage, how does the modern reader respond? The immediate reaction is likely to be unease, even embarrassment The insistent rhythms have a palpable design on us, pressing us to feel emotion. The construction of the scene—all ages

226

brought to contemplate Nell's death—and the biblical echoes, these imply a weight of religious meaning that the winter burial of Nell does not support. There is something taking place in Dickens's imagination, and in the minds of the original readers who responded enthusiastically, that we cannot share, that excludes us. But it is not that we feel as we might, say, at our exclusion from obscure allegory in a medieval account of death: we feel alienated by the *obviousness* of the symbolism, by its use of religious and romantic imagery that offers no resistance to our understanding, as through a broken net. Emotion is not only the substitute for thought, it denies substantive levels of intellectual engagement.

The simple reaction is to reject the death of Little Nell as not only inaccessible to the modern sensibility, but as a palpable artistic failure. But let us scrutinise our response more carefully. It is well known that on its first appearance *The Old Curiosity Shop* (1840–41) sold 100,000 copies (*David Copperfield* sold 25,000). It overwhelmed intelligent and apparently firm-minded readers such as Edward Fitzgerald, Daniel O'Connell, Sydney Smith, Hood, Landon, Francis Jeffrey and Macready. It was claimed to be equal to or greater than the creations of Shakespeare.[1] Even within a few decades of this success, an equally intense reaction set in, and by the end of the century it was left to Oscar Wilde to make the quip that has become better known than the novel itself, 'He must have a heart of stone who cannot read the death of Little Nell without laughing.'[2]

But there remains the obstinate fact of that original printing of the 100,000 copies. What was the response of the first readers? And can this be relevant to our own attitude towards Dickens's novel? Let us look honestly at our reaction to the death of Nell. Pressed to relate our experience of reading this, few would deny that the passage does have a strong impact, even if the impact is revulsion. We are also likely to relate this to a sense of an historical dimension—that it is 'Victorian sentimentality', or 'degenerate Romanticism'. Our sense that it is 'bad' is significantly different to our rejection of sentiment, in, say, a contemporary Mills and Boone popular romance. The novel captures, like a fern in amber, an emotional construct of a past period, and this conditions our response either for better or for worse. If our reaction is that Victorianism is to be rejected, we will reinforce our embarrassment in ways that go beyond the text itself. If we are enthusiasts for the Victorian period, we may add appreciation to the passages that overrides an 'objective' literary response. The impact of Wilde's witticism is significant here. Implicit in his sarcasm is a whole attitude to what we loosely could call 'Victorian emotionalism'. It categorises the book in a way that implies comprehensive rejection even though the death of Nell takes up a minute portion of the novel as a whole. My point is that it is naïve for the modern reader to assume that he *can* read a Victorian novel with the response one brings to contemporary fiction. The subtly shifting significance of words, the difference in moral and imaginative attitudes implicit even in tone and syntax construction, the general assumptions about the nature of the period—all these condition our reading experience. Why and how?

The assumption of most essays in this volume has been that Victorian fiction is directly accessible to the twentieth-century reader. I wish to take a radically opposed line in order to explore whether this is an adequate approach. One would not seriously attempt to understand Shakespeare without some understanding of the Elizabethan idiom. The Victorian period appears so close to us that we often forget how different was its frame of mind. Moreover, I would claim that the process of learning the Victorian idiom is continuously taking place in a largely 'invisible' way. The revival of interest in the nineteenth-century novel has been inseparable from a rediscovery of ways to 'read' Victorian paintings, buildings, printed ephemera, historical perspectives and much else. Let us take this one step further—let us, as an experiment, see if we can understand the emotional construct implicit in the original popularity of the death of Little Nell.

For G. H. Ford,[3] *The Old Curiosity Shop* provides an extreme case of the limitations of critical interpretation. The huge original popularity of the novel came because Dickens was reliving the personal emotion he felt for the death of Mary Hogarth who died in his arms at the age of seventeen. This would have a poignant immediacy to readers experiencing the high death-rates of the early Victorian period. Little Nell was born out of the last impulse of the Romantic movement, which had begun with Wordsworth's children, unspoilt by society, and 'trailing clouds of glory' from immortality, and which by 1840 was about to disappear, leaving Nell to increasing derision from a disillusioned age. In London Nell, like Wordsworth's Poor Susan, was surrounded by the material ugliness of the city, yet dreamily preserved her own spiritual integrity. She travels through the country, finding freedom and peace in nature, experiences the nightmare of the Black Country, and, like Lucy, finally becomes one with nature. 'Under the porch, where she had sat when Heaven in its mercy brought her to that peaceful spot, she passed again; and the old church received her in its quiet shade.'

Yet a good deal about Nell—her sufferings and trials, the intense sense of grief generated by her death—goes beyond the Romantic image of the child, and Ford's explanation that the Victorian sensibility went dead to the wavelength of Romanticism is not enough to account for the novel's declining fortunes. We must look closer at the period in which the book appeared. We find that the popularity of Little Nell was paralleled by a host of Victorian poems and stories about the death of little children, and by the whole range of funeral ephemera and cemetery sculpture explored by recent studies such as John Morley's *Death, Heaven and the Victorians* (1971) and J. S. Curl's *The Victorian Celebration of Death* (1972). The Victorians not only accepted death, they built it into Victorian living. When sanitary precautions moved burials out of the overcrowded vaults and churchyards, new civic churchyards, beginning with Liverpool and Kensall Green in the late 1820s, were constructed as necropolises embodying *the triumph* of death. Studying Undercliffe Cemetery, Barnsley, Stuart Rawnsley and Jack Reynolds found that the planning reflected the structure of the living society of the town, and its social values.[4]

The deaths of children, partly because of their frequency, were seen as a particular case. Rather than being a cause for mourning, they were urged to be a particular instance of God's grace; the child was taken to God with all his or her innocence, uncorrupted by the world. As Jesus rather sharply told the weeping mother in the anonymous 'The Lost Jewel'—

> 'Is thy spirit filled with anguish?
> Is thine eye with weeping dim,
> Cease, oh Mother; thus to languish,
> Cease, for I had need of him.'

The Romantic interest in the innocence of children fused with the Evangelical movement's insistence that life was a pilgrimage undergone under the constant eye of God, and that living should be a constant vigilant preparation for death. Tracts such as Leigh Richmond's *The Dairyman's Daughter* (1814), which sold over two million copies in eighteen years, described the deaths of the faithful, in particular children, and urged the reader to be ready to follow good examples of how to die.

Nell is in many respects akin to the Evangelical heroes and heroines of contemporary religious tracts. Her journey with her grandfather is at the start explicitly compared to that of Pilgrim in Bunyan's work; her visit to the races parallels Vanity Fair, the Black Country, the Valley of the Shadow of Death. She contemplates graveyards. Through her life she prepares herself increasingly for death. Although Dickens only decided to 'kill' her when the story was advanced, as Forster saw, her death was implicit in Dickens's 'own conception', for such a 'gentle pure little figure and form' could only be preserved from taint by death.[5] She moves from fears and trepidations as to the world around her, towards an acceptance so complete that even the fearful burial hole she is shown in the church where she is to lie leaves her unmoved, and the menacing shadows of life that surround her at the beginning in the Old Curiosity Shop are in the end transformed into the Gothic regalia of death in Tong Church. Her death is linked to the Nativity. The novel was written, as were the tracts, with the didactic purpose of instructing the bereaved. 'Oh! it is hard to take to heart the lesson that such deaths will teach, but let no man reject it, for it is one which all must learn, and is a mighty universal Truth' (ch. LXXII).

The difficulty we have in accepting Nell, however, is not that she is a figure from an Evangelical or Methodist tract, or that she is a figure from late Romanticism. The problem is that she moves uneasily between the two. Nell is more personalised than Wordsworth's innocents; she is a domestic heroine, not an outcrop of creation. Yet she does not conform easily with Evangelical faith. Richmond's heroine in *The Dairyman's Daughter* dies in appropriate autumn warmth: 'the air was mild and the declining sun occasioned a beautiful interchange of light and shade upon the hills'. As she died, 'We knelt down in prayer—the Lord was in the midst of us, and blessed us.'[6] Nell dies in mid-winter, and although this prefigures her Nativity into another life, the cold and white reinforce the sense throughout the book of her sad isolation. The reason for this ambivalence may be found in the religious temperament of the early Victorian era. G. M. Young has written that 'the Evangelicals gave to (Victorian England) a creed that was, at once, the basis for its morality and the justification for its wealth and power.' Yet, at the same time, by the accession of Victoria to the throne in 1837, the 'religious impulse was hardening into a code.'[7] Dickens was proclaiming faith in the divine providence of child-deaths with the energy of one undermined by doubt. If the popularity of *The Old Curiosity Shop* may be linked to late Romanticism, it is because this offered an emotional evasion of theological questioning, the comfort of sentimentality.

The modern reader will wish to reject this evasion. Yet this is not necessarily to reject the concern with the ritualisation of death that is often associated with it. The success of John Morley's exhibition of Victorian funeral ephemera in Brighton in 1971, documented in his above-mentioned book, suggests that it can relate to the modern age beyond an amused fascination with the bizarre. The appeal lies in the way the Victorians celebrated archetypal concerns with death and burial which the modern period, not the nineteenth century, tends to evade. And, paradoxically, the Victorians were enabled in their expression of views of death by their sense of the material; their images may be crude, vulgar, but they are imaginatively substantial. Even Nell, who so often appears a phantom in the novel, as she moves towards death is associated increasingly with the artefacts of the church; dead, she is one with 'tomb and monument . . . pillar, wall and arch', held silent in the moonlight. Moreover, in her death we come to see that it is related to her experience of life in the earlier part of the novel.

For under the intrusive sentimentality that surrounds Nell—even in her name and the diminutive 'Little'—there is a consistent and haunting awareness of the void that lies the other side of surface reality. Her first appearance comes in the context of the narrator's vision of the waste land of the city, 'that constant pacing to and fro, that incessant tread of feet wearing the rough stones smooth and glossy . . . the crowds for ever passing or repassing on the bridges.' 'Waking or in my sleep' he sees Nell herself dreaming, in 'the old dark murky rooms—the gaunt suits of mail with their ghostly silent air—the faces all awry, grinning from wood and stone—the dust, and rust, and worm that lives in wood. . . .'[8] The grotesque images of the Old Curiosity Shop are, as she goes on her wanderings, externalised in the bizarre peepshow of the world she meets—Punch and Judy, performing dogs, stiltwalkers, giants, dwarves, wax-works. The effect at times resembles that of *Alice in Wonderland*, and the modern reader's response may be complicated by an awareness of Carroll's novel; Mrs Jarley even talks like the Red Queen. As in *Alice*, adult reality is shown to be bizarre and arbitrary. Miss Monflathers brings 'eight chosen young ladies' from her Boarding and Day Establishment to see the wax-works, and is quite startled by the 'extreme correctness' of Mr Lindley Murray composing his English Grammar, Hannah More, Cowper and Byron. Yet Nell knows that the day before, Murray had been Grimaldi the clown; Hannah More, a 'murderess of great renown'; Cowper was Mr Pitt, and the Lord Byron that so flutters the girls (a sly dig this), had been Mary Queen of Scots (ch. XXIV). Surface reality is a dream in which only Nell, frequently shown musing or asleep, is awake. Her death is the final acceptance of this vision.

Interwoven with Nell's story, often clumsily, Dickens portrays the opposite sense, the substance of life. This contrast is emphasised not only by having Nell's story told largely in the country; that of Dick Swiveller, the Brasses, Kit Nubbles and the Garlands in the city—Dickens also employed two illustrators. Cattermole mainly depicted the dreamy and other worldly perspective of Nell; 'Phiz' the vital London life. Unusually, their woodcuts were integrated closely into the text itself, emphasising the contrast between the two visions. If Nell sees the show of Vanity Fair from backstage, Dick and Kit stand in front of the footlights. Nell's awareness of the illusion of theatre—she sees Punch with his wig being nailed on, the performing dogs being cruelly disciplined—is contrasted with the glorious acceptance of the magic of Astley's Amphitheatre by Kit Nubbles and his family on their night out. Dick Swiveller goes further—he lives in a self-created world of fairytale, melodrama and popular song. He assumes the 'manner of theatrical ravishers' when helping Barbara through the crowd; calls Sampson Brass 'the Baron Sampsono Brasso', and Sally Brass's servant, 'a small slip-shod girl in a dirty coarse apron and bib', who might as well have been clothed in a violin case, becomes 'the Marchioness'. Yet this transforms the girl not only in Dick's imagination, but in fact; he saves her from her oppressed life with Sally, and in turn she saves Dick when he is ill and penniless. It is a finer statement about the saving grace of the imagination than the more-noticed example of Sleary's Circus.

Quilp straddles both worlds. The 'demonic' Quilp is the Quilp of Nell's Nightmare, a gathering of shadows. But the Quilp who eats hard-boiled eggs in their shells and downs bumpers of rum without winking, the sexually fascinating Quilp, is part of the life-accepting world. It was Quilp above all who had the potential to interlock the two halves of the novel, but he fails to do this. This is because the decorum of the book, and the limitations in the character of Nell herself, prevent the sexuality and sadism implicit in Quilp from being realised. To work out the full implications of Nell's innocence in a material world, we require a full confrontation between the two main characters. As it is, Quilp only kisses Nell on the cheek—'what a nice kiss that was—just upon the rosy part'; his relationship to his own young wife is expressed by him keeping her up all night, sitting, the tip of his cigar glowing rosy red; and instead of direct physical violence, Kit is only tortured in the form of a wooden effigy. Quilp and Nell come closest in their deaths, for both withdraw into increasing solitude, Quilp with rage, Nell with acceptance. Nell dies in the peace of the country, Quilp in the cold highway of the river grasping at a boat that passes him by. *The Old Curiosity Shop*, then, is ostensibly about the sufferings and death of its child heroine, but the story was transformed by Dickens's imagination into a more complex exploration of the relationship of a death-centred vision to one of life. The intensity of the modern reader's reaction to the death scenes of Nell, then, can be pursued behind artistic failure to an issue of contemporary relevance—the failure itself becomes implicated in the crisis posed by the experience of a child's death.

By itself, however, this analysis is inadequate. It assumes that, if we read the novel with understanding, we arrive at a contemporary issue expressed in the Victorian idiom. But what we need to understand more fully than I have indicated so far is what is meant by 'idiom'. It is more than style, language, or religious or moral attitudes. A sensitive and experienced reader can date a Victorian novel—or painting—to within a few years, not by accidentals or knowledge of the author, but by a sense of the changing structure of reality implicit in the artistic medium. Difficult as it is to analyse this unique 'feel' or 'fingerprint', it is a central part of our reading experience of Victorian fiction, and one which has not been explored elsewhere in this volume. At the risk of generalisation, let us therefore examine some further aspects of the nineteenth-century novel's imaginative world.

In her essay, 'Against Dryness', Iris Murdoch has seen the strength of the Victorian novel as lying in the *density* that it gives to the experience it portrays. In the twentieth century the impact of existentialist thought and concern with psychology has driven our awareness into the area of the individual consciousness. Experience becomes symbolised, and loses its solidity. This account of life is ultimately solipsistic. 'We are not isolated free choosers . . . but benighted creatures sunk in a reality whose nature we are constantly and overwhelmingly tempted to deform by fantasy. . . . Through literature we can rediscover a sense of the density of our lives.'[9] This density refers to much more than the ineluctable solidity of 'things', but it is a good point from which to start exploring the Victorian consciousness as shown in fiction. For today we have become so thoroughly conditioned by a sense of the relativity of experience, the symbolic significance of objects, and the transience of the material, that it is difficult to comprehend a world in which the material had meaning in itself.

The Victorian frame of mind, on the other hand, was intrinsically 'materialistic'. Victorian science, unlike that introduced by Einstein and the Quantum Theory, was firmly based on Newtonian principles of the constancy of matter. Social theory, from Utilitarianism and the sociology of Comte, to Marx, Engels and social Darwinism, was also founded on measurable facts. The same attitude can be seen in the fundamentalism of Victorian orthodox Christianity, and its concern with the Biblical account of creation; or in Victorian psychology's interest in phrenology and animal magnetism, which could be charted by diagrams. Victorian society experienced an England physically changed by urbanism and the railways. The class struggle was conducted in economic terms, and it was visible in the dramatic contrasts between rich and poor, a social iconography of dress and possessions. For Ruskin, since the physical world was created by God, the artist's religious task was to accept and represent it: he 'should go to Nature in all singleness of heart, . . . rejecting nothing, selecting nothing, and scorning nothing; believing all things are right and good, and rejoicing in the truth.'[10]

The Victorian writer responded with fascination towards his material. The four large volumes collated by Myron Brightfield,

Early Victorian England in its Novels (1968), are remarkable not only for the physical detail with which they illustrate a wide range of social concerns, but also for the sense that most of this description was not so much to inform, as to give the pleasure of having the known reality observed—a confirmation of the material. At its worst, this interest leads to the stolid lack of vision that limits so much in the Victorian cultural world; at its best, it gives its art and fiction its sense of substance. Dickens's London is not merely metaphysical, it can be measured with the feet; its houses, river, fog, and the densely observed paraphernalia of city life, take on a reality as potent as that of the human characters. At the end of the century, Hardy's heroes and heroines are conditioned by real miles on real roads, and irreducible facts about soil and weather.

Victorian fiction is full of iconography and what we might call 'the symbolic'. But this remains, for the modern reader, curiously substantive—not just home, but the hearth; not death, but the death-bed. For Trollope's Archdeacon, tables could take on social values beyond themselves, yet these values are rooted in surface qualities of wood, construction, colour:

> Now there was something peculiarly unorthodox in the arch-deacon's estimation in the idea of a round table. He had always been accustomed to a goodly board of decent length, comfortably elongating itself according to the number of the guests, nearly black with continual rubbing, and as bright as a mirror. Now round dinner tables are generally of oak, or else of such new construction not to have acquired the peculiar hue which was so pleasing to him. He connected them with what he called the nasty, new-fangled method of leaving a cloth on the table, as though to warn people they were not to sit long. In his eyes there was something democratic and parvenue in a round table.
>
> (*Barchester Towers*, ch. xi)

Any comparison with twentieth-century fiction is of course invidious, the range of possible comparisons is infinite. However, consider the role of the table in this paragraph from D. H. Lawrence's *Women in Love* (1916):

> The food was very good, that was one thing. Gudrun, critical of everything, gave it her full approval. Ursula loved the situation, the white table by the cedar tree, the little vision of the leafy park, with far-off deer feeding peacefully. There seemed a magic

circle drawn about the place, shutting out the present, enclosing the delightful, precious past, trees and deer and silence, like a dream.

(ch. 8)

The white table has a symbolic significance here which makes it continuous with experience of Breadalby. The colour has a totally different *kind* of meaning to the darkness of the Trollope tables. Our awareness is subjective; in the nineteenth century the centre of reality is placed firmly outside the individual observer.

The way in which we apprehend external reality is conditioned by its place in time. A modern symbol such as the lighthouse in Virginia Woolf's novel, functions independently of time; the effect say, of the two pound notes Magwitch returned to Pip in *Great Expectations* comes from the fact that they exist at a particular moment, as embarrassingly real as the dusty half-pence the plasterer gives to William Dorrit in the Marshalsea. They can also be burnt. In the flame all that Pip meant by the offered notes is obliterated and forgiven; Magwitch drops the ashes into the lamp tray. Our awareness of reality is inevitably affected by our sense of 'time': if we posit for the Victorians a different sense of the material, we would expect also a different concept of time, and there is evidence that this was so. Jerome Buckley,[11] for instance, has demonstrated that the differences between twentieth- and nineteenth-century scientific method proceed partly from radically different temporal awareness. Victorian science was founded on concepts of constant sequential time—uniformitarian geology, nebular astronomy, evolutionary biology. In the modern age the clock has been exploded; time is relative, and such a perception has made possible such principles as those of entropy, the second law of thermodynamics, or mathematical continuous function.

As with a sense of the material, the Victorian sense of the time had its impact on Victorian fiction. 'Time', Mendilow has written, 'affects every aspect of fiction: the theme, the form, and the medium, language.'[12] Looking at the nineteenth-century debate about the form of the novel, in contrast with modern fiction theory, we find very little concern with temporal progression, and this is because it was taken for granted. As Carlyle said, with fine dogmatism, 'all Narrative is, by its nature, of only one dimension; it only travels forward towards one, or towards successive points. . . .'[13] For

Dickens, time was 'the magic reel' from which the story un-wound.[14] The sense of the inescapable pressure of advancing time, complicated but not denied even by an exception such as *Wuthering Heights* (1847), was intensified for the Victorians by the form that much fiction took. Reading a novel in parts over two years, a story serialised in a periodical, or even a novel in three volumes successively borrowed from a circulating library, was to 'live with' a fiction in a way foreign to most modern reading habits. In *Pickwick Papers* (1836–37), the monthly parts actually reflected the season and weather in which the original parts came out.

Victorian concepts of time found their ultimate expression in attitudes to death. The fact that the nineteenth-century concern with dying was to do with the frame of mind as much as with the social reality is shown by the statistics of death. From their literature, one might assume that the Victorians suddenly faced a huge increase in the death-rate, brought about in particular by urban conditions. The reverse is true. Indeed the urban expansion was made possible by a dramatic *decline* in the death-rate by the turn of the century: between 1720 and 1820 this had almost halved.[15] Yet once this has been said, the Victorians still faced a shockingly high mortality by modern standards, particularly in the case of children. When Victoria came to the throne, by the English national average, forty per cent of the population died before they reached the age of six. Few families did not know personally the death of a child, and most families knew the deaths of several. Moreover, while to-day such occasions occur usually hidden behind screens in hospital, the nineteenth-century pattern was for the death to take place at home, in the midst of family and friends. The multiplicity of death-beds in Victorian fiction was fact.

The experience of death, however, was mediated, not through the occult, but through a confirmation of the actual. We have seen how *The Old Curiosity Shop* is constructed around a dialectic between perspectives of 'life in death' and 'death in life'. As a very different approach to basically the same crux, we may take the example of Mrs Gaskell's *Mary Barton* (1848). This is an aspect of that novel that has not attracted much critical notice, although in the first eight chapters there are nine deaths, if one includes those indirectly reported. Some of these are intimately and poignantly observed, including that of Jem Wilson's child who has to be taken from its mother so that it will lose the will to live, and so escape from its terminal pain: 'We mun get him away fra' his mother, or he'll have a hard death, poor li'le fellow' (ch. 7). We learn details of laying-out and mourning, and the merits and de-merits of funeral rites. We see the way in which the community reacts to the deaths of adults and children. The modern reader's acceptance of these pasages comes from a complete lack of super-imposed emotion or moralising. The use of dialect allows the Man-chester people to speak isolated from authorial comment; Mrs Gaskell's sharp observation enables her to convey the futility and isolation felt in the face of death with economy and tact:

> 'Oh Lord God! I thank thee, that the hard struggle of living is over.'
> 'Oh Ben! Ben!' wailed his wife, 'have you no thought for me? Oh Ben! Ben! Do say one word to help me through life.'
> He could not speak again.
>
> (ch. 6)

The tissue of deaths that runs through the first chapters of the book come through to us with no sense of morbidity.

The full significance of the death-themes, however, may well be missed by a reader who is not alert to the way Mrs Gaskell plays these off against a portrayal of patterns of Manchester material life. One of these is finely drawn in the tea-party of Chapter 2. The scene is described with the sharp detail of a pre-Raphaelite painting—the blue and white check curtains about the longish window; the ledge with the two unpruned geraniums; the cup-board with the gleaming crockery, left open to show off its con-tents; the coal-hole covered with gaily-coloured oil-cloth; the dresser; the deal mock-Pembroke table; the bright-green japanned tea-tray with its print of embracing lovers; the crimson tea-caddy; the stencilled patterns on the walls. It can stand as an illustration for Manchester social history. But observing its setting in the story, and the tea-party itself, with its savoury-smelling eggs and Cum-berland ham, we become aware that we are also being offered something close to an icon of the 'home', with its security and order. With variations, it is a scene that we meet with often in Victorian domestic painting and fiction. Another example might be Peggotty's boat house in *David Copperfield*. In *Mary Barton* the domestic scene is threatened from two directions. There is the fear of industrial depression—Barton had already lost a son by starvation in bad times in the past. There is also the immorality embodied in Mrs Barton's sister, Esther, which is directly associated with death. Grief at Esther having fallen and 'gone on the streets' complicates the danger of a bad childbirth, and within a day of the tea-party, Mrs Barton is dead.

Immediately, the assurance of the rituals of home turns to desolation. Barton hears the bedroom drawer scraped open by a neighbour—this time to find burial clothes. Soap and water are used to wash the body. Barton's hand blunders against the un-washed crockery left from the family feast, and he is crushingly reminded of the domestic routine that has been broken. But not destroyed completely. The order that Mrs Barton had created is now taken over by Mary: the home is a model of Barton's moral world down to the removal of Esther—the brass nail reserved for her bonnet is pulled out and thrown away. It is destroyed by economic depression and unemployment. The possessions lovingly recorded in the tea-party scene are shown being sold—the furniture the tea tray and caddy, all go, until there are no blankets for the beds or coal for the fire (ch. 10). At this point the various themes of the book are strikingly brought together. Left with a room that is no longer a home, Barton takes opium and goes to a trades union meeting. It is a foggy night. Emerging from the meeting, he meets Esther, her face 'deadly pale around the vivid circle of paint' (ch. 10). The trades union meeting prefigures actual death—the murder of Carson and Barton's grief-stricken end. Esther prophesies the possible death of Mary, seduced and forced onto the streets. Esther not only appears 'deadly-pale', but her death at the end is juxtaposed to Mary's marriage. Significantly, Esther appears dead before the actuality: 'Whether she was indeed alive or dead, they know not now.' Death in Mary Barton, then, comes as part of the observed world of Manchester. But it is also the denial, by the evils of poverty, the breakdown of the family, and industrial failure, of a possible domestic and communal order.

The comparative failure of the novel, as has often been noted, comes from the shift in the story's direction after the murder of Carson in Chapter 18. The focus shifts from John Barton and the strike conditions, to Mary; social observation gives way to the melodrama of the false conviction of Jem Wilson, the chase to find the crucial witness, and the trial and last-minute rescue. Moving into the world of melodrama, Mrs Gaskell also transmuted the theme of death. Melodrama, with its ritualisation of Good against Evil, placed death in a metaphysical context. Usually the actual death is averted at the last minute, but not before it has dramatised the themes of salvation and damnation. Thus in Douglas Jerrold's *Black-Ey'd Susan* (1826), possibly the most popular of all nineteenth-century melodramas, William, about to die for the heroic act of saving his wife from rape by his own captain, stands facing his ship-mates and raises his hand in Christ-like benediction, praying 'Bless you all'. Barton's death is given similar Biblical meanings. Carson (and the reader) has been prepared for this by his reading of the crucifixion story. The scene of Barton's death is given the ritual of a passion play. There is a step upon the stairs; Carson stands a moment framed in the doorway, then hurries forward to raise the 'powerless frame' in his arms. Barton folds his hands; Mary kneels at their feet, asking, 'Pray for us', and completing the *pieta*. The theological implications of this end are evident. Like Stephen Blackpool dying in an abandoned mine-shaft in *Hard Times*, Barton has been crucified by man's inhumanity to man. By taking the murder on himself he has 'become sin' on behalf of his fellow-workers, and Carson's change of heart suggests a redemptive outcome, in more understanding industrial relations. It is also clear that this kind of symbolism is out of key with the kind of narrative the first part of the book offers us, and this contributes to our sense of disjunction at the heart of the novel. There is a general loosening of emotional control—as we see also in the court scene, 'Poor Jem! His raven hair (his mother's pride, and so often caressed by her fingers), was that, too, to have its influence against him?' (ch. 32). But in general, Mrs Gaskell handles the issues of death in ways more accessible to the modern reader than we find in *The Old Curiosity Shop*. In his own work, Dickens too, moves towards the interfusion of a sense of death with that of experienced reality. Consider for example, the treatment of death in a work contemporary with *Mary Barton*. In *Dombey and Son* (1848), Paul, like Nell, is born to die, but not because of his innate goodness. He is deprived of the strength to live by the ambition and pride of his father, who refuses to accept his son's humanity. The death scene itself is the most remarkable Dickens constructed, and its success on the stage today in the performances of Emlyn Williams witnesses its continued power. The images of death are all taken from Paul's actual experience. The river of life bearing him to the sea of death; the Homeric boat across the water to the afterlife—these are part of the visible bedroom scene, where the actual river reflects its quivering light onto the wall. Even the vision of the mother as he dies is there already in the portrait that Paul has been studying. The scene progresses objectively realised through Paul's senses—a hurry of coming and going, faces glimpsed, a breath felt on his cheek, Florence grasping him, the 'floating' of his final weakness blending with his dream of being in a boat on the river as the light pours in through the window. Again, the movement towards death is conveyed, not through a scene of dimming reality, but through an intensifying of it. 'How green the banks were now, how bright the flowers growing on them, and how tall the rushes.' The scene unmistakably echoes Wordsworth's lines in 'The Immortality Ode'—'Our souls have sight of that immortal sea / That brought us hither,' and also the Evangelical Apocalypse —the fact of Death will last until 'the wide firmament is rolled up like a scroll.' Yet it is firmly located in a middle-class bedroom in London.

Recognising such dimensions implicit to the reading experience can distract from the immediacy of our response; it can substitute literary archaeology for novelistic reality. That is one pole. But the other extreme is equally limiting. By failing to realise the issues involved in communicating with fictional modes that *are* different to our own, in effect we do not read in the fullest sense. Between intellectual pedantry and cultivated ignorance I would pose a third approach to reading—*that of the informed imagination*. After occupying this position true evaluation can begin.

NOTES

1. G. H. Ford, *Dickens and His Readers* (Princeton, 1965), ch. iv.
2. Hesketh Pearson, *Oscar Wilde* (N.Y., 1946), p. 208.
3. Ford, *op. cit.*
4. S. Rawnsley and J. Reynolds, 'Undercliffe Cemetery, Bradford', *History Workshop Journal*, 4 (Autumn 1977), 215–21.
5. J. Forster, *The Life of Charles Dickens* (1872), chapter vii. Malcolm Andrews, 'Introduction', *The Old Curiosity Shop* (Harmondsworth, 1972), p. 29.
6. Louis James, *Print and the People* (Harmondsworth, 1977), p. 291.
7. G. M. Young, *Victorian England: Portrait of an Age* (1936), p. 4.

8. *OCS*, chapter 1. It is hard to believe that T. S. Eliot did not recall Dickens's opening when writing the lines in *The Waste Land* (1922):

> Unreal City
> Under the brown fog of a winter dawn
> A crowd flowed over London Bridge, so many,
> I did not think death had undone so many.
>
> (11. 60–64)

9. Iris Murdoch, 'Against Dryness', *Transition*, XVI (January 1961), 16–20.

10. John Ruskin, *Modern Painters*, Pt. II. Sec. VI, Ch. III; *Collected Works*, ed. E. T. Cook and A. Wedderburn (1903), II, pp. 623–24.

11. J. H. Buckley, *The Triumph of Time* (Cambridge, Mass., 1967).

12. A. A. Mendilow, *Time and the Novel* (N.Y., 1965). See also Frank Kermode, *The Sense of an Ending* (1966), ch. ii.

13. Thomas Carlyle, 'On History', *Fraser's Magazine*, II (November 1830), p. 45; see also Richard Stang, *The Theory of the Novel in England, 1850–1870* (1959); Miriam Allott, *Novelists on the Novel* (1959).

14. *The Old Curiosity Shop*, Ch. LXXIII.

15. Anthony Woods, *Ninteenth Century Britain, 1815–1914* (1960), p. 5.

12

A Note on Serialisation

by MALCOLM ANDREWS

Discussions of the effects of serial publication of Victorian novels on their authors and readers[1] usually draw attention to the author's peculiar opportunities for cliff-hanging suspense, as, for instance, when Thackeray has Becky Sharp counter old Sir Pitt's marriage proposal at the end of *Vanity Fair*'s fourth number with the revelation that she is already married, and the reader must wait a month before the husband's identity is revealed. Or it may be pointed out how the author can modify his story in response to his readers' complaints or recommendations, as when Trollope records in his *Autobiography* how he wrote Mrs Proudie out of the Barchester Chronicles after overhearing two clergymen in the Athenaeum complaining of his habit of reintroducing the same characters in his fiction. In this brief note I want to consider two or three consequences of serialisation which are perhaps not sufficiently taken into account, and which seem especially pertinent to the critical focus of these essays.

We might remind ourselves of some of the facts. Someone paying his shilling for the first monthly instalment of *Bleak House* when it appeared on the bookstalls in March 1852 had no alternative to waiting a full year and a half before he could reach the end of that novel. We can finish it now in a matter of days. At least, the cases where we don't have this freedom are rare: we might accelerate unduly to avoid a library fine; or, in the academic context, there is that intellectual dyspepsia familiar to those who find themselves cramming a huge rich novel into a day or two's forced reading to meet a supervision deadline (might this be a consumer version of Thackeray's fevered scribbling as the printer's boy shuffles impatiently outside his door?). The mention of these cases is not wholly facetious. As has been stressed elsewhere in this book, we should surely consider rather more carefully than we do the circumstantial variables in the reading experience as we establish and develop our aesthetic criteria.

I want here to suggest some aspects of the particular circumstances of serial publication, and will return to the example of *Bleak House*. We may assume that for most people the main incentive in reading a novel for the first time has to do with story and plot—what is going to happen next? It was the same for *Bleak House*'s first readers; but serial publication imposed peculiar curbs on that reading momentum. The pattern might have gone something like this. The monthly instalment of four chapters or so would be bought on the day of publication, read to a circle of family and friends that evening, browsed over during the next few days (there were copious advertisements as well as the two 'Phiz' illustrations), and then shelved. Three weeks later, perhaps on eve of issue of the next instalment, it might be brought down again and scanned to refresh the memory and restore the sense of narrative continuity. This enforced delay between instalments of a story put pressure on the writer to give the monthly number as far as possible its own integrity as well as establish its place in the whole design. Dickens had a dawning awareness of this quite early in his career:

> it was necessary—or it appeared so to the author—that every number should be, to a certain extent, complete in itself, and yet that the whole twenty numbers, when collected, should form one tolerably harmonious whole.[2]

An important consequence of this, particularly in Dickens, is the rich detailing of the picture to give substance to the individual instalment. Now the modern reader trying to make fairly rapid progress through the novel to pursue plot (and few plots are more complex and compelling than *Bleak House*'s) often finds this density of detail an encumbrance. This would not have been so for the original reader who, perforce, had ample time to read and absorb the whole wealth of detail in the picture before moving on. John Dixon Hunt has very clearly shown how Dickens, 'exactly like the best of the graphic satirists . . . involves us in "reading" his scenes'.[3] This kind of reading, exploring and absorbing details that lie, as it were, to the side of the main narrative path, sets up a kind of tension with the more conventional reading that follows the linear progression of story. Monthly instalment publication frustrated the latter reading, and encouraged the former—what one might call the 'lateral' reading; and Dickens was supremely able to take advantage of this. Now, however, it is usually only on the second or third reading that we most fully appreciate this aspect of his art: I wonder if anyone else shares my experience, that each time I return to *Bleak House* it takes me longer to re-read? On this re-read one gives oneself more licence to browse in his fictional world, in the way that the original readers knew very well: one is bound (literally?) to savour the various ingredients in a monthly ration of thirty-two pages much more than one does in consuming fifty to a hundred pages a day. George Eliot, for one, was convinced that the slow plan of *Middlemarch*'s publi-cation was 'of immense advantage . . . in deepening the impres-sion'.[4]

This notion of browsing applies to another type of serial publica-tion: that is, the issuing of instalments of a novel in a magazine, where it takes its place alongside a miscellany of other writings, which would be absorbed in a kind of extended 'lateral' reading and consequently become involved in the response to the novel. The chronological successor to *Bleak House*, *Hard Times*, was first read just like this, in the pages of Dickens's weekly miscellany *Household Words*. Two or three chapters of the novel would appear on the first two or three pages of the magazine, thereby, as Joseph Butwin argues convincingly,[5] enjoying the status of a leading article as well as a signed novel. This would be followed by half a dozen articles, poems, short tales, etc. to complete the twenty-four-page issue. Thus, when the opening three chapters of *Hard Times* appeared in the 1 April 1854 issue of *Household Words*, it was followed by, among other items, an article on 'Oranges and Lemons'—a fanciful documentary about their exotic places of origin, importation details, their aroma in Covent Garden Market, etc.; a sentimental and somewhat melodramatic story of mishaps among the Devonshire scythe-stone quarrymen; a poem, 'Our Coachman'—a jolly, colourful portrait of the driver of the Prus-sian diligence; and an earnest article on 'Rights and Wrongs of Women', recommending their staying at home and tending to family and hearth rather than venturing into public office:

And there are books to read, and then to discuss by the fireside with her husband, when he comes home in the evening—though perhaps his attention may sometimes wander from the subject to her little foot, peeping out from under the flounces over the fender . . .

That opening, then, to *Hard Times*, with its relentless emphasis on Facts, on the bare monotonous vault of the schoolroom, on the emphatic square wall of Gradgrind's forehead, and on the general sense of a grim mechanical crushing of tender young imaginations, is set in a context of writings that emphasise colour, exoticism, sentimentality, jollity, and soft domesticity. The novel's original readers therefore, browsing through the whole of that 1 April number would be well aware of the way in which Dickens's new novel was designed to be thrown into sharp relief by the familiar contextual material of his miscellany.

The novel that followed *Hard Times* in *Household Words* was Mrs Gaskell's *North and South*. Dickens did not allow it to lead off the weekly issue: instead, its weekly ration of two chapters was sandwiched somewhere in the middle. But here again, readers would be aware of an interesting interplay between journalism and fiction. In the 7 October 1854 issue, Chapters 10 and 11 of *North and South* were published. Chapter 10 provides the first occasion for us to hear Mr Thornton's controversial views on industrial relations and the dynamics of the class system in the north. The lead article in that same *Household Words* issue was by Dickens, and it was his address 'To Working Men', urging them to summon their intelligence, their energy, their numbers, and their 'power of union', and call upon the middle-class to unite with them to force reform upon the Government.

In these two examples the context works in almost opposite ways to reinforce the reader's response to the novel. The impact of *Hard Times*'s opening is accentuated by the sharp contrasts offered elsewhere in the magazine; whereas Thornton's creed acquires unusual topical interest when associated with Dickens's fiery leader.

One final point, that has to do with the original reception of the serialised novel, should be mentioned here. A large proportion of those first readers could not themselves read. In this case, the monthly or weekly instalment of chapters would be read aloud, at least once, maybe twice, in the month; and this in itself makes another great difference. One of the most frequent responses to some Dickens readings that I have given is that, whatever the dramatic quality of the reading, to have Dickens read slowly and deliberately makes for a very different experience of the text: quite simply, there is more time to absorb what was written. This more public reading aloud is, like serial publication, yet another case in which someone other than the private reader is controlling the pace at which the text is delivered and received.[6]

Is it not always an open question as to who knows better the pace at which a novel should be read, its reader or its author?

NOTES

1. One of the best of these discussions can be found in Kathleen Tillotson's *Novels of the Eighteen-Forties* (Oxford, 1954), esp. sections 8–10 in the 'Introductory' Part I.
2. Dickens's Preface to the 1837 edition of *Pickwick Papers*.
3. John Dixon Hunt, 'Dickens and the Tradition of Graphic Satire', in *Encounters: Essays on Literature and the Visual Arts* (London, 1971) edited by John Dixon Hunt.
4. Letter of 4 August 1872, quoted in Kathleen Tillotson, *op. cit.*, p. 34.
5. Joseph Butwin, '*Hard Times*: The News and the Novel', *Nineteenth Century Fiction* XXXII (1977) ii, pp. 166–87.
6. Reading aloud is intimately related to rhythm, and for the relation of this to pace see Gregor, pp. 109–10.

Interchapter 4

It was suggested in Interchapter 2 that 'the contemporary reader' is an elusive or even chimerical figure. Is there any purpose then, in attempting to understand 'the Victorian reader' and recapture his reading experience? That question, of course, bears on a familiar and fundamental critical controversy that can never be resolved and that it would be idle to re-open here. It might, however, be useful to draw attention to some minor caveats and special applications relevant to our immediate concern.

Louis James's account of the changing fortunes of *The Old Curiosity Shop* and Stephen Lutman's reference to the shift in styles of book-illustration are incidental reminders of the extreme diversity of the seventy-year period that we encapsulate in the term 'Victorian'. Who can doubt that if the Queen had died in 1850, or 1860, or 1870 the era named for her successor would later have been seen to have a sensibility, an artistic and literary character all its own? To generalise about 'the Victorian novel' is to risk falsification.

That problem is made subtler by its interaction with another. The very nearness of the Victorian age encourages us to be indiscriminating in our responses to it. If the past is 'a foreign country' this particular province seems almost accessible. We have talked with people who grew up there. Many of us live and work in Victorian buildings, and regularly use Victorian artefacts. We are familiar with photographs of Victorian towns and villages, great men and ordinary citizens. The fictional inhabitants of the period speak a language that is often indistinguishable from our own. Since we have so many windows opening on to the Victorian age easy assumptions come naturally. 'Layers of time' nestle together to form a compound lens. Our grand-parents were Victorians and so was Mr Pickwick. Can we not know him as familiarly as we knew them? Thackeray and Hardy were Victorians, and their novels seem to provide a direct contact with the wars against Napoleon.

When the perspective is so vast it must be that the immediacy of response is delusive, that we are trusting too heavily in impressions founded upon an arbitrary smattering of evidence.

It is interesting to find a contemporary critic of Dickens discounting in advance the possibility that we could truly come to terms with his novels:

> All the oddities of London life he has sketched with inimitable vigour; but class characteristics and local peculiarities are of a very transient nature. Fifty years hence, most of his wit will be harder to understand than the allusions in the *Dunciad*; and our grand-children will wonder what their ancestors could have meant by putting Mr. Dickens at the head of the novelists of his day.[1]

The reviewer may have come to the wrong conclusion, but his intermediate comment deserves consideration. Is the *Oliver Twist* or *Little Dorrit* we read the novel Dickens wrote, or must it inevitably be a twentieth-century reconstruction?

It cannot *simply* be the latter. A novel of any interest presents not only a fictional world but a way of looking at that world. To read, say, *David Copperfield* or *Middlemarch* is necessarily to submit, at any rate partially, to a Victorian sensibility. No doubt there will be passages that prompt a 'modern' judgement at variance with the author's apparent intention. At certain junctures there can be something like a chemical reaction between the narrator's assumption and our own discrepant response. But the very noticeableness of such instances should remind us how much more natural it usually seems to accept the novelist's values. To an extent we become involuntary Victorians.

But a reading of any seriousness is also likely to involve a degree of conscious effort. At the simplest level the student of *Bleak House* who does not understand the term 'crossing-sweeper' or the student of *Mary Barton* who knows nothing of the Chartists will miss a significant aspect of the novel's meaning. In such areas the theoretical problem we have been speaking of translates itself, for the teacher or the editor, into a practical one. He will want to ensure that the students to whom he owes a responsibility are not disabled by ignorance. Accordingly he will supply, in fact or in effect, a footnote at the appropriate point.

Such help is plainly useful in that it relieves the prospective reader of an obvious disqualification. But is the gain significant?

The footnote may be virtually meaningless in isolation. A diction-ary-definition of 'crossing-sweeper' or an explanatory paragraph on the Chartists will say little to the reader who knows nothing about the Victorian city or Victorian working-class life. The 'historical' dimension of such a novel is plainly something too rich and com-plex to be 'dealt with' by the assembled footnotes of a scholarly edition. Indeed, to look at the assembly of notes in isolation from the text is to have a very sharp sense of the peculiar nature of the information that is thought necessary for a 'fuller reading'. Is there something in the nature of the novel that makes it 'note-resistant' in a way that doesn't seem to be the case with the poem or the play? Is it because it offers to document details which belong to a world where such documentation can never be anything but partial?

The provision of footnotes may even place a disturbing filter between the reader and the text, altering emphases and propor-tions. By consistently underlining the author's references to (say) railways or slums or sex or the place of women an editor may un-consciously superimpose his own political or social views on a given novel. The very stress on historical facts can itself be false to the complex fictional treatment of those facts. To put the point com-paratively: a reading of Gissing can more aptly be supplemented by factual information than can a reading of Dickens, who is much less concerned with documentary detail as such. It is easier to pro-vide a statistical account of Victorian slums or dust-heaps than to respond sensitively to Dickens's stylised transcription of those realities. Tom-all-Alone's relates more fully and more subtly to the fictional landscape of *Bleak House* than to some documented and photographed Victorian slum. On the other hand, of course, the student with *no* knowledge of the actuality, will be unable to gauge the degree or the purpose of the stylisation.

Victorian fiction is not unique in posing such problems, but it poses them with particular force and definition. The quoted refer-ence to *The Dunciad* supplies a negative comparison that helps to explain why this should be so. To understand 'the allusions' in that poem may be a difficult exercise but it is surely a limited one —a familiar species of literary archaeology. Coming to terms with a Victorian novel, as all three essays in this section in their various ways imply, is a much more intricate matter involving an imagin-ative apprehension of past atmospheres, furnishings, clothes, tastes, customs, beliefs, courtesies. We expect to *partake* in these novels. The 'historical' understanding essential to the reading of earlier literature is often, in effect, a formal pre-requisite. A certain grasp of the concept of courtly love or of the great chain of being provides a necessary ticket of admission to many a great poem or play. But with the Victorian novel the case is different. We seek not merely to enter and tour the building but to inhabit it.

The imaginative process involved is problematic in the extreme, but we are granted some insight into it. Every film, every television dramatisation of a Victorian novel represents, at least in theory, the detailed physical embodiment of someone's mental vision of the work concerned. Yet in most cases the effect is 'wrong'. This can be so even where casting, acting, dialogue and direction are unexceptionable. The drama somehow declines into costume drama. A miniature example of this declension may be found on the front covers of many a modern paperback edition of a Victorian novel— the covers of the New Wessex Hardy, for example. There in a genuine Dorset landscape stands a figure in genuine Victorian dress. What is it that makes the effect closer to that of a television advertisement than to that of a Hardy description? Is it the brightness of colour, the sharpness of focus? No doubt such factors contribute their anachronistic nuances. But the real issue is perhaps more fundamental. If at one extreme our imaginative response to a novel may be inadequate, or flatly mistaken, it may be that the other extreme is never reached at all, and never can be reached. It may be that the reader's vision is always incomplete, always partly in shadow. The filmed transcription is false in its very exhaustiveness and pictorial clarity.

The implications of this argument are dispiriting at first sight. In trying to come to terms with the 'Victorianness' of a Victorian novel we are obliged to embark on a journey that is necessarily inconclusive. We can be demonstrably 'wrong' in this area but never demonstrably 'right'. Perhaps the commentator quoted above was correct in his estimation of the transcience of Dickens's world, and the London we seem to see in the novels is only a pseudo-reality that we half create. But if all this is true there is still much constructive work to be done. The journey back towards the nineteenth-century is no less fascinating and rewarding for the fact that we will never arrive. And in attempting it we can hope to become at any rate better readers than we were before.

NOTE

1. The *Saturday Review*, 8 May 1858. Quoted by Philip Collins in 'Dickens and London', *The Victorian City: Images and Realities*, ed. H. J. Dyos and Michael Wolff (London, 1973), p. 546.

13

'The Flash of Fervour':
Daniel Deronda

by RUTH RAIDER

> '. . . for God's sake, don't go into any eccentricities! I can toler-
> ate any man's differences of opinion, but let him tell it me with-
> out getting himself up as a lunatic. At this stage of the world, if
> a man wants to be taken seriously, he must keep clear of melo-
> drama.'
>
> (ch. 59)

Sir Hugo, affable Englishman that he was, knew it was easier to
spot melodrama than to describe it. Certainly he spotted that
Daniel's plan to rush off to Mainz in search of a chest of abstruse
Jewish papers was not quite the thing for an Eton–Cambridge man
to do. Since, for Sir Hugo, un-English eccentricity was the criterion, he would have had a thing or two to say to King Lear about
the sensible disposition of property. Sir Hugo knew his wills. As
Michael Irwin points out,[1] neither violent actions nor exaggerated
styles of heroic or pathetic rhetoric need disqualify a book from
being taken seriously; but the fact that he and other writers in this
group feel the need to make careful distinctions about the times
when melodrama does and does not work[2] testifies, I think, to a
residual unease about the moments when fiction seems patently
stranger than life. In a book such as *Armadale*, the details may
scintillate and entice but when we realise that Collins had no
designs on us except to keep us reading, that he doesn't want 'to
be taken seriously', as Sir Hugo would put it, we are amused or
bored, but we are not disturbed.

No one doubts the seriousness of George Eliot's intentions. Sensational events and ostentatiously 'poetic' styles, which occur
throughout her work,[3] are frequently in the service of her didactic
intentions. In her earlier novels the more startling instances of

the violent and sentimental—Hetty's reprieve in *Adam Bede* and the death of Maggie and Tom in *The Mill on the Floss* for instance —seem to be desperate attempts to end her books and she is aware of the weakness of her endings. In *Daniel Deronda*, however, sensational incidents and elevated styles are far from her last resort. Barbara Hardy[4] points to the many 'sensational' aspects of the book, the 'tangled and intricate intrigues, the lost fathers and unknown mothers, the melodramatic confrontations, the mysterious past passions, the illegitimate children' and she sees the 'tension, mystery, dread and strangeness' as 'part of the psychological experiences of the reader'. We may feel some reserve about the success of such details as the painted dead face in the Offendene panel that appears to Gwendolyn at opportune moments or the hysterical guilt feelings Gwendolyn has before and after her husband's death, but we can agree that this is a book of extremes, of narrowed options and peculiar actions.

George Eliot saw the book as a tendentious one. She had been hard on the English upper class and hard on the prevalent anti-Semitism in English society and she was disappointed at the blandness of the reaction which merely praised Gwendolyn and Grandcourt and dismissed the rest of the book As she wrote to Harriet Beecher Stowe, she had expected from the beginning that the Jewish part of the book 'would create much stronger resistance and even repulsion than it has actually met with.'[5] I believe that it was precisely her desire for extreme and provocative contrasts that led her to the deliberate choice of heightened 'literary' styles in the Zionist parts of the book, a choice, given her critical bias towards realism and lively, idiomatic speech, that she made nervously and self-consciously. From the styles available to her in the Bible, biblical commentary, medieval Jewish poetry, and from popular fiction and drama, she attempted to create a heroic mode. Where her styles collide rather than merge—as in Mordecai's prophetic denunciation of the present godless generation to the Dickensian magpie child, Jacob—we have unintended comedy. Where her intentions of presenting idealised Jews such as Mordecai and actual Jews, such as the depressed Mr Ram or the degenerate Lapidoth, collide, we do not feel her fairness. Rather we feel a kind of unease we do not feel with Mrs Stowe's completely idealised Negroes in *Uncle Tom's Cabin* because Mrs Stowe's characters excite—or fail to excite—the emotions. Eliot's Jews, more austerely presented, are full of ideas and represent ideas; they call first to our judging minds.

Frequently George Eliot provokes a kind of resistance in her readers that she had not intended: we argue not only with the 'bad' Jewish parts but also with the 'good' Gwendolyn ones. We find ourselves questioning the way in which Gwendolyn is 'saved "so as by fire"', as Eliot describes Gwendolyn's progress in her letters;[6] and we find ourselves unexpectedly admiring the ambition and scope of the part of the book that is fictionally less alive. Perhaps part of our reaction is due to our admiration for the courageously extreme experiment she appears to be attempting. In later readings we may find ourselves more and more alive to the breadth of her learning, the intensity of thinking and feeling, and the complexity of intentions in the Zionist parts of the novel. It is not always easy or rewarding to try to separate specifically fictional interest from general interest. If melodrama frequently causes unstable reactions in the reader, the highly intellectualised melodrama of *Daniel Deronda*, even where one may wish to distinguish between intellectual and humanly intelligent, may cause notably drastic swings of sympathy and interest with each reading.

In theory at least, fictional interest always came first for George Eliot. Early in her career, in 1853, her comments on Mrs Gaskell's book, *Ruth*, suggest a severely realistic approach. The book, she said, would not be 'an enduring or classical fiction' because Mrs Gaskell[7]

> seems constantly misled by a love of sharp contrasts—of 'dramatic' effects. She is not contented with the subdued colouring—the half tints of real life. Hence she agitates one for the moment, but she does not secure one's lasting sympathy: the scenes and characters do not become typical.

At that stage she would not even grant the intensifying red slash on a subdued canvas that Michael Irwin suggests as an analogy for the possible heightening effects of the highly dramatic, used discreetly.[8] Throughout her career she inveighed against any effect that oversimplified life, but she was much less consistent in practice than in theory. Even though she rejected the idea of fantasy as 'vague forms, bred by imagination on the mists of feeling, in place of definite substantial reality', she resorted to fantastic plots.[9] In a letter she wrote to Frederic Harrison ten years before she wrote *Deronda*,[10] she spoke of the severe effort involved in making 'certain ideas thoroughly incarnate, as if they had revealed themselves to me first in the flesh and not in the spirit'—and even the phrasing suggests that the inspiration is initially abstract—since she believed that

> aesthetic teaching is the highest of all teaching because it deals with life in its highest complexity. But if it ceases to be purely aesthetic—if it lapses anywhere from the picture to the diagram —it becomes the most offensive of all teaching. Avowed Utopias are not offensive because they are understood to have a scientific or expository character; they do not pretend to work on the emotions, or couldn't do it if they did pretend.

In none of her works does the co-existence of picture and diagram assert itself more aggressively than it does in *Daniel Deronda*. The reader is moved between the Gwendolyn and Zionist sections much as one is moved on a roller coaster in a fairground, except that the experience is rarely exhilarating. In both the Gwendolyn and Zionist sections we are strongly aware that the author is unusually 'exempt from cerebral lassitude', to use James's phrase; in both plots we are aware that the author is making intellectual demands on us. Of course all serious novels make us think, but few nineteenth-century novels make us so self-conscious about the fact that we *are* thinking and arguing while reading. The ideas and our arguments with the ideas become conspicuously part of our experience of the novel. In attempting to give an account of the arguments we have with the book's peculiar mix of honesty, evasiveness, and high intent, we feel naturally led to the sources of some of her ideas and her use of sources.

The central political idea, the utopian one of the new Israel, is crucial to the fiction, since it determines Daniel's fate; yet it leads us away from the fiction as firmly as it leads Daniel out of England. If Eliot did not quite go along with D. H. Lawrence's view that New Jerusalems were stale buns for Aunties,[11] her reservations about 'avowed Utopias' suggest that she did see their fictional difficulties. In *Daniel Deronda* she makes no attempt to body forth the New Jerusalem beyond Mordecai's spectacularly uninviting remark that it will be the Belgium of the East. She uses the conception merely as a lodestone for personality: it gives Daniel his sublime mission and, according to the Rabbis who wrote to her, gave back some self-respect to the Jews of the Exile. Of course her avoidance of speculation about the new Israel may avoid one kind of didacticism, but it raises other problems, problems of the *deus ex machina*. She felt that critics had been unjust to her *Mill on the Floss* because she had been careful to avoid didacticism, or, as she put it, 'because I don't *load* my dice so as to make their side win', and, as late as 1876, she insisted that her fictions were 'experiments in life' and that she had become increasingly suspicious of ideas that did not come 'clothed in human form', although parts of that letter suggest that she felt strongly pulled towards direct teaching. About *Romola*, the novel closest in spirit, subjects, and method to *Deronda*, she confessed that it was her 'way (rather too much perhaps) to . . . urge the human sanctities through tragedy— through pity and terror as well as admiration and delights.'[12]

It is less frequently the sensational events—the visions, drowning, unlikely meetings and recognitions—that we experience as unacceptably melodramatic than it is the moments when people are speaking together. When Grandcourt dies no one demurs at the obvious convenience of his death or its violent manner partly because we have last seen him at his most sadistic, partly because we have seen him throughout as a walking dead man. The actual death seems merely expressive of what we have accepted, even desired. Grandcourt is eminently murderable; his death is no loss to the race. But when Gwendolyn reacts with histrionic guilt to her husband's death, her reaction throws doubt back on the event:

> . . . she said, in the lowest audible tone, 'You know I am a guilty woman?'
>
> Deronda himself turned paler as he said, 'I know nothing.' He did not dare to say more.
>
> 'He is dead.' She uttered this with the same undertoned decision.
>
> 'Yes,' said Deronda, in a mournful suspense which made him reluctant to speak.
>
> 'His face will not be seen above the water again,' said Gwendolyn in a tone that was not louder, but of a suppressed eagerness, while she held both her hands clenched.
>
> 'No.'
>
> 'Not by any one else—only by me—a dead face—I shall never get away from it.'

. . .

'I have been a cruel woman! What can I do but cry for help? I am sinking. Die—die—you are forsaken—go down, go down into darkness. Forsaken—no pity—I shall be forsaken.'[13]

The reaction of the reader is likely to be that a murderous impulse towards such a man is a natural impulse and that Gwendolyn has been exceptionally lucky in not being tied to him for life. Instead we are given Daniel's pieties about her guilt being a sign of her recoverable nature. The theatricality of the speech highlights the shakiness of the thought. Even if her tragedy creates her conscience, as James suggests when he speaks of Gwendolyn's story as the very stuff of life,[14] the tragedy is not the tragedy of her husband's death but that of a young girl's miscalculations about what is valuable and how to get it. The earlier Gwendolyn, so pleased about her intelligence, would be more likely to be livid at her own stupidity than crushed into a submissive lump by her own wickedness. There is much 'typicality' in the picture of the stifling marriage but the movement forward to her salvation seems to build on hysteria. The conscience that has been so formed is a much more feeble and doubtful article even than Isabel Archer's breezy certitudes at the beginning of James's *Portrait of a Lady*, although Isabel also has a lot to learn about true conscience as James makes clear.[15] Both girls seem entrapped by increasingly theatrical postures and attitudes.

Gwendolyn's problematical 'salvation' seems to arise out of Eliot's increasingly less subdued and realistic view of life, a shift signalled by the appearance in her letters of a category called 'the ideal'. The ideal corresponded to a 'romantic and symbolical' fiction, allied to Hawthorne's romances, of which she was a great admirer. By the time of *Romola* she had become less rigid in her theory that reality was always seen in 'half tints' and was ready for bolder effects, a more passionate selection of details. The reader might find it difficult to make the fine distinction between the sensational and the symbolical in the ending of *Romola* when the exhausted Tito floats down the river to land just in front of his enraged guardian, Baldassare, who chokes Tito and, just to be on the safe side, sits on his body all night. It is fairly clear, however, that she had Hawthorne in mind when she wrote in 1863 that the 'various *strands* of thought' she had had to work out had forced her into a more ideal treatment of *Romola* than [she] had foreseen at the outset' but the 'Drifting Away' (of Romola in a boat) and 'The Village with the Plague' (which Romola saves singlehanded) had always been parts of her original conception.[16]

The word 'forced' may suggest some unease about these 'idealised' scenes, but she was determined that these 'romantic and symbolical elements' were not an evasion of real life. To the end of her life she was somewhat puzzled by the public's cool reception of *Romola* and its rapturous reception of *Middlemarch*. She believed that *Romola* was her best, her *truest* book, but 'truth' was now more akin to Wordsworth than to verisimilitude. In 1877, after re-reading *Romola*, she wrote that 'there is no book of mine about which I more thoroughly feel that I could swear by every sentence as having been written with my best blood, such as it is, and with the most ardent care for veracity of which my nature is capable.'[17]

At times *Daniel Deronda* seems part of an implicit conversation with *Romola*: Mordecai is the unworldly, entirely passionate visionary to Savonarola's visionary worldliness: conceptions of a theocratic state exist in both books and in both the practicalities involved in the establishment of such states are entirely ignored. In *Romola* the utopian element appears in Romola's tender care for Tessa and Tito's children; in *Daniel Deronda* it is in the orgy of reverential tenderness in which Mirah, Mordecai and Daniel luxuriate. There are scenes in the two novels which are almost ironic commentaries on each other. Romola meets her dying, long estranged brother, Fra Luca[18] and rejects what he stands for; Mirah meets her long lost saintly brother, Mordecai (ch. 47) in a scene that seems like Little Nell meeting an Old Testament prophet, and she is ecstatic. It seems as if the earlier book made Eliot want to try related 'experiments in life'. In both novels there are similar ideas of the kind of reality fiction may properly imitate, ideas which permitted greater latitude in her use of 'symbolical' scenes. We might well cavil about the effect, but Romola's salvation of the villagers exists as the ideal of heroic self-sacrifice working its way through the real world. In *Daniel Deronda* the idea of a new kind of heroism—a combination of perception, empathy, and passive resistance—coexists with, and frequently competes with, her passion for verisimilitude and for the half-tints of life.

One result of such conflict which is fictionally disastrous but oddly interesting is that there often seems to be an inverse relationship between the plausibility of the plot or character and the fierce care for documentation. The reader cannot help but feel the opposing tugs of melodrama and verisimilitude. Eliot wrote many times to Frederic Harrison to clarify the legal implications of the will in this book and his answers determined Daniel's improbable relation to Sir Hugo[19] (just as he helped her verify the possibility of the extremely unlikely legal situation in Felix Holt). In 1875 she wrote to Leslie Stephen to inquire about the resignation of scholarships in Cambridge, the move she had originally planned for Deronda.[20] He told her that the usual motive was that a better fellowship had been offered by another College or the student preferred a non-academic job, so she makes Daniel miss his opportunity by helping a friend. Stephen remarked later on Eliot's care in getting the details of Cambridge life right. He added that some of the touches in Deronda appeared to have been drawn from one of her friends, Edmund Gurney, 'a man of remarkable character, and as good-looking as Deronda.'

There might well be such touches, but the essential suggestion appears to have come from D'Israeli's Coningsby,[21] a book which she appears to have thought of as popular rubbish. The young Coningsby, nephew of the Duke of Monmouth, uncertain about his parentage, terribly good-natured, somewhat reserved in his friendships, not passionately engaged in his studies at Combridge, looking about for his role in life, does suggest Deronda, just as the Monmouth–Rigby relationship reminds us of Grandcourt and Lush. It is as if Eliot were trying to retrieve a serious novel from what she thought of as a trivial one. When she made Daniel lose his chance of a fellowship, Stephen remarked that 'In the Cambridge atmosphere of Deronda's day there was, I think, a certain element of rough common sense which might have knocked some of her hero's nonsense out of him.' At first it seems that Eliot is merely insisting on Daniel's good nature when she has him sacrifice his chance by helping a friend, but this seems more likely her attempt to disassociate him from 'rough common sense' which for her was linked with the more blasé attitudes which she found, and disliked, at Oxford and Cambridge. After all the main target of the book was the genial, philistine common sense of the English upper classes who drifted from gambling halls to archery meetings to balls to country houses in search of a motive and in fear of eccentricity. Daniel's strength, for Eliot, is in his fastidious rejections of whatever might cramp his fullest development (in this case, Cambridge, later, all of England). Nothing that smacks of selfishness (the world of art, the academic life) or compromise (politics) will suffice. Only 'social captainship' of a peculiarly unlikely and uncompromising kind will do. There is something fascinating in the ambition of her conception but it seems more deeply unreal than local sentimentality about Daniel's friendships, for it is impossible to imagine any real motive or situation which will allow all the elements of Daniel's personality, or any personality, to click so neatly into place. Where she appears to have wished to balance worldly wisdom against the more deeply wise unworldliness of Daniel, she has in fact created in the reader full sympathy with Sir Hugo's genial worldliness:[22] '. . . my dear boy, it is good to be unselfish and generous; but don't carry that too far. It will not do to give yourself to be melted down for the benefit of the tallow-trade; you must know where to find yourself.' Quite against Eliot's desire we end in one of the book's many single-edged ironies. Once the reader begins to respond to the book's play of ideas and also begins to suspect that his responses and the author's intentions are out of phase, he is led to inquire more closely into the ideas he is responding to and this starts him thinking about Eliot's ideas outside of the immediacy of their dramatisation.

Certainly the Zionist parts of the novel give the reader the impression of authorial intentions gone awry since it suffers from an abysmal collection of bad styles as well as the same combination of documentation and unreality. The basic unreality is that Daniel is granted his insistence on the perfect, unsought-for vocation. We are forced to question her stance of disinterested historian because of her peculiar treatment of the Jews and her odd selection of Jewish sources. While she admires much about the Jews, she does not admire the jealous God of the Old Testament.[23] Writing to a Jewish admirer, Eliot spoke of her 'deep impersonal historic interest in Judaism' without which she couldn't have written the novel.[24] Certainly there is little in the characterisation to suggest that her interest was anything *but* historic: there seems to have been virtually no attempt to work from observation of actual contemporary Jews. In the Hand and Banner discussion (ch. 42) of Zionism, the views of the puppet-like workmen are drawn from German historians; those of Mordecai from the *Kuzari* of Judah ha-Levi, who wrote in the Jewish Renaissance of medieval Spain.

Kalonymos, the Jew who recognises Deronda, and whose name comes from medieval Spanish Jewry, speaks in the self-consciously poetic manner of a sub-Tennysonian Ulysses: 'Me you will hardly find, for I am beyond my threescore years and ten, and am a wanderer, carrying my shroud with me. But my sons and their children dwell here in wealth and unity . . . when I am in the East I lie much on deck and watch the greater stars. . . .' The Cohens come from Dickens. Daniel was brought up as an Englishman; Mirah is ignorant of Judaism; Lapidoth and the Princess are renegade Jews. The fact that these Jews exist on the fringe of Jewry eliminates the need for much direct knowledge of Jews. Even Mordecai, the great Jewish prophet, is considered a heretic by Rabbis who describe his writings as a 'New Book of Mormons'. Daniel, as Mordecai's disciple, cheerfully announces that he'll modify old Jewish beliefs. Since Daniel's knowledge of these beliefs seems both recent and scant and is apparently heavily indebted to a chestful of recondite untranslated papers left to him by his grandfather, most Jews would find Daniel's revision of Mordecai's Book of Mormons a puzzling affair. We might feel that Eliot is a cavalier historian even more than a disinterested one, for all her earnestness. God is merely a makeweight in Mordecai's call to Jewish unity; what really interests him is the doctrine from the Kabbalah about the transmigration of souls, an idea that is hardly central to Judaism. Mordecai stresses mystical blood ties, but to most Jews what is more important is the idea of a peoplehood in God. What is central to Zionism, where it is to be distinguished from pure nationalism, is the deep Jewish belief that Jews are a Chosen, a God-sensitive people, who must play out their drama of alienation and reconcilement with God and the dénouement must be in the Promised Land.

The reader feels how much Eliot was torn between a fascination which Jewish specialness and the desire to defend them by making them seem as much like Christians as possible in their beliefs. The Judaism has been eviscerated by an agnostic writer who is, as she believes, addressing English bigots. When Daniel enters the Judengasse, what we get is a vague levelling down of all religions to some vaguely Good Impulse:

Deronda having looked long enough at the German translation of the Hebrew in the book before him to know that he was chiefly hearing Psalms and Old Testament passages or phrases, gave himself up to that strongest effect of chanted liturgies which is independent of detailed verbal meaning—like the effect of an Allegri's *Miserere* or Palestrina's *Magnificat*. The most powerful movement of feeling with a liturgy is the prayer which seeks for nothing special, but is a yearning to escape from the limitations of our own weakness and an invocation to all Good to enter and abide with us . . . He wondered at the strength of his own feeling; it seemed beyond the occasion—what one might imagine to be a divine influx in the darkness, before there was any vision to interpret.

Beyond this vague religious uplift, there is no spiritual vision to interpret within the book. Eliot wrote, in 1866, after visiting a synagogue, that she 'fairly cried at witnessing the faint symbolism of a religion of sublime far-off memories.' Besides the use of historians (Graetz, Zunz, Jost, Delitzsch) in the Hand and Banner discussion, in which assimilationist positions get short shrift compared to Mordecai's impassioned Zionism, the 'faint symbolism' is all that is documented. What holds the reader's interest more and more is the sense of how far the disinterested historian has stretched the ideas she found in her Jewish sources. Because the central tenets of Judaism have been so vitiated, Daniel's Zionism seems mere gullibility and Zionism itself seems a form of national megalomania. The peculiar evasiveness of her documentation— she virtually eliminates God from her Judah ha-Levi borrowings[25] for example—merely underlines the unreality of the original conception, the idea that a young man could fastidiously reject all the roles his society offered for possible service and magically be provided with another world which he can call traditional and define as he wishes. What the American pioneers noticed fairly quickly was that what they brought to their new country was themselves: politics quickly followed. Several critics have suggested that the Zionist section nearly bursts the bounds of nineteenth-century realist fiction. It does, but partly by the unfortunate strategem of overleaping the bounds of plausibility.

Eliot's evasiveness makes the reader turn more and more critically to the fiction and can easily create an irritation which finds critical formulation in F. R. Leavis's account. It is not possible to deny his description of 'the wastes of biblicality and fervid idealism ('Revelations') devoted to Mordecai , , , the copious and drearily comic impossibility of the working-men's club (ch. 42)' or 'the utterly routing Shakespearean sprightliness of Hans Meyrick's letter in Chapter 52',[26] but we might want to resist the more general remarks that all the writing directly connected with the 'prophetic afflatus' is unreal and impotently wordy, a sign of Eliot's emotional immaturity; that the emotional intensity masks an essential relaxation, and that the higher flights of prose seem to be inspired by emotional drunkenness. The highest flights don't seem to be inspired at all, but Henry James seems more right to put his reactions to *Deronda* in a three-sided conversation. Our reactions to the book are not that straightforward, even if irritation is quite likely a part of our reaction. We might agree that tenderness is not the most convincing base for 'social captainship'; we might even add that the unreality of the Jewish sections arises because there are no real Jews in the book despite all the fussing about Jewishness. At the same time we might wonder whether any inadequacy in a book gives so deep an insight into the author's psyche and we might want to protest that it is not relaxation but strain we feel throughout the Zionist parts of the book.

The difficulties caused by her themes are intimately meshed with the thematic difficulties caused by the extreme risks she took with style, as we see when we look more closely at passages and their effects. There are times when the writing, pre-eminently that of sentimental melodrama, seems to dictate absurd sentiments which don't seem integrally connected to 'prophetic afflatus'. Here 'poetic' styles replace the allegorical scenes of earlier books—of Romola floating, of Maggie and Stephen Guest drifting, down the river—to represent the poetic reality 'deep down things', in Hopkins's phrase, and the attempt goes wrong partly because she was not a great poet in the high styles.[27] A realistic and a heroic mode are meant to be balanced against each other, to comment on each other, much as the two worlds of Henry VI, Part I, comment on each other, with Prince Hal moving between them.

One reason for thinking that she chose an elevated style rather than lapsed into one comes from the letter she wrote to her publisher, John Blackwood, who made nothing of Mordecai:[28]

> I thought it likely that your impressions about Mordecai would be doubtful. Perhaps when the work is finished you will see its bearings better. The effect that one strives after is an outline as

strong as that of Balfour of Burley for a much more complex character and a higher strain of ideas. But such an effect is just the most difficult thing in art—to give new elements—i.e., elements not already used up—in forms as vivid as those of long familiar types. Doubtless the wider public of novel-readers must feel more interest in Sidonia than in Mordecai. But then I was not born to paint Sidonia.

We might wonder in advance whether the elements offered by Scott and D'Israeli can, in combination, yield an authentic high poetry. Certainly as she tries to subtilise the elements, to create a 'new thing', she gets into difficulties. It is worth looking briefly at Chapter 47, when Mordecai meets Mirah for the first time, to watch the odd compound of modes, and the tense, vain effort to create psychological plausibility and complexity:

> when they were seated awaiting Mirah, he uttered no word, keping his eyelids closed, but yet showing restless feelings in his face and hands. In fact, Mordecai was undergoing that peculiar nervous perturbation only known to those whose minds, long and habitu-ally moving with a strong impetus in one current, are suddenly compelled into a new or reopened channel. Susceptible people, whose strength has long been absorbed by a dominant bias dread an interview that imperiously revives the past, as they would dread a threatening illness. Joy may be there, but joy, too, is terrible . . .

The use of analysis and epigram reminds us of the brilliant Chapter 48 between Grandcourt and Gwendolyn, but seems almost a parody of it. Here we have elaborate explanation of what doesn't seem to need it and the effort is that of being forced upward into thoughtfulness. The passage moves into Mordecai's priestlike in-tonings ('Yes, dear child, I shall not be long with you in the body' . . . 'The Eternal Goodness has been with you') which quickly jars against the Dickensian Little Dora–Little Nell coynesses of Mirah (' "Yes, and how you answered her—'Mother!' and I knew you loved her." Mirah threw her arms round her brother's neck, clasped her little hands behind it, and drew down his face, kissing it with childlike lavishness. Her hat fell backward on the ground and dis-closed all her curls.') This seems the only time in her career that Eliot tried so self-consciously and nervously to create a style which is a compound of the vatic, the melodramatic, and the analytical (carried over from the Gwendolyn sections). There's a lot of

D'Israeli's Sidonia in this book for all Eliot's scorn of that novel. The result seems a pastiche of all styles, and we are faced with a wealth of motives and tones but no characters.

Her unease about what she was attempting can be felt virtually everywhere in the Daniel and Zionist sections and the nervousness itself seems to do more damage than profound personality disorders. So in Chapter 35, when Daniel and Gwendolyn are together at Diplow and Daniel removes his hat, Eliot rushes in to explain his motives. Daniel suffers as much from her tense fidgeting as he does from her favour. It is this habit that gives us the feeling that each time we are meeting him is the first time. Very late in the book we are still being reminded of Daniel's oft reiterated characteristics: 'To estimate the effect of this ardent outpouring from Deronda we must remember his former reserve, his careful avoidance of premature assent or delusive encouragement, which gave to this decided pledge of himself a sacramental solemnity, both for his own mind and Mordecai's.'

The style of sentimental gush seems to take over and create absurdities where none were required by any unrealities of theme or situation. Therefore when she tells us that Daniel was shy of proposing to Mirah, partly because all lovers are timid, partly because he's unusually sensitive, and partly because he is still a virgin, we get total tweeness: 'how much more may that energetic timidity possess a man whose inward history has cherished his susceptibilities instead of dulling them, and has kept all the language of passion fresh and rooted as the lovely leafage about the hillside spring!' We feel fortunate to have been spared his actual speech. This tone so suffuses the end that it creates a sense of conspiracy with Daniel's travel plans that is probably not totally intended. Earlier she had chitted Rex for wanting to migrate to the colonies when he was disappointed by Gwendolyn; and she had been amused by Gwendolyn's plans to emigrate when the family lost its money. We get the impression that she is totally uncritical of Daniel's plans to go to the East because the rosy haze has obscured her reminder that he is going with an income, plus £16,000 pounds in reserve, and that he plans only to sound out opinions and then return to England. He is, then, only crazy north northwest.

In no other book does she work in such long stretches of contrasting style. If one compares Chapter 47 (Mirah's first meeting with Mordecai) with Chapter 48 (Grandcourt inflicting his will, in both senses, on Gwendolyn), there is an overpowering impression that the two styles were meant to be separate to emphasise the poles of selfishness and altruism. One of the appeals of the Jewish subject might well have been that their attitudes and idioms were so exotic to most English people that there was no need to strain after verisimilitude. In her letters she expresses no anxiety about the speech of the Jewish characters, where her knowledge was scanty. Yet she was very pleased when people said that her Grand-court-Lush conversations were brilliantly realistic: '. . . several men of experience have put their fingers on those scenes as having surprising verisimilitude, and I naturally was peculiarly anxious about such testimony where my construction was grounded on a less direct knowledge.'[29] We know that she can create vividly real middle-aged Englishwomen, not only from the superb Mrs Davilow in this book, but from all her novels. Surely it was a matter of choice and not necessity or relaxation that made her create Mrs Meyrick in the bathetic style of sentimental melodrama. The results are unintentionally funny, as when Mrs Meyrick warns Mirah that she must not expect to recognise her long lost mother:

> you must expect some change after twelve years . . . See my hair; ten years ago it was bright brown. The days and months pace over us like restless little birds, and leave the marks of their feet backwards and forwards, especially when they are like birds with heavy hearts—then they tread heavily.

These stomping birds mark off Mirah's world of sentimental piety.

Indeed the dramatic and bathetic are so clearly marked off, the tempo is so deliberate, that in reading we feel almost no fluidity between the styles. Drama very rarely emerges from melodrama as in Ian Gregor's description of the way the dying Fanny sets off the resentful Bathsheba in Far From the Madding Crowd.[30] Only once in the Zionist section do we get the kind of fluency in which drama grows out of melodrama. In Chapter 62, when Mirah's degenerate father approaches her on the street and impudently forgives her for deserting him, we actually experience her 'shame and grief, repulsion and pity' as dramatic; it may well be the scene from which James drew Kate Croy's opening collision with her father in Wings of the Dove.

Where a merger is attempted, it is usually not of styles but of attitudes, with odd results. We get the ironic attitudes of the Gwendolyn section in the language of Mirah and the Meyricks in the passage in which Daniel, Mirah, and the Meyrick girls discuss the virtues of self-sacrifice in Chapter 37:

After the first expression of sorrowful surprise she went on— 'But Mr. Hans said yesterday that you thought so much of others you hardly wanted anything for yourself. He told us a wonderful story of Bouddha giving himself to the famished tigress to save her and her little ones from starving. And he said you were like Bouddha. That is what we all imagine of you.'

'Pray don't imagine that,' said Deronda, who had lately been finding such suppositions rather exasperating. 'Even if it were true that I thought so much of others, it would not follow that I had no wants for myself. When Bouddha let the tigress eat him he might have been very hungry himself.'

'Perhaps if he was starved he would not mind so much about being eaten,' said Mab shyly.

'Please don't think that, Mab: it takes away the beauty of the action,' said Mirah.

'But if it were true, Mirah?' said the rational Amy, having a half holiday from her teaching: 'you always take what is beautiful as if it were true.'

'So it is,' said Mirah, gently. 'If people thought what is the most beautiful and the best thing, it must be true. It is always there.'

'Now, Mirah, what *do* you mean?' said Amy.

'I understand her,' said Deronda, coming to the rescue. 'It is a truth in thought though it may never have been carried out in action. It lives as an idea. Is that it?' He turned to Mirah, who was listening with a blind look in her lovely eyes.

'It must be that, because you understand me, but I cannot quite explain,' said Mirah, rather abstractedly—still searching for some expression.

'But was it beautiful for Bouddha to let the tiger eat him?' said Amy, changing her ground. 'It would be a bad pattern.'

'The world would get full of fat tigers,' said Mab.

Deronda laughed, but defended the myth, 'It is like a passionate word,' he said: 'the exaggeration is a flash of fervour. It is an extreme image of what is happening every day—the transmutation of self.'

No one would call this a dazzling passage, but it is an attempt to bring the values of Sir Hugo ('Don't give yourself away, my boy!') into Mirah's world in order to test some of the higher flights about heroic self-sacrifice, the idea which Eliot sees at the heart of things. The remark about 'fat tigers' belongs to the same category as Lapidoth's question about his 'sepulchral son, Ezra' or Klesmer's observation that Mirah is not an angel but a pretty Jewess, or the Princess Halb-Eberstein's strong denunciation of the constraints that Jewishness places on the women. But here, as in other instances, the questioning voice gets lost in the stiltedness and sentimentality of the speech, in Mirah's 'lovely eyes' and Daniel's stiff efforts to be amused and to be Orphic at the same time. Eliot is not weighed down here with bookishness, as Henry James suggests, nor does she seem exactly relaxed in a bath of emotion, as F. R. Leavis suggests. The passage is tense with the effort to be extreme and to be extremely fair at the same time. It nearly comes alive and misses. We feel more uneasy than dismissive about it. All of the unhappy styles of the Zionist section could be described as an effort at the single passionate word, the 'flash of fervour', the extreme image of the real.

We feel equally uneasy when the idea seems unexceptionable and the expression remains a high and hopeless rhetoric which attempts to convert the reader—by main force—to a proper responsiveness to the poetry of the present moment. We are begged and bullied and irritated by the notion that our spiritual distinction depends on our agreement with Daniel as he recognises heroism in improbable places and persons, when he feels the same reverence for the shabby Mordecai he would have felt for one of the children of Agamemnon. When Daniel is deeply affected by Mordecai's 'hectic gaze' (ch. 42) we get the characteristically insistent defensive passage, in which Eliot identifies recalcitrant readers with the dull Flemings and, by implication, with phlegmatic Englishmen:

> . . . this consumptive Jewish workman in threadbare clothing, lodged by charity, delivering his words to hearers who took his thoughts without attaching more consequences to them than the Flemings to the ethereal chimes ringing above their market-places—had the chief elements of greatness: a mind consciously moving with the larger march of human destinies, but not the less full of conscience and tender heart for the footsteps that tread near and need a leaning-place; capable of conceiving and choosing a life's task with far-off issues, yet capable of the unapplauded heroism which turns off the road of achievement at the call of the

nearer duty, where effect lies within the beating of the hearts that are close to us, as the hunger of the unfledged bird to the breast of its parent.

Underneath this magisterial style, laced with abstractions and torpid, sometimes mixed, metaphors, is an idea that is not essentially sentimental: heroes, she claims, may exist in the present; we lose much by our fearful blindness to the extraordinary here and now, our preference for the past or for some utopian place where all is clearly labelled.

While no one would defend the writing, few, I think, would deny the generosity of mind that is evident in such a passage. What she had hoped for was the kind of effect that only Edward Dowden appears to have felt among contemporary reviewers, since his was the only article that she and Lewes thought properly sympathetic, and we cannot help sympathising with his position: [31]

> When we speak of *Middlemarch* as more realistic, and [*Daniel Deronda*] as more ideal, it is not meant that one is true to the facts of life and the other untrue: it is rather meant that in the one the facts are taken in the gross, and in the other there is a passionate selection of those facts that are representative of the highest (and also of the lowest things . . .) . . . If 'knowledge of the world' consists chiefly in a power of estimating the average force of men's vulgar or selfish appetites, instincts, and interests, it must be admitted that in such knowledge the author of *Middlemarch* and *Felix Holt* is not deficient; but there is another knowledge of the world which does not exclude from recognition the martyr, the hero and the saint.

In our own reading we may feel sympathetic with this without being able to agree that the book is an unqualified success or anything near it. There is a great deal of life in both the Gwendolyn and Zionist sections and a great deal of courage about taking on large issues. What I think most readers feel is the uneasiness of that life not least because of the complexity of good intentions that have gone awry. First there is the attempt to forge a style for a novel deeply concerned with ideas out of the materials of popular romance and melodrama; then there are competing ideas of the nature of the reality to be imitated: there is the world of half-tints associated with normal life and there is an ideal, evolving concept of the reality deep down things. What is being evolved is a conception of heroism as empathy and tenderness, a heroism of perception. When she requires that her hero act in the public world rather than the Jamesian word of generous imaginings inhabited by Lambert Strether, the results seem absurd. Every episode in which Daniel is involved increases his apathy and seems to demand rejections. The entire apparatus of Jewry—or George Eliot's version of Jewry—seems to have been dragged in to help a repressed young man become a little less repressed. When Prince Hal moves away from Falstaff's tavern world and towards the world of kingly power, he pays a real price and gets real power. Daniel pays no price: everything is a gift but the gift is unreal; as unreal as the gift relationships Bernard Sharratt describes in Morris's *News from Nowhere*.

NOTES

1. Michael Irwin, p. 15.
2. The essays by Doreen Roberts and Ian Gregor are instances.
3. See the chapter on George Eliot in Mario Praz's *The Hero in Eclipse in Victorian Fiction*. Praz traces many instances of melodrama throughout her works to support his claim that among great Victorian novelists only Dickens used melodrama more frequently.
4. Barbara Hardy, Introduction to the Penguin edition of *Daniel Deronda*, p. xxvii.
5. *Letters*, ed. Haight. George Eliot to Harriet Beecher Stowe, 29 October 1876, VI, 301. See also Eliot's letter to John Blackwood, Vol. VI, 304: 'I expected to excite more resistance of feeling than I have seen signs of, but I did what I chose to do . . .'
6. GE to John Blackwood, 18 November 1875, VI, 187.
7. GE to Mrs Peter Taylor, 1 February 1853, II, 86.
8. Michael Irwin, pp. 22–3.
9. GE to Mrs Peter Alfred Taylor, *ibid.*
10. GE to Frederic Harrison, 15 August 1866, IV, 300.
11. D. H. Lawrence, from his preface to Frederic Carter's *Dragon of the Apocalypse*, *Phoenix*, I, 294.
12. GE to Frederic Harrison, 15 August 1866, IV, 300.
13. *Deronda*, Chapter 56.
14. Henry James, 'A Conversation'. Reprinted in *Henry James: Selected Literary Criticism*, ed. M. Shapira.
15. See Stuart Hutchinson's comparison of the two girls on p. 275.
16. GE to Mrs Peter Alfred Taylor, 19 August 1852, II, 52.
17. GE to John Blackwood, 30 January 1877, VI, 335.
18. *Romola*, Chapter 15, 'The Dying Message'. Compare Mirah's first meet-

ing with Mordecai, after long absence, with Romola's reunion and last meeting with her brother: 'Romola was not prompted to speak again. It was useless for her mind to attempt any contact with the mind of this unearthly brother; as useless as for her hand to try and grasp a shadow.'

19. See GE to Frederic Harrison, 1 January 1875, VI, 105; GE to Harrison, on 7 January, 110–111; on 19 February, 126, 2 June, 149–50; 18 June, 152. Originally she had planned that Daniel would be the illegitimate son of Sir Hugo.

20. GE to Leslie Stephen, 6 May 1875, VI, 140. Stephen's remark is in the footnote and comes from his article on Eliot in the English Men of Letters series.

21. There is a passage about Coningsby at Cambridge which reminds one of Daniel and it is one among many such: '. . . neither a prig nor a profligate, but a quiet, gentlemanlike, yet spirited young man, gracious to all, but intimate only with his old friends, and giving always an impression in his general tone that his soul was not absorbed in his university.'

22. *Daniel Deronda*, Chapter 16.

23. GE to John Sibree, Jr., 11 February 1848, I, 246–47. Her early bigotry can be a relief after the defence of the Jews in *Daniel Deronda*: 'The fellowship of race, to which D'Israeli exultingly refers the munificence of Sidonia, is so evidently an inferior impulse which must ultimately be superseded that I wonder even he, Jew as he is, dares to boast of it. My Gentile nature kicks most resolutely against any assumption of superiority in the Jews . . . I bow to the supremacy of Hebrew poetry, but much of their early mythology and almost all their history is utterly revolting. Their stock has produced a Moses and a Jesus, but Moses was impregnated with Egyptian philosophy and Jesus is venerated and adored by us only for that wherein he transcended or resisted Judaism. The very exaltation of their idea of a national deity into a spiritual monotheism seems to have been borrowed from the other oriental tribes. Everything specifically Jewish is of low grade.' Although she adapted to the idea of the fellowship of race and continued to love Hebrew poetry, there is no way that the jealous God of the Jews could have increased in appeal.

24. GE to Abraham Benisch, 16 December 1876, VI, 317.

25. See William Baker's treatment of the Jewish sources in *Daniel Deronda* in his monograph, *George Eliot and Judaism*, Salzburg Studies in English Literature, ed. J. Hogg, 1975. I am indebted to Dr Baker for lending me this monograph and for conversations about the Jewish material in the novel, but I believe there is little similarity in our critical views of it.

26. Leavis, *The Great Tradition*, Chapter II, part iii.

27. See Mario Praz's excellent discussion of George Eliot's imagery in *The Hero in Eclipse in Victorian Fiction*: 'Images and allegories of this kind reveal a pedestrian, a Biedermeir imagination; no light of poetry ever emanates from them . . . We shall never find in her those rapt, in-

spired images which throw a beam of light upon an entire situation. . . .' His chapter is a careful demonstration of the quality of her imagery.

28. GE to John Blackwood, 25 February 1876, VI, 223.
29. GE to John Blackwood, *ibid.*
30. Ian Gregor, p. 99.
31. Edward Dowden, 'Middlemarch and Daniel Deronda', *The Contemporary Review*, February 1877. Reprinted in *A Century of George Eliot Criticism*, ed. Haight, p. 116.

I would like to thank Rabbi and Mrs Cohn-Sherbok, and Mrs Morris Shapira for their help in the preparation of this chapter.

14

Beyond the Victorians: *The Portrait of a Lady*

by STUART HUTCHINSON

According to the Preface, *The Portrait of a Lady* began with 'the conception of a certain young woman affronting her destiny.' It's undoubtedly appropriate to argue that such affronting, especially in the nineteenth century, was a characteristically American pre-occupation. Unlike the heroes and heroines of several earlier English novels, Isabel does not confront: she does not journey through her book face to face, either for support or as a burden, with her established identity in an established world. Instead she is neces-sarily and instinctively, as both Richard Chase and Richard Poir-ier[1] have observed, the author of her own life. In claiming this authorial prerogative. Isabel within the novel is a surrogate for James himself. Two years before *The Portrait of a Lady*, the central implication of James's book on Hawthorne had been that because America lacked the established diversity of public life available in England (and to this extent lacked identity), the American imagin-ation was necessarily forced in on itself. James, like Isabel, came to the Europe of established, impersonal tradition to find relief from this burden of personal and national self-absorption. He came, as man and writer, to find what he termed 'completeness', declaring in his *Notebooks* for the early 1880s that the American writer, to be 'complete', '*must* deal, more or less, even if only by implica-tion, with Europe.'[2]

Such a parallel between James's career and Isabel's own might seem to provide inevitable further grounds for Leavis's criticism of *The Portrait of a Lady*. According to Leavis, James, in contrast to George Eliot with Gwendolen Harleth, so idealises Isabel that 'be-yond any question we are invited to share a valuation of Isabel that is incompatible with a really critical irony.'[3] Yet it seems to me that in wanting James to treat Isabel as George Eliot treats Gwendolen, Leavis is fundamentally wrong-headed. Gwendolen can be presented so substantially because she can be seen against a society of firmly established manners and opportunities. *Daniel Deronda* is, in James's phrase, 'full of the world'[4] but, as far as the realisation of Gwendolen is concerned, it is a circumscribed world. In it she has only two possibilities. She can become a governess, or she can marry Grandcourt. Such defined limits give George Eliot an enormous advantage over James. They make possible that encompassing and pervasive certainty with which she offers to us her worldly wisdom about Gwendolen. As modern readers, however, how we wish George Eliot had let her characters off the hook of her didacticism. How we wish she had forsaken the advantage she holds over them and let Gwendolen and Maggie Tulliver before her express their undoubted strengths in a less confining arena. In short, how we wish a George Eliot woman had been allowed to seize something equivalent to the opportunities George Eliot seized for herself.

In *The Portrait of a Lady*, the characters affront a less firmly established world than is confronted in the Gwendolen Harleth parts of *Daniel Deronda*. Nor does James himself lay claim to George Eliot's didactic certainties in his treatment of his characters. As the title of his novel indicates, his intention, with regard to Isabel especially, is to exhibit rather than to moralise.

He wants to present his own portrait of Isabel's portrayal of herself. As compared with *Daniel Deronda* therefore, what is seen or said about a character in *The Portrait of a Lady* is always relative. There is much less confidence in the possibility of conclusive wisdom. James's only advantage over Isabel and the rest of the characters is that he can see their case from more angles than they can see it from themselves. *His* portrait invites us to appreciate these angles, and in the first half of what follows I shall offer a guide to them. In the second half, which begins with a consideration of Chapter 42, I make some comments on where *The Portrait of a Lady* eventually leaves us. Because it is written by a nineteenth-century American, and because of its closeness to the twentieth century, *The Portrait of a Lady* foregoes Victorian affirmations. The price it pays, however (together with several twentieth-century novels) is that it eventually leaves the reader, along with its heroine, *'en l'air'*[5] amid its self-reflections.

But first Isabel as she presumptuously affronts her destiny. Take the moment at the end of Chapter 2 when, in reply to Ralph's observations that Mrs Touchett has 'adopted' her, she replies that she is 'not a candidate for adoption', and that she is 'very fond of my liberty'.[6] We will all be inclined to underline these pronouncements. It would be a simple reading of the novel, however, to judge Isabel literally by what she says. As Richard Poirier shrewdly observes, the opinions Isabel spouts are often 'merely trial balloons.'[7] As they occur dramatically, her proclamations are quite uncalled for by Ralph's humorous comment, and he is completely thrown by them. They are the words of a young woman who, 'with a certain visible eagerness of desire to be explicit', is as concerned to present herself to herself as to other people. What 'really critical irony' could be brought to bear on Isabel here that James doesn't bring? James knows that Isabel's is an absurdly portentous response to Ralph's casual remark, and that its emphaticalness betrays the young woman's deep uncertainty about herself, even as it demonstrates her admirable ambition. As the novel develops, he will show that Isabel will eventually ensnare herself just because, in pronouncing about liberty and other ideals, she is never wise enough to know how they might genuinely be experienced. But Isabel can only be taught by experience. Unlike Gwendolen Harleth, she is not faced by choices which with reference to authority can be defined as good and evil. As an expression of the country she comes from, she is in a position to create herself. What draws James and the reader to her is precisely the fact that, unlike her sisters and the Miss Varians (whose conventional fates we read about at the beginning of Chapters 4 and 6), she has the imagination and the guts to want to use her freedom. Despite her own occasional 'sense of her incoherence', (ch. 13) she will try to realise what she understands to be her best revelations. For James, and eventually for Isabel herself, the most critical irony that can be brought to bear against her is that the best she is capable of should lead only to Gilbert Osmond. This outcome amounts to a crippling self-knowledge for Isabel. Nor can she ease the consciousness of how she has wasted her life by blaming, in the Victorian way, the worst part of herself. Hers is indeed a tragedy which reaches forward into the twentieth century's promise of 'Great Expectations' all round: one may live to the best of oneself, with the greatest opportunities, and yet arrive 'in a dark, narrow alley with a dead wall at the end' (ch. 42).

It's with a sense of her wanting to be the artist of her own life that we should view Isabel's responses to both Goodwood's and Warburton's proposals of marriage. In these scenes we see how James's portrait of Isabel's portrait of herself encompasses other figures. It has not been sufficiently appreciated how the other characters in their different ways share her problem. Both Goodwood and Warburton within their contrasting public orbits are triumphant, and yet both personally are desperately unfulfilled. Their proposals are their affronting of their destinies: Warburton's case making us aware of what we also see in Hardy's work (think of Henchard, Jude and Sue), that towards the end of the nineteenth century such challenging of experience to give one an identity is no longer a peculiarly American obsession. Both Goodwood and Warburton, by marriage to Isabel, want to provoke into reality imagined possibilities, the realisation of which in any other way renders them impotent. Goodwood pursues Isabel (she is his Sue Bridehead) because in post Civil War America she is, with her indifference to the nation's public energies in which he is embroiled, an exceptional spirit. In his portrait of their relationship she would bring beauty into his life. She would give expression to the needs of his frustrated soul: 'he had never supposed she hadn't wings and the need of beautiful free movement—he wasn't, with his own long arms and strides, afraid of any force in her' (ch. 16). As for Warburton, who has lost that belief in himself which in an earlier generation his confrontation with his 'station' would have guaranteed, he admits half-jokingly that he needs a woman to tie 'round my neck as a life-preserver' (ch. 1). An alliance with a 'young lady . . . from a queer country across the sea' (ch. 12) would substantiate in his own eyes and the world's his radical posture. Indisputably (think of his sisters' reaction!), it would be a dramatic burning of his boats in which hopefully his unresolved state would be settled.

To understand the proposals in this way is to perceive how James has solicited our sympathy for Isabel's response. She refuses both suitors because she is determined not to foreclose the possibilities of her life so early by confronting destiny and becoming a wife. Moreover, in the two men's determination that she should count for so much in their lives, we can recognise something of that 'aggression' (chs. 12, 16) she ascribes to both of them. How is she supposed to live up to the different roles they create for her? What kind of 'beautiful free movement' must she perform for Goodwood? How must she represent for Warburton, who is needled by Henrietta, that 'queer country across the sea?' To the final chapter ('I never knew *you* afraid') Goodwood is never to understand that if he is not afraid of Isabel, she is afraid of herself. To the end Warburton, who finally confronts his destiny in a marriage to 'a member of the aristocracy' (ch. 54), never grasps that Isabel is not in Europe to give herself, but to find herself. Yet the sympathy James solicits is not only for Isabel. What distinguishes James from his fellow nineteenth-century American novelists is that he has learned from the European novel how to realise the contrasting positions of his characters in a more substantial way than by allegory and symbol. Counter-balancing Goodwood's and Warburton's portraits of Isabel are her portraits of them. She would do greater justice to the personal positions of both men if she did not persist in seeing them in metaphoric and conceptualised terms. She ought to understand that proposals are by their very nature a threat to one's freedom and that in marriage people usually do want to complete themselves by taking what they find in the other person. It's ominous that what she terms the two men's 'aggression' is also her sense of their masculinity. As the first paragraph of Chapter 17 makes clear Isabel, in her reaction to potential sexual encounters, vibrates not in anticipation of offering accommodation, but in the triumph of having rejected. She has just seen Goodwood off, and her excitement over her 'victory' (an excitement which supplants sexual excitement) is modified not at all by her wondering earlier 'if she were not a cold, hard, priggish person' (ch. 12).

This last quotation is only one line from Isabel's attempted portrait of herself after Warburton's proposal. It's only one example of her capacity for self-analysis and self-disapproval. No-one has ever more consciously wanted to do the 'right' thing than Isabel. In this sense she contrasts with several Victorian heroes and heroines. Just as *The Portrait of a Lady* begins with its characters having come from a promised land, whereas Victorian novels usually end with the characters about to step into one, so Isabel enters her novel already possessing, and possessed by, the sincere, moral ambition earlier Victorian characters are finally left with. Unlike

Daniel Deronda, The Portrait of a Lady shows that such ambition may also betray. This is why Isabel to some extent needs from Ralph advice which is exactly the opposite of the counselling Deronda gives Gwendolen:

> Take things more easily. Don't ask yourself so much whether this or that is good for you. Don't question your conscience so much—it will get out of tune like a strummed piano. Keep it for great occasions. Don't try so much to form your character—it's like trying to pull open a tight, tender young rose. Live as you like best, and your character will take care of itself. Most things are good for you; the exceptions are very rare, and a comfortable income's not one of them . . . You've too much power of thought —above all too much conscience. . . . It's out of all reason the number of things you think wrong.
>
> (ch. 21)

These are the words of a man who has thought a great deal about that problem of conscious living with which all the main characters of the novel are burdened. Ralph too wants to be the author of his own life, but he must feel he is sharing the task with a partner (his illness) who will always have the final say. Deprived as he sees it of his true freedom in actuality, he affronts it in imagination. Isabel, 'living as you like best', will enable him to enact 'the requirements of my imagination' (ch. 18). In her he can live by proxy. It is indeed he, and not James, whom the reader identifies as strongly inclined to idealise Isabel. She herself becomes aware of his peculiar, parasitic involvement in her, and this knowledge is later to make her tragically resistant to his advice about Osmond. But Ralph's attitude to his cousin is not entirely self-serving. It is also an affirmation of faith in the virtue of human nature made by a man whose personal lot has given him little cause to go in for such generosity of spirit. When Ralph, by paraphrasing Iago ('I should like to put money in her purse'), glances at the immorality of the authorial power he is assuming over Isabel's life, we are reminded how, understandably, he might have become poisonous. Ralph, however, always resisting the darkness, replies in the same chapter to his father's doubts about Isabel by asserting what for many will be at least a working creed: 'She's as good as her best opportunities' (ch. 18). Of course he means what he will recognise as good and best. At this stage he has not learned James's wisdom, that to liberate someone is not to require them to do something

of which one will approve. Ralph is an author who wants his character always to fulfil his hopes. He has too much at stake on Isabel.
His putting money in her purse is after all a substitute for making
love to her.

But a great deal is lost for us all in Ralph's humiliation by
Isabel's marriage. With its roots in American idealism *The Portrait
of a Lady* has the authority to challenge our fondest hopes. What
are people if they are not as good as their best opportunities? It's
because Isabel by her marriage has been forced to face the implications of this question for herself, that she is wary at the end of
further new schemes for life. But Ralph, even as a 'mere lattice
of bones', clings to his belief in the best possibilities. Acknowledging his culpability ('I believe I ruined you'), still further surprised
by how Isabel actually behaves ('Are you going back to him?'), he
can yet say: 'I don't believe that such a generous mistake as yours
can hurt you for more than a little' (ch. 54). Throughout the book,
Ralph's optimism and humour are the equivalent to, and the
vehicle for, the buoyancy of tone with which James delivers to us
a novel containing so many stories of personal disappointment.
Like James, Ralph remains completely unembittered. Unlike George
Eliot and Tom Tulliver with Maggie, James and Ralph have no investment in making Isabel 'pay' for what she has done. Life is
simply worth more than this kind of morality. One pays in so far
as one has the capacity for awareness. Isabel is to become aware
that 'she has thrown away her life' (ch. 42), and who can say how
this self-knowledge will determine her future? Ralph is indeed
very close to James despite being completely placed by the author.
Watching Ralph perform in the world of *The Portrait of a Lady*
James understands how drastically more compromising it is to try
to fulfil the requirements of one's imagination in life, than it is by
writing a novel. What beneficial contribution to others can the
authorial imagination make? James's study of Ralph's dealing with
Isabel is a bleak answer for a young novelist to offer to this question.

Though it's hard to believe anybody can be ready for the kind
of windfall she receives, Isabel, with 'too much power of thought
—above all too much conscience', was perhaps the last person to
burden with a fortune. In her case, moreover, 'Great Expectations'
do not come with the promise of an established social life which
she simply has to fit into. In fact her inheritance encourages her

sense of superiority to the way people, whatever their ideal conception of themselves, actually find accommodation in the world. She is right to conclude that the lives of the American expatriates in Paris are 'though luxurious, inane' (ch. 20); but in her belief that 'the world lay before her—she could do whatever she chose' (ch. 31), she fails to undestand that we are all compromising expatriates just because this kind of freedom has long been lost. Since her fortune has come to her without strings, and without her knowing by whose intervention, it confirms her too ready desire to believe in her own absoluteness. Furthermore, she is by now modelling herself on Madame Merle who at this stage in the novel always appears to Isabel's innocent, admiring eyes completely uncompromised: the very 'portrait of a lady' in the flesh as it were.

Her imitation of Madame Merle already signals a move in the direction of Osmond and is a repression in herself of those outgoing qualities which are writ large in Henrietta Stackpole. Hence her bitchy, self-congratulatory approval of Madame Merle's response to Henrietta: 'Madame Merle genially squeezed her into insignificance, and Isabel felt that in foreseeing this liberality she had done justice to her friend's intelligence' (ch. 26). It's true that Isabel and we have had earlier in the novel what the Preface recognises as 'indubitably too much' of Henrietta, who must exasperate Isabel with her confident belief that she knows all about her friend. Henrietta knows some things, but the following words are not the lessons to teach an Isabel who has already rebuffed Goodwood and Warburton: 'You must often *dis*please others. . . . That doesn't suit you at all—you're too fond of admiration, you like to be thought well of' (ch. 20). Even so, as one more character with reference to whom we must create our portrait of Isabel, Henrietta's career undoubtedly brings 'a really critical irony' to bear on James's heroine. Unlike the uncompromising Isabel she is bravely, if at times insensitively, making a life for herself amid the ways of the world. Also, in her relationship with Bantling, she concedes to her sexual nature. As Ralph puts it, 'It seems to me she's doing very well, . . . going over to Paris with an ex-Lancer!' (ch. 19). But while James's affection for Henrietta is entertained by her adventures with Bantling, Isabel is amused only in order to feel superior. She is not aware that in so far as she is not to have such basic good times with a man her life will be poorer.

Isabel indeed is never to be as naturally in love as even Rosier and Pansy are in love.

When, therefore, Martin Green observes disparagingly that 'the relationship between Isabel and Osmond is dangerously thin in sexual or affectionate emotion, dangerously strong in impersonal appraisal,'[8] we can reply this is a view James's portrait prompts the reader to take. For Isabel, even being in love is distanced by being placed in the story she is telling herself about herself: 'to prefer Gilbert Osmond as she preferred him was perforce to break all other ties. She tasted of the sweets of this preference, and they made her conscious, almost with awe, of the invidious and remorseless tide of the charmed and possessed condition, great as was the traditional honour and imputed virtue of being in love' (ch. 35). How wonderfully James captures here Isabel's ardent, theoretical nature. She accepts Osmond not only because he alone seems to have established a life of personal, uncompromised value, but also because, in contrast to Goodwood's and Warburton's complicating pressures, he initially makes no demands even when he proposes: 'You may heed it now or never as you please' (ch. 29). For his part, his despairing, desolate soul ('I'm sick of my adorable taste' [ch 22]) is briefly uplifted by the opportunity to ally himself to, and to capture, an unblemished idealism he still can envy. Very soon after the marriage, however, because by its very nature such idealism is a condemnation of what his life amounts to, Isabel becomes contemptible to him.

2

But it's from Chapter 42, when Isabel sits through the night meditating on her relationship with her husband, that we learn nearly everything about the marriage. For James, writing the Preface more than twenty years after the novel's publication, this chapter was 'obviously the best thing in the book'. 'Reduced to its essence,' he observes, 'it is but the vigil of searching criticism; but it throws the action further forward than twenty "incidents" might have done.' There can be few readers willing to accept these judgements without demur. For a start, Chapter 42 has to perform functions unmentioned by James. It has to throw the action *backwards* to the early years of the marriage, restore to the reader his close relationship with Isabel, and thereby rescue the reader from the sense of dislocation he has felt since the end of Chapter 35 when he left Isabel on the verge of marriage. All readers, as they began Chapter 36, will have been more prepared for some direct treatment of Isabel's early married life than they are for what they get: a defiantly announced date revealing that three years have passed, and a re-introduction to Mr Edward Rosier whom, in James's unblushing words, 'the reader will perhaps not have forgotten!' Why is it that James has not given us directly the first three years of the marriage? We undoubtedly miss what is not presented. We may decide that James was incapable of writing the required scenes. Indeed I think this is the case, and yet I want to argue that it's not simply a matter of lack of talent for creating objectively a certain kind of experience. James doesn't do Isabel's and Osmond's first three years of marriage, because he never believed in the marriage as a possible sustenance for Isabel. In this respect James throughout the novel is ahead of Isabel, just as he is always capable of seeing her portrait from more angles than she can see it from herself. He always knows she will find no form of life to match her conceptions. Even when Isabel, by her marriage, hopes she has found such a form, therefore, James can give the enactment of her hopes and the process of disillusion only a distanced treatment. He is much more firmly on ground he believes in when, in Chapter 42, he can present her reflection on her own failure, a failure which for him was inevitable

The Portrait of a Lady is in fact the expression of James's development as a novelist as much as it is the story of Isabel. Up to the marriage, we engage with a novel of manners in which the heroine is searching for a public life to match her personal ambition. She never finds what she seeks and consequently, in despair of the life she had hoped for, she turns relentlessly inward. Of equal significance, however, is the fact that James, the novelist, goes with her. After the marriage, The Portrait of a Lady loses its forward momentum. It's no longer concerned with possible choices to be made in an observed public world. Like Isabel, it has lost whatever faith it had that such a world can offer fulfilment.

Following The Portrait of a Lady and the realistic apprehension of the surface of things in much of The Bostonians and The Princess Casamassima, James's lasting pre-occupation was to be with the consciousness of his characters. Disillusioned by what civilisation offered the affronting individual, he was convinced that it was in the consciousness that the individual must really live. Chapter 42 may be seen as one of the signals in his career of the onset of this conviction. His preference for the chapter affirms the conviction. If the chapter then can be said to throw 'the action further forward than twenty "incidents" might have done', it's not towards a Victorian self-knowledge for Isabel which will coincide with her accepting the completion of herself in some defined social position; instead it's deeper into the irresolvable and essentially private life of the consciousness.

For Isabel in particular the chapter amounts to the recognition, which nothing in the rest of the novel will alleviate, that for the foreseeable future she has come to the end of herself: 'She had taken all the first steps in the purest confidence, and then she had suddenly found the infinite vista of a multiplied life to be a dark, narrow alley with a dead wall at the end.' The best of herself has led to Osmond. But she does not understand her situation completely and James, despite his endorsement of Isabel's commitment to self-reflection, continues to exhibit her critically. It's James and not Isabel who appreciates that the other lives she hears from her 'realms of restriction and depression' are 'easier and freer', because those living them have never had so much as to think their way. It's James who lets the reader see that Isabel's life must remain impoverished in so far as it continues to be an aesthetic enterprise. Consider this reflection on her marriage: 'The finest—in the sense of being the subtlest—manly organism she had ever known had become her property, and the recognition of her having but to put out her hands and take it had been originally a sort of act of devotion.' Such a reflection reveals Isabel to be a sort of collector of experience. She knows now that Osmond isn't the property she had invested in, but she doesn't understand that to see a man in this way is not to take him as a husband. Had Osmond even been what she imagined, marriage to him on these terms would have been a queer affair.

Like the rest of the novel, Chapter 42 is James's portrait of Isabel's portrait of herself. Our relationship to Isabel in the chapter remains dynamic. She may still grow to understand herself as well as James lets us understand her. She has much to learn, and not only factually. After her marriage, she more than ever desires to imitate Madame Merle and to make, as she is convinced the older lady does, 'her will [the] mistress of her life' (ch. 40). But she has yet to appreciate out of what shameful sense of failure, and consequently with what 'courage' Madame Merle maintains her posture. She understands these things when the two 'ladies' meet for the last time in Chapter 52. The encounter is one of those moments a novel of *The Portrait of a Lady*'s developed length can give us. It depends so much on the reader's memory of Isabel's and Madame Merle's early exchanges, for example in Chapter 19. Then Isabel was all innocent admiration for what she conceived simply as her new acquaintance's 'talents, accomplishments, aptitudes'. Madame Merle, for her part, was then agreeably refreshed and entertained by the virginal ambition of a young woman she was able to handle with one stained hand behind her back. But in Chapter 52 Isabel understands out of what abyss of disappointment and unfulfilment Madame Merle's manner has matured. Now she comprehends that if she is to portray herself to the world as a lady, it may be only to conceal a similar abyss in her own life.

It's Isabel's self-recognition in Madame Merle at this moment, her seeing 'it all as distinctly as if it had been reflected in a large clear glass', that diffuses the outspoken revenge she is very tempted to take on the older lady. Or rather, the self-recognition confines the revenge to silence, to leaving Madame Merle, 'the cleverest woman in the world', in the 'unprecedented situation' of 'knowing as little what to think as the meanest'. Again James asks us to contemplate all the angles of *his* portrayal of the scene. Undoubtedly, Isabel's conduct towards Madame Merle, prompted by the mess she recognises they have both made of their lives, is charitable on both their behalfs. Later in the chapter, she can even tell Pansy: 'You must never say . . . that you don't like Madame Merle.' Yet Isabel's silence does leave Madame Merle in a position of 'helplessness', and we are told by James that Isabel would never 'accuse' Madame Merle because 'she would never give [Madame Merle] the opportunity to defend herself.' Isabel's continuing pride, which has always defensively cut her off from the advice and sympathy of others, cannot let Madame Merle have her moment. Indeed, in so far as Isabel sees all of this meeting 'as if it had been reflected in a large clear glass', she doesn't see Madame Merle. She doesn't appreciate how readily her former friend, who has been a *lover*, would give herself to some act of mutual consolation. Because Isabel cannot respond to the older lady's need, Madame Merle, when Isabel returns from seeing Pansy, finds herself striving to restore their relationship to its earlier status. To regain the superiority over Isabel she always enjoyed, she vainly tells Isabel it was Ralph who was responsible for her money. But her triumph does nothing to relieve her profound unhappiness over her life's betrayal of her own and Isabel's best hopes.

Yes, throughout the novel, James does bring 'a really critical irony' to bear on Isabel. He is always aware of the life she is separated from by her withdrawal into her consciousness of herself. This is nowhere more evident than in her extraordinary last encounter with Goodwood. If she is to grow, surely she must some day come to terms with the masculinity she feels to be 'justified' by his last embrace. But although James always exhibits and places Isabel, it's striking that the energies she frustrates are relegated to a marginal or implicit role in *The Portrait of a Lady* itself. The life given over to consciousness is restricting and self-deceiving, and yet it is after all the life to which James, like several modern novelists, gives his major attention. There is no indication in the novel at large that public experience can be equally significant. This is why the novel has such a double attitude to Isabel's marriage. On the one hand it expresses her particular failure to match private and public realities. But on the other, it apparently represents all forms of civilisation amid which the affronting self vainly searches for fulfilling accommodation. Resignedly, therefore, Isabel returns to Osmond and to her public role as the very portrait of a lady. Concealed within this role she can create herself as introspectively as she once did in Albany. The difference is that now she has a real knowledge of the disillusion and alienation awaiting her beyond 'the bolted door' (ch. 3). She has eaten the fruit of a knowledge which for James was inescapable.

In a famous letter of September 1867 to T. S. Perry, James wrote: 'We are Americans born . . . I look upon it as a great blessing; and I think that to be an American is an excellent preparation for culture . . . we can deal freely with forms of civilisation not our own, can pick and choose and assimilate and in short (aesthetically &C) claim our property where we find it. . . . We must of course have something of our own . . . and I take it that we shall find it in our moral consciousness, our unprecedented spiritual lightness and vigour.' What a momentous fate James announces here! Given such opportunities what could the Americans James describes ever settle for? They would always be ardent for completeness, while the inevitable sense of incompleteness resulting from a life so deliberately pursued would have nothing traditional to fall back onto. If, like James and Isabel, they were also not visionary, the self-reflection to which Isabel is always prone, but for which her experience really gives her material, would be the only solace. For James himself, indeed, *The Portrait of a Lady* embodies self-reflections of a kind Isabel has yet to encounter. With only these possibilities before her it seems, we leave her *'en l'air'*.

NOTES

1. Richard Chase, *The American Novel and its Tradition* (New York, 1957); Richard Poirier, *The Comic Sense of Henry James: A Study of the Early Novels* (London, 1960).
2. F. O. Matthiessen and Kenneth B. Murdock, eds., *The Notebooks of Henry James* (New York, 1961), p. 245.
3. F. R. Leavis, *The Great Tradition* (1948; rpt. Harmondsworth, 1962), p. 126.
4. See James's *'Daniel Deronda*: A Conversation'.
5. 'The obvious criticism will be that it is not finished . . . that I have left [the heroine] en l'air.' *Notebooks*, p. 18.
6. All quotations from *The Portrait of a Lady* are taken from the New York Edition, 1908. The numbers in brackets refer to chapters from this edition.
7. *The Comic Sense*, p. 215.
8. *Re-appraisals: Some Commonsense Readings in American Literature* (London, 1963), p. 157.

15

News from Nowhere:
Detail and Desire

by BERNARD SHARRATT

> To anyone not deeply interested in the social question it could
> not be at all an attractive book. It is true that it is cast in the
> form of a romance, but the author states very frankly in his
> preface that he has only given it this form as a sugar-coating to
> the pill, and the device of making a man wake up in a new world
> has grown so common, and has been done with so much more
> care and art . . . that by itself this would have done little for it;
> it is the serious essay and not the slight envelope of romance
> which people have found interesting to them.

A literary critic today might well find this an apposite judgement
on William Morris's *News from Nowhere*. The book has certainly
attracted attention as a 'serious essay', as an almost unique instance
of the utopian imagination at work within the marxist tradition of
social critique,[1] but for readers and critics attuned to the assumptions and conventions of nineteenth-century literary realism the
work clearly offers a thin experience: one could easily articulate
their predictable unease at the lack of complex characterisation,
the absence of any delicate exploration of moral sensibility, the
paucity of densely felt life.[2] Yet it is precisely in its oblique relation
to the more central instances of 'the Victorian novel' that *News*
provokes critical consideration. Our very puzzlement as to whether
to read it as 'a novel' at all might alert us to some of the limits
of current critical conceptions of 'the novel'. What one can loosely
term a Jamesian approach to fiction,[3] can be contrasted with, and
even supplemented by, a 'sociology of literature' which concentrates
on 'popular fiction', yet there are some nineteenth-century works
which seem unamenable to bracketing either with George Eliot,

Dickens and Thackeray in an extended great tradition or with G. W. M. Reynolds, G. P. R. James, Mrs Marsh and the cheap fiction of the Parlour or Railway Library. *News from Nowhere*, like perhaps Peacock's conversation novels, Butler's *Erewhon* and Mallock's *The New Republic*, seems to straddle and implicitly challenge our current critical categories and methods. That *News* did once enjoy a steady popularity, at least among politically conscious workers, can be accounted for largely in terms of its explicit content[4], but now, with a re-awakening of interest in the political or ideological significance of literary form,[5] it is perhaps the relation of *News* to the formal procedures of Victorian fiction that might win it a certain critical place; its very oddness as a 'novel' might prove illuminating.

News itself includes a number of comments about Victorian fiction which indicate Morris's own awareness of standing askew to a dominant tradition. In the second chapter Dick says of Boffin, the dustman whose name recalls Dickens, that 'he has a weakness: he will spend his time in writing reactionary novels, and is very proud of getting the local colour right, as he calls it; and as he thinks that you come from some forgotten corner of the earth, where people are unhappy, and consequently interesting to a story-teller, he thinks he might get some information out of you.' Dick's comment alludes to two central strands in Victorian fiction, often intertwined and mutually supportive: the attempt to achieve a densely matted convincingness which ostensibly offers the reader an indubitable depiction of a believably 'real' world (its 'local colour' authentic), and a concern with the fate of individuals, their personal trajectories from unhappiness to happiness, or sometimes vice-versa. Both these facets of nineteenth-century fiction—which one might label, in shorthand, 'realism' and 'romance'—are criticised more explicitly elsewhere in the text. When Walter, in Chapter 24, has an unhappy story to tell he eschews any convincing density of detail, any nuanced elaboration, offering us only the bones, the basic shape of the tale: 'I will make it short enough, though I dare say it might be spun out into a long one, as used to be done with such subjects in the old novels'—and Morris's own compression of a whole historical novel, on 'how the change came', into a mere thirty pages (Chapters 17 and 18) perhaps exemplifies the same impatience with 'the long novel', a concern for the clearly intelligible structure of events rather than the vivid picturing and complex patterning of incidents.[6] Old Hammond's answer to Clara in Chapter 16 is even more directly sceptical of the 'realist' programme:

> It is true that in the nineteenth century, when there was so little art and so much talk about it, there was a theory that art and imaginative literature ought to deal with contemporary life; but they never did so; for, if there was any pretence of it, the author always took care . . . to disguise, or exaggerate, or idealise, and in some way or other make it strange; so that, for all the verisimilitude there was, he might just as well have dealt with the times of the Pharaohs.

In Chapter 22 Ellen is complementarily contemptuous of novelists who selectively focus on the fate of privileged people:

> I say flatly that in spite of all their cleverness and vigour, and capacity for story-telling, there is something loathsome about them. Some of them, indeed, do here and there show some feeling for those whom the history-books call 'poor', and of the misery of whose lives we have some inkling; but presently they give it up, and towards the end of the story we must be contented to see the hero and heroine living happily in an island of bliss on other people's troubles; and that after a long series of sham troubles (or mostly sham) of their own making, illustrated by dreary introspective nonsense about their feelings and aspirations, and all the rest of it; while the world must even then have gone on its way, and dug and sewed and baked and built and carpentered round about these useless-animals.

Ellen's outburst is a response to her grandfather's admiration for nineteenth-century fiction; ironically, Morris so formulates this conservative defence of Victorian art as to make it suggest a quasi-'marxist' emphasis on the connection between the economic structure of a society and its fiction and also hint at a possible ideological distortion of the past when viewed through literary spectacles:

> I have read not a few books of the past days, and certainly *they* are much more alive than those which are written now; and good sound unlimited competition was the condition under which they were written—if we didn't know that from the record of history, we should know it from the books themselves. There is a spirit of adventure in them, and signs of a capacity to extract good from

evil which our literature quite lacks now; and I cannot help thinking that our moralists and historians exaggerate hugely the unhappiness of the past days, in which such splendid works of imagination and intellect were produced.

The case against nineteenth-century fiction suggested in these
comments would, obviously, have to be argued further; the implication that realist romance is 'reactionary' is not elaborated, but
at least Morris indicates that his hostile stance is not merely a
temperamental response—though it is well known that he was personally blind to the great achievements of European realism and
much preferred the saga and epics of older civilisations.[7] Given
these comments and this attitude to 'realism', it is clear that Morris, in writing News, is not setting out to rival the great realists in
their own terms; it is also unlikely, I presume, that anyone would
attempt to read, let alone judge, News according to the canons of
'realism'. It is perhaps worth elaborating a point made earlier: a
critic who attempted to treat the 'characters' in News along lines
similar to, for example, the way Stuart Hutchinson elsewhere in
this volume discusses the characters in James's The Portrait of a
Lady—in terms of their motivations and decisions, their genuine
comparability to the complexity of people we might know outside
of fiction—would be deeply and obviously mistaken. Equally,
another aspect of the kind of critical analysis which has derived
from James's own practice, as novelist and critic, would seem
curiously inapposite in a discussion of News. What I have in mind
is that kind of criticism which regards the literary work as to be
discussed primarily in terms of its formal qualities, so that an
article on The Portrait almost inevitably subordinates any consideration of the moral dilemmas explored in that novel to a commentary on James's 'handling' of those dilemmas. The fine line
which divides these two emphases may even be the subject of
Portrait itself (the relation between James's use of 'portrait' and
Wells's half-accurate accusation that 'life isn't a studio' would be
relevant here—though Wells fails to register that it is surely
James's characters who sometimes see life as a studio), but it is a
fine line which haunts any critic influenced by James or by Leavis.
The obverse side of this point is that perhaps any novelist who
strives for the kind of complex and nuanced unity inculcated by
James will be drawn towards the microcosmic (the terrain of in-

dividuals, of moral subtleties, of personal and close relations), but be less able to deal with, to encompass adequately, the different complexities—and simplicities—of social and political movements; the absence of convincingly political novels within the English great tradition is germane here (one immediately thinks of the limitations of *Daniel Deronda*). Insofar as *News from Nowhere* both attempts to provoke discussion, inescapably, about its political *content* and tries to cope with the whole social and political domain, it was almost bound to be found wanting by Jamesian critical standards, and, conversely, to find Jamesian novelistic practice inadequate or inappropriate to its purpose.

Yet at the same time *News* doesn't offer itself as simply a socialist *tract*, a reverse variation on the purely didactic 'cautionary tale' so beloved of Victorian propagandists against the tastes, habits and aspirations of the 'lower classes'. It offers itself as a story, as fiction, and as the work of an artist, a craftsman with words who was, within a few years, to be seriously suggested as the successor to Tennyson as Poet Laureate. Clearly, *News* has to be classed *more* with the flood of tract publications than with *Daniel Deronda* or *Portrait*, yet its peculiar mingling of didactic intent with a kind of one-dimensional but vivid imagining might remind us rather of the conventions of cartoon-art or perhaps even of the strategies of satire. If we were to regard *News* as, in a way, the 'obverse' of a satire, as depicting the 'norm' which would operate covertly or implicitly in a political satire, the relation of the text to both the *details* of the Victorian society it distances itself from, and to the *principles* which structure *any* capitalist society—competitiveness, antagonism, private profit-seeking, exchange-value, rather than collaboration, mutual help, communal benefit, use-value—might be somewhat clearer. Its own relation as a literary text to the local devices and general principles of 'realist' fiction might even be discussed along analogous lines.

However, rather than seek to 'categorise' *News*, it seems more fruitful to take the hint offered not only by the content of the comments on nineteenth-century fiction quoted earlier but also by the very fact of their being included in the text itself, and to explore the *effect* of that inclusion on our awareness that there do indeed seem to be elements of both 'realism' and 'romance' in *News* itself. A way of putting the point would be that our awareness of some of the 'formal' aspects of *News* may even be *part* of its political 'content'. One effect of these comments is to enforce some critical reflection on the reader's part about the text he or she is actually reading and its relation to a perhaps more familiar fare in fiction; the reader, faced with these comments, is necessarily reminded that *News from Nowhere* is also a fiction, yet insofar as it dissociates itself from the fiction of its own period it appears to demand to be read in a different kind of way.[8] It is this prompted *doubleness* of response that invites analysis, and it is convenient to focus on two of the interests that permeate this collection of essays: the formal function of detail and the process of reading.

The opening chapter is an intriguing instance of how the reader's response can be made peculiarly ambivalent by the details offered. The first words of the text, 'Up at the League, says a friend', begin a pattern of oscillations in the rest of the chapter, with variations on the phrase 'says a friend' intrusively and awkwardly repeated; as we read we treat this 'friend' as a transparent device, collapsing the 'friend', the 'he' about whom the friend speaks, and the authorial voice itself into one, and that one is clearly to be taken as William Morris himself; that multiple identification is almost, but not quite, admitted at the close of the chapter:

> Our friend says that from that sleep he awoke once more, and afterwards went through such surprising adventures that he thinks that they should be told to our comrades and indeed the public in general and therefore proposes to tell them now. But, says he, I think it would be better if I told them in the first person, as if it were myself who had gone through them; which, indeed, will be the easier and more natural to me, since I understand the feelings and desires of the comrade of whom I am telling better than any one else in the world does.

The effect is curious: we almost *over*-react to the obviousness of the device, the grammar of shifting pronouns almost tempts us into so eluding their refusal of first-person attribution that we end up almost believing that when the 'I' does finally speak in its own voice that 'I' is telling a reluctant truth rather than organising a fiction; yet at the same time the very clumsiness of the authorial prevarications reminds us emphatically that this is indeed fiction *despite* the circumstantial and autobiographical authenticity of what we are told—the League, the debates, the tube-train, the station five miles walk from the house on the Thames, the new suspension bridge (built by Bazalgette in 1887), all have a real and documentable existence in the London of 1890. This opening chapter already establishes a fluctuating relation between the text and the 'real' which is to permeate the whole work.

Some other moments of definite reference to the extra-textual 'real' can be simply listed: the location of the guest-house on the site of Morris's own Hammersmith home, the mention of the Hammersmith Socialists in Chapter 3, the memories of actual childhood in Epping Forest included in the same chapter, the final detailed description of Kelmscott Manor (Morris's Oxfordshire home) in the last chapters, including comments on his own work ('still hung with old tapestries, originally of no artistic value'). Such moments are obviously aspects of the general device of superimposing the imagined future directly onto a present topography intimately known, and this is, of course, a variation on familiar realist techniques (Hardy's Wessex and Dickens's London map easily but not exactly onto their respective actual terrains), though the geographical details act in this text as a constant reminder of the very fictiveness of the work: it is the disparity as much as the identity, the departure from reality as well as the accurate observation, that we are constantly invited to recognise. Such a strategy of juxtaposition, of direct contrast between the actual now and the imagined possibility, is basic to any utopian fiction, but Morris's text brings the two worlds 'physically' much closer together than any previous utopia: almost all utopian societies before Bellamy's *Looking Backward* had been located in a geographical elsewhere,[9] and even Bellamy's Boston is utterly unrecognisable, whereas Morris's England occupies exactly the same geographical terrain as the England of 1890: Guest's route from 26 Upper Mall, Hammersmith, to Bedford Square and the British Museum (ch. 4 to ch. 8) can easily be traced in detail in a London A–Z—and the exercise is revealing: names like Primrose Hill and Kensington Gardens sound new notes.[10] The closeness of the physical identification between the now and the then serves to make more possible, more tantalisingly near, more credible, this transformed world and yet simultaneously reminds us poignantly of its remoteness, its fictional status; the recognition that the 'large open space, sloping somewhat toward the south, the sunny site of which had been taken advantage of for planting an orchard', in Chapter 7, is Trafalgar Square, with all its associations of 13 November 1887 ('Bloody Sunday', also echoed in ch. 17), is one sharp instance of this doubleness of vision. In this use of geographical detail Morris is clearly very close to certain tactics of realism yet we are being prompted to read such details in a directly political way, to be alert to their political implications. At times we are reminded that *some* elements of this future, gracious society are already present, albeit distorted or hidden, in the old now: the description of the beautiful country-side of the upper Thames, which remains beautiful across the centuries, juxtaposed with comments on the nineteenth-century country-houses as having been 'mere blots on the face of the land' (ch. 29), is one instance of this effect on a large scale, while the Pevsner-like mention of the Fleur-de-lis on the village guest-house (ch. 27) is a miniature example of the revealing and mellowing change that time itself can bring to something the beauty of which is now obscured to us. At other times a descriptive detail can pull us up sharply, as we register the historical and political distance that has been travelled: Guest's own reaction to the bridge in Chapter 2 is the paradigm of this, but a single adjective can have the same effect: that the garden in front of the Thames-side houses is 'continuous' (ch. 2) indicates a *very* radical shift in property-values. The significance of such 'local' details is self-consciously underlined for us in the explanation, in Chapter 25, as to why there are numerous birds of prey in the air (no more gamekeepers, no more game-laws, no more landed gentry . . .); Guest's working this out for himself ('did not even have to ask Dick') is obviously a nudge to the reader to think about the implications of similar 'realistic' details.

As we read *News* we do indeed find ourselves noting apparently realistic touches with an awareness of the questions and problems they raise, their presence registered not so much as 'convincing' (or otherwise) but as indicating the carefulness (or otherwise) of the author's political imagination, the precision of his political thinking. A list of various kinds of bread can prompt us to ponder on the overseas links and foreign trade of this society ('the thin pipe-stems of wheaten crust, such as I have eaten in Turin', ch. 3); a comment that the road-menders' clothes, gleaming with 'gold and silk embroidery', are 'under the guardianship of a six-year-old boy, who had his arm thrown over the neck of a big mastiff' (ch. 7) can set the mind racing back and forth on the problem of personal possessions and casual theft; that the road-menders have a 'foreman' raises the old queries of the Anarchist; that Dick, talking about children's education in Chapter 5, rather casually plays down 'book-learning' helps us to note the detail in Chapter 6 that both the shop-children are reading books—and that Dick himself in Chapter 8 knows Shakespeare well enough to recall the Bishop of Ely's house in *Richard II*. Morris is at times explicit about *not* offering a solution to a problem raised by a detail: a minor instance is the good Rhine wine in Chapter 6 ('I made a mental note to ask Dick how they managed to make fine wine . . .'), a more substantial one is the absence of any explanation of the form of fuel or power for the 'force-vehicles' (ch. 24). Our sense that we have to read with an eye open to the underlying political ramifications of such details is itself part of a wider awareness of the artificial nature of the text, our sense of the presence of Morris prompting us rather than trying to 'convince' us—and at times that prompting becomes a kind of playing with us: we find ourselves watching with amusement as Morris quite blatantly works into the text various side-hits at his own pet aversions.[11] For example, the coins with which Guest tries to pay Dick are there not only as signs of the time-shift (oxidised) or of the abolition of the cash-nexus but also, michievously, to provoke Dick's rather gratuitously insulting remarks on their ugliness compared to those of Edward III's reign (ch. 2); when we are given a glimpse of the Houses of Parliament (in 1890 the largest new building in England since the Reformation) they have, predictably, been turned into 'a storage place for manure'—Morris in 1888 had fought a long struggle against the League's Parliamentarians, and he had Dickens's backing for the imagery of 'manure'; but the preservation of the building itself is owing to 'a queer antiquarian society which had done some service in past times', and we realise that Morris's own Anti-Scrape activities have borne ironic fruit. Such moments link us back to those opening realistic details about Morris's own life and remind us of the connections between this future society and his present political activities ('Up at the League'), which include, of course, the writing of this very fiction we are reading.

None of these various uses of detail could be exactly paralleled within the confines of a text modelled according to a realist aesthetic, even though many of them at first glance offer themselves as authenticating the 'reality' of the world presented. It is clear that to attempt to read *News* as trying to build up a convincing picture or realistic representation of a future society would be to mistake the significance of such details: they lead outwards from the text towards an idea of, and arguments about, such a society, rather than inwards to a depth or density of close-meshed fictional coherence which then offers itself as a 'real' depiction of a 'real' world. Obviously, then, faced with the absence of, say, any sustained account of the processes of heavy industry (a preoccupation of some marxist futurologists), we need not regard this as a gaping and disabling hole in the utopian picture; we simply recognise that the text is not concerned to present a seamlessly complete 'world' but rather to indicate the essential elements of an adequately human society. What those essential elements are, for Morris, is best approached obliquely by a consideration of another facet of the text: the interplay between romance elements and the process of reading.

The defining characteristics of the new society are sketched in very early in the text: as Guest approaches the waterman, in Chapter 2, 'he nodded to me, and bade me good morning as if he expected me'; as Guest gets back into the boat after his over-brief swim, the waterman 'held out his hand to help me'; once Guest looks closely at the waterman he notices that he had 'a peculiarly pleasant and friendly look about his eyes.' Such details could, of course, occur in a description of a real event or pass without comment in a realist novel, as minor contributions to characterisation; here they carry a different weight, as indicating the habits and norms of the new society: it is in the attitudes, tones, expressions of people that the basic beauty of this future life is to be found. George Orwell begins his account of Republican Spain, in *Homage to Catalonia*, with a glimpse of that possible life in a casual encounter:

> As we went out he stepped across the room and gripped my hand very hard. Queer, the affection you can feel for a stranger! It was as though his spirit and mine had momentarily succeeded

in bridging the gulf of language and tradition and meeting in utter intimacy. I hoped he liked me as well as I liked him. But I also knew that to retain my first impression of him I must not see him again; and needless to say I never did see him again. One was always making contacts of that kind in Spain.

In the communist England of the twenty-second century the quality of such contacts—'the affection you can feel for a stranger'—defines the habitual and basic relations between everyone.

The point is obvious, but it also opens up onto the overall structure of the work; not only is such 'affection' part of the world suggested to us, it also provides the principle by which our relation as readers to the text is organised and controlled, and so too, in an interesting way, does the notion of never seeing the 'stranger' again. It is clear from the third chapter that the women Guest encounters fascinate him: of the three women in the guest-house 'one of them (was) very handsome'; this 'handsome one', Annie, later 'stood behind me with her hand on my shoulder'—a gesture that would clearly break the codes of Victorian propriety governing meetings between strangers of the opposite sex! As the exchange about Guest's age proceeds, we can feel his interest in this 'pretty girl', and we recognise the undertones of desire when he comments 'She blushed a little under my gaze, though it was clear that she had taken me for a man of eighty'—that inconsequential 'though' speaks loudly of silent wishes on Guest's part. When she leaves the room she takes 'at least part of the sun' with her. Annie's appearance and her—for Guest—too premature disappearance, suggests the pattern which is to follow. In Chapter 4, on the way to Bloomsbury, Guest notices 'a beautiful woman, tall, dark-haired, and white-skinned . . . who smiled kindly on me, and more kindly still, I thought, on Dick'—that touch of male envy is to be picked up later; her passing presence distracts him till she disappears from view—'and I felt that disappointed kind of feeling which overtakes one when one has seen an interesting or lovely face in the streets which one is never likely to see again.' In Chapter 6 'the pretty Annie' is briefly remembered, then Guest is quickly attracted by yet another 'very handsome woman', who agrees to look after the horse while Dick and Guest shop; Guest's admiration this time is more explicit and prompts the comment from Dick: 'Tis a good job there are so many of them that every Jack may have his Jill'; but when they come out of the shop, 'to my disappointment, like a change in a dream, a tall old man was holding our horse instead of the beautiful woman.' As the journey continues, Guest takes note of more 'young girls' and women, and we are also made aware that Dick is hoping to meet someone 'whom I particularly want to see', his blush indicating whom: Clara, who appears in Chapter 9. This, the first chapter given over to Old Hammond's long exposition of the new society and its history, is titled 'Concerning Love', and Guest's first question when Hammond offers to answer 'questions about anything' is not concerned with economics or politics but simply: 'That beautiful girl, is he (Dick) going to be married to her?' That Guest has his priorities right becomes increasingly clear as the work proceeds.

We can return, briefly, to Old Hammond later, but it is the emergence of Guest's interest in the women of the new society, as a major strand in the construction of the text, that I want to pursue. That interest remains focussed on Clara during the meal in Chapter 16 ('I thought it bad manners to stare at Clara all the time, though she was quite worth it'), but on the return to Hammersmith it is Annie who again attracts him: 'Annie shook hands with me, and hoped I had had a pleasant day—so kindly that I felt a slight pang as our hands parted; for to say the truth I liked her better than Clara' (ch. 20). He falls asleep that night with a 'vague fear'—but awakes still in the future, and Annie is the first person he meets; she 'gave me a kiss, quite meaningless I fear except as betokening friendship' (ch. 21); but Annie soon disappears again, left behind as the journey up-river begins, though her parting kiss 'almost took away from me my desire for that expedition.' The immediately following chapter provides him with a new focus of attraction, in Ellen (echoes of course of Helen), and the terms of admiration are even stronger: 'her strange and almost wild beauty.' Chapter 23 suggests hovering complications between Dick and Clara and Ellen, and Guest's male envy and sense of being *de trop* are heavily marked ('I hope you see that you have left me out of the tale'), but Chapter 24 returns to the pattern: Ellen is left behind—and 'quite a keen pang smote me as I thought how I should never see the beautiful girl again.' Ellen does however reappear, in Chapter 27 (the delay being filled with Walter Allen's tale of jealousy), and she thereby seems to be breaking the pattern, though initially Guest fears that her arrival is prompted by affection for Dick.

Guest's subsequent relation with Ellen need not be traced in detail; the growth of his love for her is clear, as is his fear of losing her. And in the end, of course, in returning to the nineteenth century, he does indeed lose her: Ellen's is the last face he sees from the future before ('like a change in a dream') he encounters, shocked, the apparently old labourer. That final loss of Ellen is, as we have seen, the last and worst of a series of disappointments related to women, but whereas the earlier brief encounters and the suddenly curtailed relation with Annie are held within a frame of promise, of possible re-encounter or resumed relation or at least another 'Jill', the separation from Ellen is sharp and final. It is a curious ending by certain standards—precisely those standards of 'happy ending' criticised by Ellen herself. Few novels which rest so much on a gradually developing love-interest would conclude on such an arbitrary separation; even utopian fictions tend to ensure that the explorer of utopia finally marries the inevitable heroine (Bellamy's Julian West, Butler's narrator). But Morris's ending is not a simply arbitrary one, nor is it absolutely dictated by the notion of time-travel: Bellamy had found a technical solution to those problems and his devices might have been improved upon— Wells's *The Time Machine* was to be written in 1894. The constant teasing or tantalising of the *reader* by the pattern of aroused but frustrated attraction and involvement, of which the loss of Ellen is the culmination, is crucial to the political impact of the book, in at least two aspects. The reader, *insofar as* he or she has 'identified with' the love-relation between Guest and Ellen and has *willed* its consummation (in accordance with the familiar expectations of popular and naïve 'romance'), is left by the ending with a final feeling of frustration. That frustration thereby serves to provoke a desire that, *nevertheless*, that relationship might be achieved—but that doesn't mean only, in Brecht's ambiguous phrase, 'rewriting the ending';[12] it means endeavouring, outside the anticlimax of the tale, to achieve the kind of society where such a relationship might be possible, it means re-establishing that future. In a curious but definite way, the desire of the lover (and by transference the desire of the reader) is coupled with, brought into the service of, the political desire that the text seeks to provoke—and the text itself makes precisely that connection explicit: 'Looking back now, we can see that the great motive-power of the change was a longing for freedom and equality, akin if you please to the unreason-

able passion of the lover' (ch. 17). By this abrupt and *un*-satisfy-
ing ending, we are left by the novel in a state akin to that of the
narrator in the first chapter: 'I understood the feelings and desires
of the comrade of whom' I have been reading; I, too, if I am a
reader attuned to the patterns of 'popular' romance fiction, have
been drawn, perhaps reluctantly, like the opening narrator, into the
text and my expulsion from it leaves an unfulfilled desire, a lost
object I seek to re-discover in the non-fictional world that remains
when the text has closed in upon itself. Secondly, and closely
linked to this effect, is a more dispersed desire played upon by the
text, a desire for the kind of (love-)relationships that seem possible
in the future world—for it is a change in human relations rather
than in forces of production (though the former is clearly not possible without the latter, as Old Hammond's account makes clear)
that characterises the new society as communist; those relations
are seen in the guest-house, in the shop and street, in every working activity, they are palpable in the touch of hands and the expressions on faces, and what is at the core of those relations is the
promise of a *gift*; the society of *News from Nowhere* is a gift-
society in the fullest sense[13]—and the most basic, and 'utopian',
gift-relationship is precisely that of love. In making of his text a
kind of finally withheld gift of satisfaction, Morris is utilising a
device familiar to psychoanalysis—this text, too, is a game of
Fort/Da[14]—and in putting sexual relations at the heart of his
utopian fiction Morris is discovering for himself an insight into
'communism' the young Marx had had: [15]

> The immediate, natural, necessary relation of human being to
> human being is the relationship of man to woman. In this natural
> species-relationship the relation of man to nature is immediately
> his relation to man, just as his relation to man is immediately his
> relation to nature, his own natural condition. Therefore this re-
> lationship reveals in a sensuous form, reduced to an observable
> fact, the extent to which the human essence has become nature
> for man or nature has become the human essence for man. It is
> possible to judge from this relationship the entire level of develop-
> ment of mankind. . . . This relationship also demonstrates the
> extent to which man's needs have become human needs, hence the
> extent to which the *other*, as a human being, has become a need
> for him, the extent to which in his most individual existence he is
> at the same time a communal being.

We can now draw some strands together and, very briefly, suggest a wider argument. It is clear that the device of enticing or teasing the reader into a frustrated desire that might provoke political displacement of that desire rests not only on certain romance conventions but also on the overt fictiveness of the text itself; the appropriate reaction is effected because we *know* that the work is *not* offered to us as a 'real' account, in which the ending lies outside our control and—by a deep convention of realism— apparently outside that of the author too (the 'inevitability' effect), but rather as a deliberate and challenging demand upon us, a demand we can ignore only if we treat the text as a different and more familiar kind of fiction, as indeed 'pure fiction'. Yet at the same time, in playing variations on the realist use of detail and in utilising, in its own structure of expectations, one of the primary components of the pleasure of reading romance fiction, *News from Nowhere* is clearly, in these aspects, at least a second-cousin to the tradition from which it dissociates itself. In other aspects, of course, *News* makes a much sharper break with the conventions of nineteenth-century fiction: the expository chapters given over to Old Hammond loom large in our reading experience (and in familiar objections to the work); there is, as one could show, a certain element of teasing here too—in the arrangement of this long discourse and in the fact of it being there at all. But the essential point to make is that once 'organicist' or 'Jamesian' criteria of fiction are left aside and we read rather with an awareness of fictiveness, of the conventions of fiction—some older than the nineteenth century (the long discourses in Homer, the sagas, the Old Testament), some established in twentieth-century fiction (the long argumentative conversations in *Magic Mountain* or *The Glass Bead Game*)—the eighty or so pages devoted to Old Hammond need cause no more of a formal problem than catechetical exposition does in Plato.[16] The content of these chapters may well arouse different degrees of interest in different readers, but in 1890 (after Bellamy's success) and in the pages of *Commonweal*, Morris could presume a high level of prior interest. But, of course, the critical objection is often to the 'awkward' inclusion of these chapters in an otherwise mainly, if thinly and unsuccessfully, 'realist' work—by which is meant the latter half of the tale. Yet, as I have tried to suggest, both the realist and the romance elements in *News* are so handled that the overt fictiveness of the text modifies our response to them in a self-reflexive way; we are made aware of them as conventions of fiction which are being manipulated by the author for purposes which stand askew to the familiar effects of fiction. The Old Hammond chapters can then be seen as another instance of this acknowledgement of the limits, and the undermining of the conventions of, 'Victorian fiction': we are being invited to recognise that since so much of fiction is implicitly didactic, we might as well settle back and read some explicitly didactic exposition; these chapters, one might say, bring together Morris's equivalent of all those quasi-authorial comments on morals, the organisation of society and common sense wisdom which operate as the voice of truth in the hierarchy of voices that constitutes the realist mode.[17]

In certain respects, then, we can see that *News from Nowhere* comes close to some of the preoccupations of 'modernist' fiction: there is the same sense of the artefact declaring itself as made, constructed, self-conscious of its own devices; there is an element of using the conventions of fiction as part of its own material; there is a playing upon the relation of the reader to the text as a text rather than as a depiction of a world.[18] Clearly *News* is not a modernist masterpiece before its time but we can now read it with a certain hindsight and recognise in its mingling of conventions and its self-awareness, its deliberate breaking of certain expectations, its cavalier attitude to the preoccupations of other nineteenth-century novelists, a serious response to the dominant tradition of fiction in its own day. We should also, obviously, recall the more basic point about *News*, that Morris was content to bracket it with his historical handbook for militants, *Socialism: its growth and outcome*, as a 'more or less propagandist' work;[19] the fact that a work of fiction intended primarily as a contribution to militant socialist propaganda should have challenged and tried to both undermine and modify some of the conventions of fiction need not surprise us if we remember that in all of Morris's many activities —his work in textiles, tapestry, embroidery, wall-papers, furniture, stained-glass, printing, architecture—he was constantly aware of the relation between the formal qualities of a work of art and its social, and finally political, use; it was from Ruskin that Morris, in his early PRB days, first learned that the relation between detail and form is always politically significant: two years after writing *News* he reprinted on the Kelmscott Press that crucial chapter of *Stones of Venice*, 'The Nature of Gothic'. And forty years after

303

Morris, Brecht too was to recognise that a political challenge necessarily involves an aesthetic challenge, and he too set out—more
explicitly, more coherently, and more successfully—to create a
political, propagandist art which was aware of its own devices, its
own artificiality, and which took as its material not only the
political dilemmas of its day but also the popular and dominant
forms of art, precisely in order to undermine them.

A brief essay can only sketch a case, but—to use again Morris's
own words in his review of Bellamy[20]—though it may still be true
that 'to anyone not deeply interested in the social question it could
not be at all an attractive book', it may also be possible for a critic
to find interesting both the 'serious essay' and the 'slight envelope
of romance' in *News from Nowhere*, since in important aspects of
the text—and not least the deliberate slightness of the envelope—
the two cannot finally be separated.

NOTES

1. *Cf.* E. P. Thompson, *William Morris: Romantic to Revolutionary* (London, 1955) and Paul Meier, *William Morris: the Marxist dreamer*
   (Hassocks, 1978). The Postscript to the second edition of Thompson's
   book (London, 1977) surveys work on Morris in the last twenty years.
   News from Nowhere was first published serially in 1890, in *Commonweal*, the paper of the Socialist League.
2. *Cf.* the useful comments in the Introduction to *News from Nowhere*,
   ed. J. Redmond (London, 1970), pp. xxiv–xxv. Redmond, however, seems
   to deny the appropriateness of *any* 'literary criticism' to *News*.
3. 'Jamesian' is perhaps the most appropriate term in this context, bearing in mind the relevance, for the critical issues raised by the propagandist intention of *News*, of the exchanges between James and H. G.
   Wells about the purposes and function of fiction; *cf. Henry James &
   H. G. Wells*, ed. L. Edel and G. N. Ray (London, 1958), especially
   James's letter of 10 July 1915, pp. 265–68.
4. In the 1930s, Harold Laski found copies of *News* 'in home after home
   of the miners', even when most of the furniture had been sold; *cf.* Paul
   Thompson, *The Work of William Morris* (revised edition, London,
   1977), p. 239. For some rather caustic comments on the influence of
   Morris's 'dream of socialism' on some Glasgow socialists, *cf.* Harry
   McShane, *No Mean Fighter* (London, 1978), pp. 30, 33.
5. *Cf.* e.g. Terry Eagleton, *Criticism and Ideology* (London, 1976), especially Chapter 4.
6. This is not to deny that this sketch of the process of the socialist

revolution in England is, in some of its political and strategic details, remarkably specific, but a full analysis is impossible here.

7. On Morris as a literary critic, *cf.* Paul Thompson, ch. 8; for Morris's list of his 'Best Books'—and his dismissive comments on James—*cf.* E. P. Thompson, 1977 edition, pp. 659–60.

8. Other instances of the text being aware of its own fictiveness include the Sterne-like Chapter 13, 'Concerning Politics'. Even the title, in the pages of *Commonweal*, would indicate a certain playfulness.

9. *Cf.* Meier, vol. I, Part Two for a survey of previous utopian works.

10. It is perhaps also worth noting that the river-trip in *News* traverses much the same well-known territory as that in the widely-popular *Three Men in a Boat*, published in 1889.

11. In his review of Bellamy's *Looking Backward*, which provided the immediate stimulus for writing *News*, Morris remarked that 'the only safe way of reading a utopia is to consider it as the expression of the temperament of its author'; *cf.* May Morris, *William Morris: Artist, Writer, Socialist* (Oxford, 1936), vol. II, p. 502.

12. Bertolt Brecht, *The Good Woman of Setsuan*, Epilogue.

13. *Cf.* the development of Marcel Mauss's notion of 'the gift' in Richard M. Titmuss, *The Gift Relationship* (London, 1970).

14. *Cf.* S. Freud, *Beyond the Pleasure Principle* (1920), Standard Edition, vol. XVIII, p. 14*f.*

15. K. Marx, 'Economic and Philosophical Manuscripts' (1844), in *Early Writings* (Pelican Marx Library, 1975), p. 347. The obvious problem of the retention of male domination in *Nowhere*—or Marx—cannot be debated here.

16. Morris's tactic is worth comparing with Mallock's in his *The New Republic*—which also, it seems, influenced Wells's *Boon*, the immediate occasion for the break with James.

17. For a sketch of the analysis of 'realism' implied here, *cf.* Colin Mac-Cabe, 'Realism and the Cinema: Notes on some Brechtian theses', *Screen*, vol. 15, no. 2 (Summer 1974), pp. 7–10.

18. A certain congruence between Morris's preference for pre-Renaissance literature and elements of 'modernism' in his own fiction is perhaps not surprising, in view of the general argument advanced in Gabriel Josipovici's *The World and the Book* (London, 1971).

19. Meier, vol. I, p. 268, citing a letter from Morris to Hyndman, (22 Dec) 1890.

20. My opening quotation is taken from that review, *cf.* May Morris, vol. II, pp. 501–2. Considering Morris's own concern with the criteria of 'care and art' in literature, it would indeed be surprising if he had merely lapsed into the same faults he had criticised in Bellamy.

Interchapter 5

There seems to be an interesting paradox in each of these essays, as they seek to register different kinds of dissatisfaction with, or transition from, the Victorianness of Victorian fiction. Realisation in terms of the here-and-now, that basic strength of George Eliot, is at once the restriction against which her fervour rebels in *Deronda*, and the measure by which Ruth Raider nevertheless finds the 'Jewish novel' lacking, however she may respect the fervour itself. Henry James finds a way forward from the Victorian to the modern novel, but the very achievement of a contemplative art (James's 'portrait' of Isabel's 'self-portrait') so exclusively concerned with private consciousness, is seen by Stuart Hutchinson as a register of loss and unfulfilment. Morris's desire for a changed person and a revolutionised community results, for Bernard Sharratt, in an art whose 'thinness' is essential to the strategy of its critique of Victorianism; but which therefore, though the conclusion isn't drawn, can hardly avoid being thin, and unsatisfying, as an experience.

Yet it is because these fictions so register how things fall apart, that we become so sharply aware not only of where we are going (the twentieth-century arts of myth and fable; the novel of consciousness; the attacks on Victorian 'realism' as embodying re-restrictive, or reactionary, or delusive conceptions of human being); but also where we have been, and how much we have lost. In the 'dissatisfactions' of George Eliot, Henry James and William Morris, a last set of questions about what it is for a modern reader to read a Victorian novel may begin to pose themselves.

After Henry James, novels tend to impress on us a sense that their authors have already comprehensively read their own work. Compared with James we can already feel mere infants in literacy; from Joyce to Pinget the author magisterially precedes his readers, subtly pre-constructs a medley of possible 'readings', provocatively invites a variety of overlapping 'interpretations'. This tendency has been reinforced by the academic industry which surrounds every author with myriad attendant commentaries—like this book. The emphasis on the organic (the detail instantiating and shaping the whole) has encouraged a plenitude of tiny critical *aperçus*, multiplied our provisional points of view, spawned that curious phenomenon we have found ourselves nicknaming, with guilty affection, 'Super-Reader': the expert delicately, yet verbosely, alert to *every* detail and pattern, down to the *finesse* of a comma, but whose brilliance fails somehow to recall to us the books we've read. A counter emphasis upon 'the reading process', on recounting the current experience as the pages turn, rather than any microscopic scrutiny of some suspended passage, might seem to recover a more appropriate response, a more Victorian, even 'serial' reaction. But, of course, the actual reading of a novel always occurs in the now; *we* cannot read *Wuthering Heights* in 1847; only in 1977, 1978, and later. We cannot erase our own history— which includes the intervening fictions we have read and responded to. In one sense, Victorian fiction has not come to an end: the novels are still with us, every time we open them to read. But no longer, quite, as Victorian; inescapably, whatever the depth of our period knowledge or capacity for historical imagination, we make the novels our contemporaries. And yet we are never fully our own contemporaries; we each trace an idiosyncratic route through the present as well as the past, guided by taste and temperament, past training and present accident. As one effect of these contingencies, each critic bends the 'past' novel towards his or her 'present' reading. What we cannot finally do, however, is to write the texts that never happened; though we know that we might well read *Deronda*, or even *Romola*, differently, had their directions actually fostered improvements upon their attempts; and we might grasp more confidently the peculiarities of *Nowhere* had Morris somewhere found successors. We read James so well (though never so well as James?) because his, and Flaubert's progeny have made a limited though rich range of fictional practices deeply familiar, in extending and adapting them. In that sense we can indeed date the fading of other possibilities, locate a historical cross-roads between what has since been developed into a major highway with numerous feeder-routes, and a few apparently dead-end country-paths, barely explored and badly sign-posted. The field of fiction can sometimes, however, be traversed by an unexpected short-cut:

we may still find ourselves faced with a major political novel that will bring both the 'Jewish novel' in *Deronda*, and *Nowhere*, back into perspective, as the tentative precursors they might one day turn out to have been. Perhaps then we might even know how to read them as their authors did.

On the other hand, may it not be when we are most aware of the Victorian novel as another world, set off against our own modernity, that we are also most vividly conscious of what the Victorians took for granted, as we cannot. And is there not a sharp sense of balancing the loss against the gain?

As we ponder their sense of detail, their dense solidity of speci-fication, and take in just how detailed a process of imaginative realising the Victorian novelists felt was expected of them, may the 'modern' reader not be overcome as much by their sense of responsibility to a 'here and now', as by his own sense of how that depended on a particular society and a peculiar stance? Or, as we respond to Victorian characterisation, may there not be both a longing to recover an equivalently dense and mysterious conception of the human being (Iris Murdoch's pleas in *Against Dryness*) and a sense of the restricted conditioning of a class and a society fixed in time? Wilson Harris's attack on what he calls the 'novel of persuasion' has been followed by increasing hostility, on the part of 'third world' writers, to fictive criteria and expectations derived, as they see clearly, from a colonialist society. But can we separate, in our response to the detail in these novels, a sense of marvel, from a sense of otherness or alienation? *Is* realism, as Bernard Sharratt suggests, now essentially reactionary?

If we turn to 'process'—the 'into' of 'detail into form'—perhaps we only recognise just how essentially projective, proliferative, anxious to be *doing*, and energetic Victorian fiction is, when we see how quickly, in these three transitional fictions, 'doing' passes into contemplation. Yet again, can we help bringing to bear a modern scepticism about action as the realisation of consciousness and conscience? We respond, in reading Victorian novels, to differ-ent kinds of relationship. We have to balance the rich consequences of insisting that the human being must be necessarily, and fully, inner and outer, private and public, against the politics of in-dividualism and the problematic of Victorian morality. Again, Mark Kinkead-Weekes notes how the reader can feel his relation to the author through the Victorian novel as it is being written and read; whereas in modern fiction the work has a high degree of autonomy. But here again we balance formal refinement (in terms of which Victorian novels can seem 'baggy monsters') against increasing refrigeration, cold labyrinth.

As we move from a Victorian to a modern sense of form, we watch the end of 'the common reader'. No period of fiction has had conceptions of form which were so hospitable as the Victorians; so inclusive, not only of a multiplicity of detail and relationship, but of multiple kinds of reader. The more subtle and artistic framing which establishes the 'portrait' begins both to exclude kinds of reader, and to make more exclusive contracts with the readers that remain. The sense of form as political, and of art as autonomous, must do so too. The gain in formal awareness and artistic subtlety has been very considerable and rewarding, but the wide variety of readers who could happily lose themselves in Victorian novels, have been largely lost to serious fiction now.

Inevitably, critical practice reflects, and is parasitic upon, developments in fiction, though it can also sponsor re-discoveries and remind us of potentials. Yet critical practice has its own crossroads also. In some respects this collection seems itself to register transition. The very title marks an intersection of approaches, while the process which has produced it as a collaborative effort has been, more generally, not only an interaction but sometimes a very cross exchange. But of course no reader will stand—at least for very long—on the same spot as ourselves; and neither will we. This is a book for reading: so, like others, its pages will be turned fast or slow once, or more often, its details remembered or forgotten, its form registered and rejected. Even as we write this, we already hear some of us asking, with a certain sharpness: 'Whatever happened to melodrama and to suspense? . . .'

Index

anamorphism, 20, 28–9
Austen, Jane, 94–5, 104, 147; *Emma*, 128–29, 175; *Sense and Sensibility*, 20

Bellamy, Edward: *Looking Backward*, 294, 304
Bradbury, Ray: *Fahrenheit 451*, 130
Brecht, Bertolt, 304
Brightfield, Myron: *Early Victorian England in its Novels*, 234–35
Brontë, Charlotte: *Jane Eyre*, 19–20, 28, 87, 131–47, 177, 193–94; *Villette*, 17, 20, 45–8, 132, 176–83, 189, 193–94
Brontë, Emily: *Wuthering Heights*, 64–8, 92–8, 237, 307
Browne, H. K., 196–223 (passim), 232
Buckley, Jerome, 236
Butler, Samuel: *Erewhon*, 289
Butwin, Joseph, 245

Cattermole, George, 232
Carlyle, Thomas, 236–37
Carroll, Lewis: *Alice in Wonderland*, 68–9, 232
Cervantes Saavedra, Miguel de: *Don Quixote*, 55
characters, 60, 62, 102–3, 114–15, 140–44, 220; and detail, 41–2, 65, 75–6, 115–17, 150–65 (passim); and form, 41, 44–5; and memory, 111–25; as narrator, 64–6, 131–47 (passim)

Chase, Richard, 274
coincidence, 24–6
comedy, 41, 100–1, 118, 216–20
Collins, Wilkie, 33, 62; *Armadale*, 39–45, 253; *The Moonstone*, 34, 39, 45, 48, 63; *The Woman in White*, 34, 36–9, 45
Curl, J. S., 229

details, 57–8, 86, 104, 125, 129, 139, 142, 169, 216–20, 238–39, 249–50, 296–97; accumulation of, 54–5, 64–6, 216; ambivalence of, 32–3, 40; and form, 11–13, 32–48, 113, 116, 137, 306–9; and film and television, 101–2; as signals, 16, 33–5, 41, 128–29, 171
Dickens, Charles, 57, 147, 244, 248–49, 250, 265, 289; *Bleak House*, 16–19, 27, 48, 56, 58–9, 194, 198, 243–44, 249; *David Copperfield*, 21–4, 67, 72, 87, 138, 150–65, 169–76, 183, 189, 194, 196–223, 227, 238, 249; *Dombey and Son*, 26, 199, 206, 240–41; *Great Expectations*, 128, 236; *Hard Times*, 245–46; *Little Dorrit*, 25, 236; *Martin Chuzzlewit*, 68; *Nicholas Nickleby*, 67–8; *The Old Curiosity Shop*, 19–20, 23–4, 199, 226–33; *Oliver Twist*, 21, 27–8, 216, 249; *Pickwick Papers*, 59, 237; *Tale of Two Cities*, 25–6
Disraeli, Benjamin, 265; *Coningsby*, 260

311

Dowden, Ernest, 270
drama, 15, 84–5, 87, 89, 100, 103, 121, 139; and melodrama, 23, 99, 267
dreams, 39–44, 95–6, 205, 210

Eliot, George, 57, 105, 136–37, 255, 290; *Daniel Deronda*, 16, 88, 107, 253–71, 274–75, 278–79, 292, 306, 307–8; *Middlemarch*, 17, 24, 56, 60, 84, 88, 107, 245, 270; *Adam Bede*, 19–20, 254; *The Mill on the Floss*, 20, 26–7, 30, 72–90, 105–9, 254, 257, 275; *Romola*, 258–59, 307; *Felix Holt*, 260, 270
endings, 65–9, 73–4, 87–90, 104–10, 181–83, 188–90, 254, 286–87

Faulkner, William, 175
Fielding, Henry: *Tom Jones*, 16, 18, 55
Flaubert, Gustave: *Madame Bovary*, 120
Ford, G. H., 228, 229
form: and detail, 11–13, 32–48, 113, 116, 137, 306–9; and plot, 38–48, 157–58 (*see also* novel)
Forster, John, 163
Fowles, John: *The French Lieutenant's Woman*, 61, 182

Gaskell, Elizabeth: *Life of Charlotte Brontë*, 147; *Mary Barton*, 19, 237–40, 249; *North and South*, 23, 246; *Ruth*, 255; *Wives and Daughters*, 133
gesture, 37, 212, 214
Gissing, George, 250; *New Grub Street*, 20, 56
Green, Martin, 282

Halliday, A.: *Little Emily*, 200
Hardy, Barbara, 63
Hardy, Thomas, 129, 235, 248; 'The Dorsetshire Labourer', 120; *Desperate Remedies*, 19; *Far From the Madding Crowd*, 18, 20–1, 29–30, 98–101, 102, 104, 267; *Jude the Obscure*, 24, 27, 109; *A Laodicean*, 111; *The Mayor of Casterbridge*, 17, 24–6, 102–4, 111–25; *A Pair of Blue Eyes*, 21, 111; *Return of the Native*, 111; *Tess of the D'Urbervilles*, 19, 23; *The Trumpet Major*, 111; *The Well-Beloved*, 111; *The Woodlanders*, 16
Harvey, J. R., 198, 199, 216
Hesse, Hermann: *The Glass Bead Game*, 302
Hunt, John Dixon, 244

illustration, 196–223, 232

James, G. P. R., 289
James, Henry, 198, 256, 264, 269, 271, 288, 292, 306; *The Ambassadors*, 160, 171; *The Bostonians*, 283; *The Golden Bowl*, 196; *Notebooks*, 274; *The Portrait of a Lady*, 88, 258, 274–86, 291; *The Princess Casamassima*, 283; *What Maisie Knew*, 152, 156; *The Wings of the Dove*, 267
Josipovici, Gabriel, 60
Joyce, James, 306; *A Portrait of the Artist*, 26, 138; *Stephen Hero*, 138

Kingsley, Charles: *The Water Babies*, 87

Lawrence, D. H., 131, 256; *The Rainbow*, 109, 131; *Women in Love*, 235–36
Leavis, F. R., 263–64, 269, 274–75, 291
Leavis, Q. D., 141–42
Lodge, David, 145–46
Lubbock, Percy: *The Craft of Fiction*, 9–11

Mallock, William: *The New Republic*, 289
Mann, Thomas: *Buddenbrooks*, 27; *The Magic Mountain*, 302
Marsh, Anne, 289
Marx, Karl, 301